About the Author

After a 12-year career in the Royal Navy, 18 months in the Foreign Office and six months selling semi-conductors, Norman Dabell finally achieved his dream of becoming a journalist and, eventually, an author. Following spells on weekly, then daily, newspapers he launched a freelance golf journalism and broadcasting career in 1989, during which he worked notably for BBC 'Five Live' and BBC Radio Ulster, the *Observer, Daily Telegraph*, all of Ireland's major newspapers and Reuters news agency. Norman has also written six successful books on golf, including an entertaining memoir of a calamitous life on tour called *Natural Hazard*.

Having hung up his laptop, he now lives with wife Sharon, also an author, peacefully (but always wary of fate) in the Highlands of Scotland.

Dedication

For my mother, Sheila Elizabeth.

Norman Dabell

PLUM JAM AND POT MESS

COPING WITH CHAOS AS A SCHOOLBOY AND SAILORBOY

AUSTIN MACAULEY
PUBLISHERS LTD.

A CIP catalogue record for this title is available from the British Library.

ISBN 978 1 78455 166 7

www.austinmacauley.com

First Published (2014)
Austin Macauley Publishers Ltd.
25 Canada Square
Canary Wharf
London
E14 5LB

Printed and bound in Great Britain

Introduction

A few years ago I wrote a book called *Natural Hazard*. It was a 20-year diary of an accident-prone golf writer, recounting the incidents and mishaps that befell me and all those around me as I travelled the world on the European Tour. I was notorious for my misfortune – and very occasionally fortune – and everyone wondered how so much could happen to one person. Well, being a hazard was nothing new to me. I was born a hazard.

My latest account is a sort of 'prequel' to *Natural Hazard*, a memoir of the 1940s to 1970s as I first stumbled through my childhood and schooldays then joined the Royal Navy, moving effortlessly from jinx to Jonah.

The story begins with a lad growing up in a rural village in the East Midlands. It wasn't an ordinary boyhood. Havoc followed me like a trusty dog. How did I survive? Was the star I was born under a lucky star or an omen of doom? What did my relations, friends and teachers do to have such a calamitous soul thrust among them?

But it is not just a litany of mishaps. Embroidered around my tale is a nostalgic chronicle.

The Second World War was still vivid in the memories for many as families picked up the pieces, having lost loved ones, lost homes. My mum and dad had survived the war but they were like millions of working class parents, raising a family on very little. The house rent took up much of Dad's pay; we shared a toilet up the yard; bathed in a tin bath once a week; walked everywhere or took a bus on rare occasions.

It was tough for me. Sweets didn't come off ration until 1953. Then there were sherbet dabs, liquorice bootlaces and gobstoppers that you could hardly close your mouth on. If pennies were short, in the summer I could go scrumping.

Life had its mysteries. I wondered whether Peter Brough's mouth was moving when Archie Andrews spoke on his radio show. And where the yellow went when I brushed my teeth with Pepsodent.

Coronation Day, pancake races, Nyoka at Saturday matinee, Uncle Mac, carnivals, fairs and football with nuggs – just some of the memories of boyhood.

It wasn't all play. Sitting the eleven-plus was a trial we all had to go through. Against the odds and the snipers, I won a scholarship to grammar school. Suddenly boyhood was over.

Sport, especially football and cricket, dominated my life. I discovered girls; they didn't discover me. An eon of shyness with the opposite sex began.

As I moved into my most formative years, my world fell apart. I lost my beloved father when I was 13, to leave me head of the family. Eventually I left school to join the Navy.

Ah, the 'Swinging '60s'. The only swinging I did was in a hammock – when I could stay in it. No, it wasn't exactly hornpipes and 'Yo, ho, ho and a bottle of rum' but, while we still ruled the waves, sailors did actually break in the middle of the day to drink a tot that might put the modern matelot on his back. The second part of my story is a 12-year stint in the Royal Navy – getting into scrapes from Plymouth to Bangkok.

It all started like this…

THE SCHOOLBOY

Chapter 1

GOOD JOB IT WAS HIS HEAD

As I hurtled over the brink of the pit and plummeted down into the quarry, my life, as they say, flashed past me. It didn't take long. I was only two years old.

After the war Britain was enduring painful years of recovery. I was blissfully unaware of all this, just enjoying a wonderful life as a toddler, living deep in the Nottinghamshire countryside.

I had gone through my paces with my new tricycle, learning how to negotiate pedals for the first time and how to stay in the saddle. Now it was time to broaden my horizons.

With my much-loved little fluffy doggie accompanying me, I pedalled down the drive. A squadron of worms had been placed across the drive's end, a ritual whenever I was outdoors. There was no way I would go past the worms. I couldn't stand the little blighters. This was all because my cousin Margaret had, in an act of devilment, once dropped a couple of worms down my wellingtons. It gave me a lifelong revulsion of worms. It was a brilliant system, a sure-fire way of keeping me away from the road outside the house.

Well this time the worms seemed to have wriggled away. I careered out into the road, a blur of spinning legs. West Leake

Lane didn't see much traffic in 1946 and a good job it didn't, or that might have been it straightaway. I pedalled up the lane, turned a corner and cruised into a spinney. In this spinney was a large pit where gypsum, the white plaster found in huge escarpments locally, had been quarried then taken away on the little 'Lady Angela' train.

Suddenly I was careering downwards out of control. My feet were whipped off the pedals and over the handlebars I went, ejected into the pit. I tasted fear for the first time. Over and over I tumbled until my head smacked into a lump of gypsum. Blackness closed in.

My escapade, though, had been seen by the driver of the Lady Angela, Tommy, and his fireman Snowy. They'd watched in horror as I shot past their train and disappeared over the pit. Tommy scrambled down the pit and struggled back up the crumbling face with me in his arms.

I gradually came to with this sooty-faced man whispering soothing words and rubbing my forehead, by now one big lump, with the butter from his lunch box. In my dazed state I thought he was offering me a sandwich.

When Tommy got me home I must have looked a proper sight, butter and blood oozing down my blouse. Mum nearly passed out, wailing about how I might be brain damaged. Snowy went up the road to the telephone box to summon a doctor. By the time the doctor arrived, though, I was on my feet, asking for my tricycle.

Everyone was amazed at not only my remarkable escape from death but on my miraculous recovery. As people would say over the years: "Good job it was his head; he might have been badly injured otherwise".

It had all begun for me in that a wooded little lane near Gotham in Nottinghamshire, on November 9, 1944. The Second World War still had a way to go before its conclusion. Apparently, when I came into the world just after midnight, the doctor who delivered me said to Mum: "You know who he looks like? Just give him a cigar and he could be taken for Churchill!" At least I didn't look like Hitler.

My mum, Sheila Elizabeth, née Elliott, was a slim beauty, of Northern Irish and English stock. My dad, Neville, of French Huguenot ancestry, was a wiry, tough Englishman. They had met at Slack and Parr's engineering company in Kegworth, where they worked on aircraft parts until Dad was called up. They were a very attractive couple, Mum resembling Elizabeth Taylor a little and Dad not unlike Gregory Peck.

They'd set up home with my maternal grandparents in Leake Lane but just before I was born, Dad got his call-up papers and had to go and do his bit in India. I was just a few weeks old when I had my first narrow squeak that was a prelude to a life on the edge.

I was in Mum's arms at the railway station when she tearfully waved goodbye to Dad, off on his journey to India. Suddenly the train guard's whistle blew shrilly and I dived out of her grasp in fright. That might have been the end of my story there and then but, as Dad looked on in horror from his carriage, Mum's lightning reactions saved me from harm. With the skill of a high class slip fielder she grabbed me just before I hit the platform.

While my dad served in the army out in India, Mum and I lived with her parents, Bob, a gentle Ulsterman and Mary, a disciplinarian who had been in service when young and who put the fear of God into me for years. Granddad Elliott never used to say much, leaving most matters to his wife. He had had a traumatic time in the Great War, in the trenches, but he never spoke about any of it, like many men who suffered the horrors of conflict.

My granddad's Christian name incidentally, was very popular in the Elliott family. Mum's brother, who died of tuberculosis during the war, was also called Bob. So are two of my cousins. Mum's sister Jessie's eldest son is Bob and Mum's brother John's boy has the same name. Bob's your uncle – and your granddad and your cousins. I'm named after another of Mum's brothers. He loved the name Norman so much he was always called Bill. My second name is Alfred, after my dad's brother. It is an apt second name, not for anything great but more about a king who burnt the cakes.

Dad came home from India in early 1946. I was totally baffled by his sudden appearance, this person who cuddled me as if he knew me. I had been told he was coming home but it didn't really register. I soon warmed to him, even though I immediately fell off the little wooden stool with doggies either end of it, that he brought home for me. He completely won me over when he went out and bought me the tricycle. It wasn't long before he was regretting his present, however.

After the pit fall I continued to be a liability down the lane. For instance, I had to be rescued, bleeding, pecked shins and all, from a couple of cockerels. "We're getting rid of those birds," Mum warned Dad, who was making a brave attempt at building up a smallholding. "What on earth were you doing anywhere near the cockerels?" said Dad, already seeing his prized birds getting plucked and heading for somebody's oven at Christmas. "I was just trying to see where our eggs come from," his bloodied and shaking son replied. "I tried to look underneath them but they wouldn't let me." Even now I would cross a raging torrent to avoid walking near a cockerel. And I'd rather pick up a python (something I once did) than a worm.

I bet everyone in the lane was secretly relieved when Mum, Dad and me upped sticks and moved to nearby Kegworth, over the border in Leicestershire in 1947. Dad took our meagre possessions off in a van he had borrowed and Mum and I piled aboard – the Lady Angela. Tommy took us as far as Kingston, where the railway line ended. It was some adventure to be standing in the cab with Tommy at the helm of the Lady Angela and Snowy shovelling in coal. It was the start of my love affair with trains I suppose. On the way, the railway line passed within a few yards of where I had my escapade down the pit.

Having got to Kingston, though, Mum and I then had quite a hike to Kegworth where we met up with Dad at his parents' home, a sprawling house in Plummer Lane. Here we were to live with my paternal grandparents, Albert (Joss) and Cecilia (Ciss).

'Nanan' (both grandmothers had this affectionate sobriquet) Dabell was a lovely lady, harassed by bringing up four sons while her husband drank away much of his pay. She never refused me anything. Her ancestry was actually on the toff's side as she was a Heaffield, former Kegworth landowners.

I never saw Nanan without her black bonnet. There was a good reason for that. She had suffered some terrible shock, no-one ever talked about it, and all her hair had fallen out. She also had part of one index finger missing, having squashed it in a clothes mangle.

We lived in Nanan and Granddad's back room, the only drawback of that being that the rest of the house occupants, including two of Dad's three brothers, had to pass through us to get to the bedrooms. Our temporary accommodation had a small bathroom. I think the water heater in it had packed in long before, so the bath would be filled with kettles of hot water. That kind of 'luxury' would soon be denied us when Mum and Dad found a home of their own.

Less than six months later we were moving in to One Plummer Lane, just a few doors away. Our new abode was a rather weirdly shaped end-of-terrace cottage, right at the top of the lane, with a sort of odd, pointed front.

The house had two bedrooms, reached by way of a steep, enclosed staircase that led to a small landing. Downstairs there was a tiny room reached by the back door, which had a sink for washing up and washing clothes and had a small pantry adjoining. This alleged kitchen was not even big enough to house an oven. The gas oven was at the entrance to the living-room, which housed our table and chairs, set only a few feet back from the fireplace. This room, with a front door, was where the family spent most of the time when we weren't sleeping.

The front part of the living-room looking down on the lane was the show area. It housed Mum's Singer sewing machine table, on which sat a wireless. The sewing machine would swing up from under its table when Mum wanted to do some sewing, which was often. Various knick-knacks, including games like Ludo, Monopoly and Snakes and Ladders were stored in a mysterious curtained alcove. It was the focal point of the house. Our 'front room' was for use on high days and holidays only. There was a small display cabinet in it which had in it a few pieces of china and silverware, including a magnificent silver teapot. It had a really nice sofa and chair in it, too. But it was pretty well off limits to everyone. We did light a fire and use it properly at Christmas time, though.

Ablutions were pretty rudimentary at One Plummer Lane. When I look back on our toilet arrangements, for instance, I have to ward off nausea. We had no indoor toilet, only a privy up the yard, which we shared with another family.

Mum used to keep everything in pristine condition, dusting everything every day and cleaning our silverware at least once a week. She had a blue fit on the day I somehow breached the front room, took out her precious silver teapot and filled it with water. I'd decided Dad was going to be home soon from work and needed a cup of tea.

Dad worked long hours and he worked hard. Most of his wages were spoken for. He didn't drink or smoke. He did like a bet, though. Dad loved horses. Mum told me with a shudder that he would sometimes spot a horse in a field when they were out for a walk courting, jump on it and ride it bareback. I suppose it was his Huguenot ancestry.

Horses were never that kind to Dad, though. He hardly ever backed a winner. And he had no luck with our clothes horse either. It was in the form of a long rack hoisted up to the kitchen ceiling by pulleys, on which hung the washing. As time went by the pulley rope got frayed and Mum warned Dad it needed replacing. He kept putting the job off, though. One day the rope broke when Dad was standing right under the clothes horse on which the bed-sheets were drying. It was a quite sturdy device and fetched Dad a real good blow on the head, leaving him lying on the kitchen floor, shrouded in a sheet, looking like some dazed Ku Klux Klansman.

I spent a lot of time at Nanan and Granddad Dabell's. I'd soon decided Nanan's doorstep blackcurrant and plum jam sandwiches were infinitely preferable to Mum's Lancashire Hotpots. Toasting bread and pikelets (aka crumpets) in front of a roaring fire at Nanan's was a particular delight, too. They had this big fireplace with ovens either side of it and grills to put kettles on.

The fire and hearth was the focal point of their house. Eventually my granddad set up his 'throne' in front of it. Joss worked for the council, mainly as a road sweeper, but he had passed out on the job a couple of times and even though some thought it might have been Home Ales bitter that caused this, he was subsequently diagnosed as having a dodgy ticker. That was it. Granddad decided to enjoy his malady. He growled out his orders from this huge armchair in front of the hearth and next to the dining table. For a good while he didn't do much, just listen to the radio, read the newspapers, talk to his canary, doze and have everything brought to him.

His downtrodden wife was at everybody's beck and call but in rare quiet moments you could see her thinking. Ciss was in her own little world. She occasionally came out with some wonderful gems. She told my uncle Eric, after a tragedy in the village when a young lad drowned in the River Soar: "You're not going anywhere near the water until you can swim." And one Christmas she'd knitted me two jumpers, a brown one and a green one. When I went round to see her on Christmas day proudly wearing the brown pullover, she said rather disappointedly: "Don't you like the green one then?"

I don't know whether it was the Great War that made Joss turn to drink. He once saved a horse, I'm told, when it fell into a trench and was drowning in mud, hauling it to safety.

Unlike my maternal granddad, Joss would tell us stories about wartime. The best yarn he told me was about when, as an army cook, he was coming home on leave during the Second World War. To his dismay his sergeant, who had been making his life a misery, got into his carriage. He was also headed for Nottingham.

Eventually the sergeant started to doze. As the sergeant slept Joss noticed money slowly starting to trickle out of his pocket. Joss furtively leant over, scooped up the coins and stowed about five shillings away. When they reached Nottingham, Joss made for the station bar to spend his ill-gotten gains before catching the bus home. The sergeant had the same idea. Joss took great delight in watching his boss order a pint – then start scrabbling around in his pockets, unavailingly searching for the money to pay for it. "Could you lend me some money to pay for a pint?" the embarrassed sergeant was forced to ask. "Don't worry sarge, I'll get these. What'll you have?" It ensured several weeks' grace for Granddad, without having the sergeant on his back.

When Dad came out of the army he worked for three years or so at Donington Park, driving and maintaining army lorries at the aerodrome there. The park would subsequently become East Midlands Airport. Just up the road from where Dad worked was the race track, which would eventually become a motorcycle and Formula One Grand Prix circuit. For a time, the famous British racing driver Reg Parnell, who drove a BRM, was based at Donington Park. We used to hear the roar of his BRM when he was practising, all the way down in Kegworth.

As 1947 turned into 1948, the winter chill set in on One Plummer Lane. I don't remember the house being excessively cold, though. The roaring fire we always had on the go from dawn to bedtime in the winter in the living-room kept the downstairs as warm as toast. Dad used to settle down in front of it after a hard day's work and doze off, occasionally stirring and muttering "Shift me I'm burning". The heat from the fire coming up kept my bedroom warm too. Just in case though, my dad's army greatcoat would be laid over the top of the blanket on my bed during the freezing nights. But because of all the weight on top of me I could hardly turn over in bed.

Kegworth was a real metropolis compared to Leake Lane. I was to discover there was paradise in the High Street just a few yards down and along from our house, in the shape of 'Lottie Stockton's Shop', an Aladdin's cave of sweets, chocolate and toys. First of all I went along to Lottie's with Mum to spend our sweet ration. I became a regular customer of the shop where you could buy sherbet dabs, gobstoppers, liquorice sticks, mint chews and a myriad other things for a mere penny. Then there was a 'penny drink'. This was a tumbler full of pop. My favourite was dandelion and burdock. I would eventually elevate to Crunchie bars and peppermint creams. I had been born with a sweet tooth.

Mum put in a lot of hours educating me at home. By the time my first day came along at Kegworth County Primary School in 1949 at the age of four, I could actually read and write. I could recite nursery rhymes off-by-heart, too. 'Baa baa black sheep' was my favourite. Mum had convinced me I *was* the 'little boy who lived down the lane'. I apparently staggered my first teacher because I could also tell the time. It was all down to a patient mum.

I didn't spend long at the sand-pit and building blocks stage. Within a month I'd left the infants classes. On leaving, I had finished playing with the children's musical instruments that were brought out of the cupboards twice a week. That was a relief. I got fed up with being left with a soppy little triangle after the drums and tambourines had been handed out.

My writing was coming on. However it was nearly the end of me. I'd gone to stay for the summer holiday with grandparents Bob and Mary, who had moved to Quorndon (Quorn) in Leicestershire, where Granddad was the council gardener and caretaker. I decided to write a letter to Mum, who was having a little respite at home, about four or five months pregnant with my brother John. Oblivious to the fact that letters needed a stamp, I determinedly marched off from

Nanan and Granddad's house in the town hall and headed for the letter box near the park to post my missive. This meant crossing a busy road in the process. As I wandered back, very proud of myself, a lorry screeched to a halt with me in the middle of the road. It was my dad, on his way back from Tilbury Docks. There was hell to pay. My grandparents really got it in the neck for allowing me to slip the net. I was bundled into Dad's lorry and whisked back to Kegworth immediately.

Chapter 2

A SHOCK FOR DAD

With my brother's arrival imminent, Dad left Donington Park to start working for a chap called Len Elliott (no relation but he was just like an uncle), driving a cattle-lorry. Len's garage, where his lorry was kept, was just a short walk up the road from our house, so it was much more convenient for Dad and easier for him to care for Mum.

Dad's brief was to ship animals to and from market, mainly cows and bullocks, sheep and pigs. In less smellier periods he took horses to showjumping. Moving animals with a sixth sense that it is their last journey is not an easy process. So Dad had a battery-powered cattle-prodder. We were on the way to Old Dalby market, a regular port of call, when I discovered the cattle-prodder under my little seat, which Dad had set up just behind him. I tapped it on the metal strip of the driver's window. At that point we were cruising downhill, a relaxed dad leaning his arm on the same metal strip. In a flash the day's relaxation ended. Dad's arm shot up in the air as he let out a yelp and he had to battle with the steering wheel to stay in control of his lorry. I'd now had my first lesson about electricity and conductors. Dad had learned one, too. He had a highly inquisitive son who would get up to anything.

Soon Dad had to look after me a lot. With John's arrival only a month or so away, Mum had my bed set up for her in the hallowed front room. Dad and I slept in the main bedroom above Mum, who would rap on her ceiling with a broom if she needed anything during the night.

It was the only time I can recall we didn't spend Christmas Day and Boxing Day in the front room. Christmas 1949 was a bit different altogether, though. I wasn't too worried about Christmas presents. I was too wrapped up in the thought of getting a new brother. I think Mum still cooked the dinner. I don't ever remember Dad cooking anything but his favourite food from army days – egg 'banjos' (fried egg sandwiches). I'm sure we didn't have them with stuffing and cranberry sauce.

The arrival of my brother John in January 1950 imposed a whole new regime on me. There were then restrictions on the time Mum had for me for a start. And Dad spent a lot of time doting on my brother while John moved from baby bottles and nappies to rompers. I soon got used to not being the centre of attention. I often watched over my baby brother to make sure he didn't choke on his bottle. Mum swears I saved his life twice when he was only a few months old.

On the first occasion he was rolling about on the bedroom rug. I looked on in horror as Mum unwittingly started to step back while admiring her new pair of high heels in the mirror – right above John's head. I screamed out and pulled him from under her feet.

The next time John was in mortal danger came when Mum was bathing him, again when he was really tiny. She was always prone to fainting fits and she passed right out while soaping John down in our tin bath in front of the fire in the living-room. John went under as Mum went into oblivion, still holding on to him. I dived forward and plucked him from her, wailing loudly until a neighbour came rushing in and took over.

With a baby and a five-year-old, Mum qualified for the nutrition that was handed out from the clinic set up in the chapel next to our house. She collected concentrated orange juice and cod liver oil, which was considered efficacious for youngsters' growth. I could manage the orange juice with impunity but spoons full of cod liver oil made me gag. When he moved on to it, though, my brother loved cod liver oil, to such a point that he was virtually addicted to it. Even Mum was baffled by this fondness. She couldn't stand the stuff either. When no-one was looking I used to allow my brother to drink my share, too. He used to gurgle with pleasure – and so did I.

The festive season of 1950 was a big occasion of course – my brother's first Christmas. It was an extra treat to see his bulging eyes as he held his first presents. I was happy enough with a stocking full of oranges, nuts and chocolates. Pleasures were pretty simple in our house. My main present was a splendid fort which I subsequently found out my dad had made and painted. My grandparents supplied the lead soldiers. I still half-believed Santa Claus brought the presents at that stage, though.

However, I was beginning to have my doubts. Santa had arrived to much fanfare at our school Christmas party but I wasn't totally convinced by him. He talked very much like our school caretaker Mr Gutteridge. And surely Santa's beard wouldn't keep slipping. But I was going along with it. Then on Christmas morning I heard this loud swishing noise on the roof, followed by an even louder 'crunch'. "Is that Santa's sledge taking off?" I shouted excitedly from the confines of Dad's army greatcoat. "No it's not, it's snow falling off the roof," Mum barked back from the next bedroom, "go back to sleep." I was so disappointed. It had been a great theory. Maybe the older kids at school were right.

I soon stopped digressing. Christmas Day was wonderful. I even had my own chocolate log. I wasn't fond of dried fruit. We spent the afternoon and evening in the front room playing board games on the floor in front of the fire. We did that every year.

As we slipped into 1951 it was decided that my bro. could move out of Mum and Dad's bedroom, where he had slept in a cot by their bed. He was bought a bed of his own and my bedroom now became our bedroom. My independence was over. John even got the army greatcoat. I got the circulation back in my legs.

We were a very happy family. Weekends were a real treat. Sunday was the day when Dad put on his best sports jacket and flannels. After reading the newspapers from cover to cover and avoiding helping with the washing up after Sunday dinner (lunch) and a cup of 'Camp Chicory Essence' (a substitute for coffee) Dad would take John and me by the hand and walk us down to Kegworth market place to a confectionary shop. In the summer he bought us a slab of Walls ice cream.

In the winter ice cream was replaced by wonderful steamed puddings. Mum was fantastic at treacle, jam and raspberry vinegar dumplings and her pièce de résistance, chocolate sponge with chocolate sauce. Puddings were about all I'd clean up my plate for. I was so thin I looked as though I'd bend like a sapling when it was windy.

I was also into fruit – apples, pears, plums, damsons, gooseberries, raspberries, logan berries, black currants and red currants – all gleaned from my uncles' orchard.

They were really my great uncles. Amos, George, Fred and Alan were all deaf and dumb due to the way they were delivered at birth, apparently. They taught me to speak to them by using the deaf and dumb alphabet on my hands. Uncle George was the housekeeper. George also used to run a little farmyard. He kept hens, mostly bantams, which were under the wing of a stroppy little bantam cock fondly called 'Don'. He was named after the famous boxer of the time, Don Cockell. Don was indeed a pugnacious little blighter, taking on anything that got near his brood, such as the myriad stable cats around and any pigeon that had the effrontery to try to eat the corn Uncle George scattered around for his charges. I once saw Don attack a dog (fast flew the Don), which had wandered into the yard. As you could imagine I always gave Cockell the cockerel a wide berth.

The uncles – Amos was appropriately the mainstay here – tended their large orchard along with several types of vegetables. Poor old George was bent double with a spinal disease he suffered as a young man and was unemployable, but he laboured away all day at home duties until his crooked body just gave out one day.

Fred and Alan worked full time. Fred, profoundly deaf, never heard the lorry that mowed him down on the road as he cycled to work.

Amos died early but Alan, the youngest, made it to retirement age. He used to love it when he saw me come in the pub when I came home on leave from the Royal Navy. Alan survived on his own for many years when his sisters grew too old to visit him on a regular basis, or, indeed, passed away. A heart attack claimed Alan not long after he had been sitting in his favourite seat at the 'Fox and Hounds'. His demise meant the end of Kegworth's own little 'Darling Buds of May' corner off Plummer Lane. The yard and stables and the huge orchard were all either ploughed up or sold off. It was the end of the Heaffield dynasty. Nowadays the only memorial to the Heaffield family is a road named after them in Kegworth.

As I moved through primary school I became more and more adventurous, my confidence building with the numerous friends I made.

My pals and I would think nothing of wandering around the countryside all day during the summer holidays, doing things that young lads did, like splattering your mate by hurling a rock into a cow pat.

Dad's family had a dog to which I was greatly attached. 'Joe' was half bloodhound, half Shetland pony. He was referred to as 'Cab'oss' (cab horse). Some of the tots from Plummer Lane used to ride on him. Joe wandered around Kegworth, fathering litters here there and everywhere. You could tell he was a stud by his huge, swinging testicles. He was my pal. He would lope alongside me on my trips away with my friends until he spotted something more interesting and go trotting off, probably to beg a titbit somewhere or sniff out a bitch. He used to come with me down to the recreation ground and then lie and snooze, in his own way guarding me, until it was time to go home. He lived in a kennel up the path of my nanan and granddad's garden. His favourite pastime when he wasn't spawning puppies was to lie under the fence next to his kennel and wait for someone to walk up the lane. As they approached his lair he would suddenly jump up and give a loud, growly bark, just for sheer devilment. Regularly, when the Slack and Parr workers knocked off and made for home up Plummer Lane they could be seen crouching low like commandoes until they had passed his kennel.

Mum would encourage me to take part in everything that was going when it came to kids' plays and pageants, although, thankfully, I think I was deemed as not looking angelic enough for nativities.

For Christmas 1951 a review involving all the Sunday Schools was put on and I was urged to take part. My role was that of a soldier who sang 'Pack up your Troubles in your Old Kit Bag' with two other 'squaddies', a little skit about army lads. The war was still on plenty of people's minds.

I did my best to learn my lines but it wasn't my delivery that made me the object of ridicule by some of the crueller members of the audience. As we took to the stage, my two comrades were both rigged out in full army regalia, made from their dads' old uniforms, sporting genuine-looking kitbags. I was in civvies – grey flannel shirt and short trousers, holding my nanan Dabell's washing bag, which only loosely resembled the proper article. Mum had given up trying to make up a uniform that would fit her scrawny framed son. I stuck out like a sore thumb. I marched around valiantly, though, and earned an accolade, as well as a photograph, in the local newspaper, for my determination. It was a prelude to many a performance that was to go not exactly according to plan for me.

That spring, Dad, who was really a farmer at heart, decided we should have a pig and some fowls and turkeys in the grounds at the back of my paternal grandparents' home.

Dad took up smallholding with great enthusiasm. He even gave up his regular flutter on the gee-gees to pay for his livestock. My brother and I kept vigils on pullet chicks and baby turkeys in their incubators and watched them mature. We were ecstatic when our pig arrived and was housed in the sty that Dad had spent hours on end building on Sundays. We christened our sow Alice. Unfortunately Alice had been proven barren, so she wasn't going to be providing us with a litter of piglets, probably a good job because there wouldn't have been much room for them in the sty.

Well, the pullets and turkeys grew and eventually were ready for selling or, perish the thought, killing. John and I made so much fuss that Dad gave in. They stayed in their runs until they were big enough to break out and scratch around in back gardens. They eventually became feral and wandered off.

Much later, when it came to have Alice taken to the abattoir, we wailed and stamped (including Mum) in protest. We'd cared for her lovingly, feeding her the best of food scraps and swill and she'd grown to an enormous size, hardly able to waddle about her sty and its yard. She was prime pork and would have made Dad a bundle. But she had become an institution, a dear friend who trusted us implicitly.

Alice, who was already a few years old when Dad bought her, eventually died of old age and we buried her under the sty. Dad wrapped his hand in. He decided to give up on livestock and concentrate on growing things that weren't likely to give him so much grief – like runner beans and sweet peas.

Religion was high on the agenda for Mum but not for my dad. He wasn't quite a fully paid up atheist but it would have taken a team of his biggest equine customers to drag him to the church door. He much preferred to read the Sunday newspapers and look after my brother while Mum and I were in church. His non-appearance in the pews used to stick in the craw of the vicar of our church, St Andrews, a haughty individual by the name of S. H. Cartwright (Dad used to say Cartwright's initials were only half the story).

In the end the vicar's arrogance and an incident with my church choirmaster in the summer of 1952 encouraged us to give up our Anglican ideals and switch to the congregation at the Wesleyan Methodist Chapel right next to our house.

The incident with the choirmaster nearly turned very serious. I had been given a small solo part to learn at Thursday evening's choir practice, a piece all about birdsong and the joys of spring. When it came to my turn to perform, though, I dissolved into a fit of giggles after seeing my good pal Mick Snape rolling his eyes and flapping his arms like a condor behind the choirmaster's back. I got a way-over-the-top smack in the face from the choirmaster, who was renowned for his ill temper. I ran out of the church humiliated. I still had a huge red and blue weal on my cheek when I arrived home. I thought I was going to be in more trouble. However, Mum, who had a fair old temper of her own, marched straight down to the church and tackled the choirmaster at his lectern, apparently threatening to give him as good as he'd handed out. It was late when Dad got home or I think he might have laid the choirmaster out. Well, the choirmaster's response was to sack me from the choir. So we sacked the church.

With the move to Methodism, I had to place some serious thought into covering up tracks from commando raids made by myself and various friends over the back wall of the chapel. The rear of the chapel had all sorts of interesting little buildings we could, with a little manipulation of locks, play in. The front of the chapel had front lawns, too. It was all perfect as a play area. That was until two incidents that got me banned from the chapel grounds.

First, while rolling down the front lawn I picked up a little more speed than intended and crashed down into the front wall, bounced back on my bottom – and felt an agonising pain in my left buttock. I'd sat on a broken bottle. I limped home with bloody trousers to let Mum sort me out. She nearly fainted when she saw all the blood, whipped me straight into our faithful old tin bath, filled it up with soapy water and disinfectant (agony) and eased out the glass. I wouldn't stop bleeding though, so a large pad was put in place and I was rushed off to the doctor. I was a rather shy kid. The doctor who inserted the stitches to stem the flow of blood was a lady doctor. I died a thousand deaths.

Then there was the day I fell on my sword. The films 'Scaramouche', 'Robin Hood' and 'Ivanhoe' filled my head at that time. I fancied myself as a great fencer. As I lunged at my opponent, again on the sloping chapel lawn, to carry out the coup de grâce, I tripped and fell forward. My wooden sword, with a whittled-down sharp end to it, plunged straight up into my eye. By a truly amazing stroke of luck the sword missed my eyeball by about a centimetre, ramming instead into the socket bone just above. Of course I poured blood. Mum was watching from the corner window of our house and witnessed the whole incident. She thought I'd blinded myself. Once again she nearly passed out.

The chapel's chief benefactor and lay preacher was a Mr Stafford. Everyone called him 'Daddy' Stafford. He had retired to Kegworth after spending many years in Africa as a missionary. He was probably the kindest, quietest-spoken man I have ever met in my life. He thought only good of everybody. You couldn't help but fall under his spell at the chapel and I was inveigled into various congregational activities, nearly all involving me singing. I had been blessed with a sweet and angelic treble voice that rather hid the devil inside me.

Chapter 3

CORONATION CAPERS

The year 1953 was a memorable and infamous one. Sweets finally came off ration for good. Until then I'd had my sweets and chocolate apportioned out to me. Suddenly I could walk into Lottie Stockton's with tuppence and buy a dozen raspberry chews or several liquorice sticks, or a packet of peppermint creams, or four gobstoppers, or a couple of sherbet fizzes, or a penny drink and a packet of sugar cigarettes... I was in heaven. Lottie Stockton eventually made so much out of me she was able to take on a full-time assistant and enjoy early retirement.

The delight of choosing my own goodies from Lottie's for the first time, though, got me into trouble. Absorbed in what to buy, I didn't notice the time. I was late for school. I arrived breathless about a minute after roll call had been taken. This was a heinous sin at our school and resulted in your name being put in a black book if you didn't have a strong excuse. If you were late again you were reported to the headmaster and your name was read out at assembly. The indignity of that was far worse than any corporal punishment. Having a whole school hall turn round and stare at you was just too hard to bear. It taught me punctuality. It also taught me how to come up with some pretty resourceful excuses. The one where I pleaded for clemency because I'd had to go back to fetch the chocolate cake Mum had packed up for me, wasn't one of them.

I have dark memories of early 1953, however. I remember being horrified, even as an eight-year-old, over the east coast flood disaster which claimed many lives. It was close to home for our family and Dad's boss Len Elliott, even though it took place more than 50 miles away.

We had started taking our annual holidays on the east coast from when I was seven years old. Len Elliott would lend Dad a car for a week and we'd hire a caravan called 'Anne' from Mr Adcock, the butcher in Gotham, who kept it at a site in Ingoldmills near Skegness. We'd already spent many happy hours there. All around that part of the east coast was badly hit.

We found out from Mr Adcock that 'Anne' had survived the flood which swamped the coast but Len was told that his holiday bungalow had been badly hit by the floods. He took me along to near Mablethorpe to see what damage it had suffered. It was a real mess. The building was waterlogged and had subsided in places. The whole area had been devastated. I can remember seeing all the debris that had been scattered around. I picked up a forlorn little toy lorry that had been parted from its owner, lying among broken furniture and sodden cushions. Len took it from me and placed it on a hedge that had withstood the sweeping water. "Some lad will be missing that; let's hope he'll find it here," said a melancholy Len.

With confectionary off ration Easter provided Lottie with fabulous revenue as I indulged in copious amounts of chocolate eggs. Before Easter, of course, it was Shrove Tuesday, or, as we called it, Pancake Day. I could take or leave hot cross buns but I adored pancakes. After school Mum would have this wonderful ritual of making – and tossing, to my delight – her delicious pancakes. We'd get through a huge stack of them, complete with lemons and oranges and sugar, sometimes syrup. Even Dad couldn't wait to get home for his share. As an aficionado of all things sweet, those days are still etched in my memory. The tradition of pancake tossing seems to have fizzled out. Every year without fail, Movietone Newsreel ran a clip of ladies in a race, tossing their pancakes as they ran the 100 yards.

Spring 1953 was also when Mrs Armstrong's 'Tadpole Party' was inaugurated.

Mrs Armstrong was your archetypal colonial. She was brought up in the Raj in India, used to servants, cleaners, gardeners, that sort of thing. She lived in a huge manor house a couple of orchards away from our house. My grandmother Ciss was her housemaid and when I was younger I would accompany grandmother during her duties. I loved exploring the many rooms in the house. My favourite room had been the nursery and play room. It had an enormous rocking horse, a wonderful fort with soldiers, old cricket bats, balls and an extensive library of children's books. I spent hours in the nursery. I learnt to avoid the rocking horse like foot and mouth, though. My first experience of it led to quite a spill. Having got up a good head of steam I nearly rocked myself out of the nursery window.

For several years I was given roaming rights of the sprawling house, gardens and orchards. It was bliss. I had a great fascination for the garden pond and what lived in it. I particularly liked dropping my net in during the spring and fishing for tadpoles.

Mrs Armstrong decided I should share my pleasure with my friends, so she came up with the idea of a 'Tadpole Party'

I was encouraged to recruit around a dozen friends to come to the 'big house'. They were given similar rites of passage as me, allowed to charge around in the orchards and grounds, climb trees and play on ropes and swings that had been set up by Mrs Armstrong's brother.

When fatigue was just about starting to set in for the rampaging band, Mrs Armstrong called everyone to order, using a real megaphone which looked as though it had seen duty on the ramparts at Poona or somewhere, to tell marauding mutineers where to get off. We were summoned to the summer house where all kinds of splendid treats were on offer, sandwiches, jellies, cream cakes, scones and Mrs Armstrong's home-made lemonade and ginger beer. I know I'm sounding a bit like Enid Blyton but that's how it was.

After the wonderful picnic came the party's pièce de résistance: a trip to the large lily pond in the garden, where said tadpoles were flitting about oblivious of the fact they were about to be scooped up unceremoniously by fishing nets and deposited into jam jars. The idea then was to take them home, find them more suitable dwellings, like fish tanks, as we watched them mature. Then, the theory was, they would be found homes in water meadows in Kegworth as they achieved frog status, thus giving us marvellous early lessons in biology.

It never quite worked out that well, although it brought us youngsters hours of fun. My haul of tadpoles, which had to be kept in a bath in dear old Nanan's wash-house because we didn't have suitable accommodation at home, found escape easy and I never did see them reach full maturity. What I can only assume was a sort of Colditz frog tunnel under the bath helped them to freedom to Plummer Lane and on to greater things. We took a dozen of the much larger tadpoles to school to watch them grow and discovered they were newt-poles. One morning we came to school and found they, too, had gone AWOL. We got a lot of satisfaction telling the girls they were on the prowl in the classroom, though. A sudden explosive revelation that a newt was crawling up a girl's shoe brought suitable squeals of terror.

The Tadpole Party survived complaints from mothers whose sons had undergone smelly duckings in the pond through over-zealous swoops for the fattest specimens (no, curiously, that fate never befell me), and went on for a good few years.

Easter time was also a great occasion for the Wesleyan Chapel, with an event called 'Sitting Up' or the 'Sermons', a day of readings, recitations and song. I had to go to practice for weeks beforehand, spoiling my burgeoning career as a sportsman. Going through endless practice in chapel while your mates were kicking a football about was not on my wish list at that time.

Come Sitting Up day, though, I managed to quell my nerves enough to make a fairly good fist of my solo piece and I got an appreciative accolade from the audience in the chapel. My thunder was completely stolen by my brother, though. When the tots did their bit, John was the star. No squeaky lisps for him. He growled all the way through the number in a deep bass voice which sounded remarkable coming from the lungs of a three-year-old. Lee Marvin later plagiarised him in his rendition of 'Wandering Star'.

For once Dad had had to make an appearance at the chapel for this service. In the week before the sermons Mum decided my dad's hair was looking scruffy – he pleaded lack of time to go to the barber's – and warned him she'd attack his locks if he didn't get something done.

I remember poor old Dad agreeing, with great trepidation to allow Mum to cut his hair. I don't know why he trusted her. By profession, as a large brass plaque proudly advertised outside our front door in Plummer Lane, she was a corset-fitter. Not a hairdresser.

Anyway, a brow-beaten Dad settled down in front of a roaring fire and Mum began clipping. She'd never cut anybody's hair before and soon there were yowls coming from Dad as sometimes hair came out in tufts because of a certain lack of sharpness of Mum's scissors and clippers she'd borrowed from one of my aunts. However, the heat of the fire took its toll on him. He'd had a really tough day with the animals and no amount of misdirected clipping could keep him awake.

Well, Mum made a right old mess of the job, cutting too much off here and then trying to even it up there. The result was horrendous. Dad looked as though he'd been attacked around the head by a swarm of drunken locusts. There were lumps and bald patches where Mum had savaged him, all over his head. She dare not wake him up and nipped off next door to confess to her friend Josie, who had to be forcibly restrained from coming in to view the mess.

Dad woke up, flicked out hair from all over his chest and neck and went to inspect Mum's handiwork. A howl from the kitchen demonstrated his evaluation. There was a heck of a barney when Mum plucked up the courage to come home. Trouble was, she kept breaking down in hysterics every time she looked at his bonce.

So it was off to Bill Orme the barber for a rescue job, first thing the next day. Dad didn't dare go to work until Bill had tidied up for him. I say tidied. Dad finished up with a crew-cut. It didn't suit him and you could see cuts and scratches on his scalp where Mum's implements had done the sort of damage a myopic Apache would have wreaked with a blunt tomahawk. He wanted to wear a hat for the Sermons but Mum wouldn't let him.

Bill the barber used to be filled with dread when I hove into view outside his shop. It wasn't me that was the problem. It was the brother I had in tow that Bill feared.

John was perfectly all right until the cape came over him and he heard the buzz of Bill's clippers. Then he turned into a screaming, whirling dervish. There was nothing Bill could do to calm my brother down, no toys, no smooth talk, not even threats. John just howled the place down and wriggled and squirmed in the chair. The only way Bill could keep contact with John's hair and the clippers was for me to try to pin my brother's arms down. It was exhausting and it rarely worked well. On more than one occasion John left with his hair half done. Bill couldn't take any more.

There was a great deal going on in 1953. One great memory was the 'Stanley Matthews Cup Final'. I was football mad. I remember the occasion quite vividly, although I had to wait until the match highlights came on the newsreel to watch Stanley turn the game around. I'd only been able to listen to it live on our wireless.

And about that time came the exciting news that Edmund Hillary and Sherpa Tenzing had scaled Mount Everest.

The biggest event of the year, though, was, of course, the Coronation. Elizabeth II was crowned on June 2 and it was quite a day. We had spent weeks at school building a huge model of the coronation. Nobody could talk about anything else. We didn't have a television at home but we kids all massed around Dunmore's Electrical Shop window in Kegworth High Street, where Mr Dunmore had kindly placed a television in the middle of his display shelves. It was blurry black and white and sometimes impossible to discern the pictures because of the condensation engendered by a dozen eager kids, but we were all spellbound.

The highlight of Coronation Day was a gala and sports meeting on Kegworth's King George VI Playing Field. Well sports loosely. There were 'egg-and-spoon' races, sack races, three-legged races and slow bicycle races laid on in the afternoon.

Curiously, I never once saw an egg balanced on a spoon in an egg-and-spoon race in all my times taking part in them. It was always a potato. I suppose eggs would have inevitably caused a right old mess. An oeuf, so to speak, would have not been an oeuf for long. Three-legged races caused mayhem. Two runners' legs, one right, one left, were tied together with the other two, outside legs, free. The object was to complete a smooth, synchronised passage to the tape, as one. It was not a race that fostered good relationships.

Then came slow bicycle racing. The idea with this was to be the last over the line rather than first. You had to advance in a series of organised wobbles to the tape, no grounding of feet. Those that could balance in limbo best, sometimes remaining static for a couple of minutes, excelled at this.

The alleged egg-and-spoon race heats came first. I didn't make the final. I was too intent on keeping my spud balanced to realise everyone was holding their spuds with their thumbs and leaving me in their wake. The three-legged race was always going to be a trial. My skinny legs were not an attraction when canvassing for a partner. I finished up with a girl who was at least a foot shorter than me. We fell over immediately and by the time we'd managed to get upright and tumble over again, our opposition had breasted the tape. I couldn't even take part in the slow bicycle race because I didn't have a bike, quite a stumbling block to entry.

The sack race was, though, more my forte. I was ace at kangaroo jumping inside my sack and stormed to victory in the final, winning a large Coronation tin of sweets. Heaven.

When the afternoon's entertainment came to a close all the kids were presented with a Coronation mug. Mine only lasted a few weeks. Mum and Dad had a right old row one day and my dad, who could show quite a temper, finished up trashing a tableful of crockery. Among the debris was my poor little mug.

Mum and Dad often used to go at it hammer and tongs, mainly about her continual demands over finding herself a job that was a little bit more demanding and lucrative than fitting plump ladies into tight corsets. He was of the old school that deemed he should be the one who went out to work. Their spats, though, nearly always ended up in laughter rather than tears.

I remember Mum hurling a plate of boiled tomatoes at Dad one breakfast-time. Dad ducked and the tomatoes hit the wall. Mum was highly embarrassed when my brother answered the door to our milkman and, as George ladelled the milk from his churn into our jug, proudly announced: "My mum's just thrown a plate of hot tomatoes at my dad. You should see the mess." No matter how she tried, Mum couldn't get rid of the stain and we couldn't afford to redecorate right away. When my friend Paul Tuckley came to our house for tea I told him it was a bloodstain, leaving it to his imagination on what had gone on between Mum and Dad. Soon there was quite a list of friends wanting to visit the Dabell household to gaze in awe at the stain.

The tomatoes on the wall incident wasn't the only time, by a long chalk, that Mum lost her temper. When riled her Irish blood would boil. One day Dad and his younger brother, my uncle Eric, and two friends were playing cards in Dad's garden shed. They'd snuck away and furtively ensconced themselves in the shed to avoid Mum finding out about their covert activity. Money was a bit tight at the time and Mum didn't want Dad losing any of ours at cards. Anyway, the boys must have been playing for a little while before Mum rumbled where they were and what they were doing. Furious, she stole up to the shed, grabbed a large boulder from my granddad's rockery – and hurled it through the shed window. "Nearly gave us all a bloody heart attack," my uncle Eric told me. "I was holding a full house as well." Dad was led off with his tail between his legs.

You couldn't stop Dad having his bet on the horses, though. I remember the local bookie, Mr Beale, riding around the village on his bike collecting betting-slips and the weekly football pools entries. Mr Beale was never allowed anywhere near our house, however. Dad used to meet him up at his mum and dad's house. I can remember Mr Beale quite distinctly. I used to feel sorry for him because he was always sneezing. It was much later in life I found out he was addicted to snuff.

For my ninth birthday, Mum and Dad allowed me to pick out my first pair of football boots from the fascinating emporium of Saddler Sutton's Cobblers and Shoe Shop. This was a dimly lit cavernous place, with a wonderful smell of leather and saddle-soap that hit your nostrils when you opened the door to old Saddler tapping away on his last. Around him and disappearing into the gloom were row after row of shoes and boots, including football boots. All were handmade by him. I loved the place and would always volunteer to take in shoes and boots that needed mending. This time my visit was more exciting than ever – that heady moment when a lad picks out his first football boots. I fell for a light tan pair that I convinced myself fitted like a glove.

Trouble was, they never really fitted like a football boot. They were fearsome objects, made of unyielding leather with a toe-end which felt like cast-iron. They sported large wooden studs called 'nuggs' which you hammered into the bottom of the boots with nails. No matter how much 'dubbin', a not unpleasant smelling polish made out of some kind of grease (pig? cow? dog?) I massaged into my boots, they stayed as stiff as the day they were bought. They were a little bit tight and chafed the sides of my toes. And with the amount of wear they got, the nugg nails soon started to come through the soles to impale my feet. After limping home with my socks awash with blood I'd hammer down the nails but they soon prodded back out.

Nanan and Granddad always gave me a 'Saturday threepence' apiece, so I decided to buy my own football kit from a jumble sale with my pocket money. I forked out fivepence for a job-lot. The lady selling wanted sixpence but I'd stopped off at Lottie Stockton's for a penny drink. My wistful eyes gained me the knock-down price. I triumphantly took home a voluminous tangerine top which I just knew Stanley Matthews must have grown out of, a large baggy pair of greyish white shorts (Persil and Mum soon had them sparkling white) that easily covered my knees and huge, woolly (rather itchy) red and white socks that ascended well past my shorts-line.

Football was a painful business at the time, and not just for nugg nails. I was drinking water from a glass pop bottle at half-time in one match when a ball got whacked at me. The bottle slammed into my top teeth, breaking off a triangular chunk. As I got older and more self-conscious I would only smile with my lips closed.

Christmas 1953 provided me with one of those memories that stays with you forever. Mum and Dad had bought me my first bike. I'll never forget the wonderful moment when I went down to the Christmas tree. My little red Phillips wasn't brand new but Dad had cleaned it up and checked it out. I'd envied all the kids who had bikes and now I had one of my own. With

Dad running along behind me holding me steady by the back of the seat, I quickly got the hang of things. Within an hour I was flying solo, scooting up and down Plummer Lane. Mum was proud of me but warned me to steer clear of gypsum mines.

Having a bike was a massive boon. The soles and heels on my shoes didn't need mending so often. I went everywhere by bike. It served me well for three years, give or take the odd puncture or displaced chain.

I was soon the master of my bike and I could thus cruise down to Kegworth Station with the lads instead of having to route march.

I was an avid trainspotter, spending hours and hours on the bridge above the station 'copping' wonderful engines carrying the names of far-off places which I'd then locate on the globe atlas in my bedroom. Basutoland, Bechuanaland, Baroda, Bihar and Orissa, Mysore, Gwalior, Kolhapur… I can reel off the names to this day. My favourite name, for some reason, was Travancore. Hadn't got a clue where it was. It sounded like a hill station in the Raj, which wasn't a bad guess. Couldn't find it anywhere on my globe, though. It was always such a thrill to line out with your little ruler a new name in your trainspotting book. Your day was only briefly interrupted by a break to absorb Mum's doorstep sandwiches and chocolate cake. We didn't even protect our 'snap' from the huge smoke furls filling our eyes and ears with wonderful gritty fumes, which signified another prized cop hurtling under the bridge. Not many trains stopped at Kegworth. In fact I think we only had two services a day. Kegworth's stationmaster must have had a cushy job.

As well as the station there was a big marshalling yard just further down the line. It was quite fascinating to break your vigil on the bridge and wander down to see our coalman loading up his lorry from the coal trucks. We were also a bit stupid. One of the more risky activities at Kegworth Station was to nip down before a train came and place a penny or halfpenny on the line. Then, after the train had gone, you shinned down to collect your flattened masterpiece.

Learning the deaf and dumb language from my uncles then came in real handy now that I had two wheels. I used to go on long bike rides with Len Elliott's daughter Kathleen. I idolised her. She was my first real, but unrequited, crush. Kathleen was an absolutely lovely girl but she was born deaf and dumb. While I say having a grasp of the deaf and dumb language came in handy, it also caused me a few problems. I'd whisk up to Kathleen as we rode and try to converse with her. Riding with no hands was rarely successful. Kathleen advised me to keep our conversations to when we'd stopped riding.

I did learn to balance a football on my crossbar and ride in football boots, though. I was by then stark staring football crazy. My Uncle Eric, the youngest of Dad's three brothers, is mostly responsible for my great love of the game. Before he went off to do his National Service I'd sit up in his bedroom with him (he's only around 10 years older than me) and go through all his footie mags, like the brilliant *Charles Buchan's Football Monthly*, and match programmes. I knew a whole stack of stuff about football when I was eight years old. Eric would test me on footballers and who they played for, each football ground's name in Britain, all the teams' nicknames. I reckon I could easily have got on 'Mastermind' when I was nine. I repaid Eric for giving me a vast knowledge of football by running errands for him. My most frequent task was to fetch him 'Carter's Little Liver Pills' from the chemist. I think they were for when he had a hangover.

Chapter 4

OH BROTHER

As 1954 wore on a sense of foreboding gripped my brother. He knew he would be starting primary school in autumn and the idea didn't appeal to him much. I was a little nervous, too. I wasn't sure what he would be getting up to.

He was a really happy kid but he had his demons. One of them was that he had grown to hate bath time. It wasn't because he subliminally recalled once nearly drowning. John had a dread of 'used' water, the type his elder brother had already bathed in.

As you will recall, we didn't have a bathroom at 1 Plummer Lane. Our bath night at first took place in the living-room. The big zinc bath that hung up outside the pantry area at the rear of the house would be hauled indoors and large steaming hot jugs of water, boiled on our gas stove, would be poured into it. Norm was then sent in first, under orders to swill himself clean as quickly as possible. Then John had to follow me in.

Bath time had taken place in front of a roaring fire in the house when John was tiny and I was too young to be fussed about being seen in the buff. It got more complicated when Mum and Dad had a shed built on some land they rented right outside our back door. This was in effect our bathroom, although it also housed bikes and garden tools. Mum did her best to smarten it up, putting curtains on its windows for privacy, but it was still a shed. It could be darned cold in the winter, even with a little paraffin heater on the go on the coldest days. The very act of transferring from the bath into the house was a test of speed and acrobatics as you tried to dive into the warmth without tripping over the bits and pieces in the shed and the back doorstep. If you took your time the icy air would hit you in your nether regions, even with a bath towel wrapped around you.

Sometimes, by the time my brother's turn came to bathe the water temperature had cooled to just above character-building. So, more jugs of the hot stuff would be added. John hated this process, often jumping up like a scalded cat as the added hot water took effect. It also stirred up the grimy suds elder brother had left behind. Now he had reached the grand old age of four, John would protest. I can see the disgusted look on his face as he dipped a toe in. It made me fairly punctual when given a set time for bathing. I knew I was under threat to go in after John if I was late from football, say, and I could only imagine in horror what he might have been up to in his trousers.

The outside toilet up the yard had no light. We used to go through the motions by candlelight much of the time. Knowing how squeamish I am over these things, it must have been sheer purgatory as I got older. In the winter it could be quite entertaining, though. Dad used to scoop out the innards from a mangold wurzel and cut out a hole in the front of it in the shape of a large mouth, then place a lit candle inside. It was a pleasant, and safe, way of lighting up the loo. The wurzel lighting didn't sit well with my brother, though, when he was finally old enough to be left in the toilet on his own. The mouth on the wurzel would give off a large, menacing-looking, flickering shadow all around the loo ceiling and walls. On his first experience of the wurzel lighting it absolutely freaked out John. A terrified bro. finished up bursting out of the toilet with trousers and underpants around his ankles, convinced he'd been visited by a ghost.

At school we had various 'seasons' for pastimes. Sledging and sliding down a long sheet of sheer ice in the playground highlighted our winter activities. Then there was whip and top season, marbles season, scrabbling for Mr Barker's hazelnuts through the school railings season, things like that.

Marbles was a passion for every boy at our school. We'd carry hefty bagsful of glass marbles, 'mibs' as we called them, sometimes augmented by a couple of Slack and Parr ball-bearings, a prized possession. The object was to scoop in the marbles into a hole from whatever distance you and your fellow protagonists had thrown to. Nearest went first. All the marbles you successfully holed, went to you. It was great when you cleaned up the whole set in one go. No-one had any sympathy for the poor wretch who trudged away with an empty bag and had a quiet sob in the toilets before going back to lessons. We were ruthless. I was pretty proficient and regularly carried around a bulging bag.

My acumen was due to putting in hours of marbles practice with my brother on our rug at home. It had circular patterns on it and one of them was picked out as the 'hole'. Unfortunately we used to choose a similar target each time we played. Eventually our target turned into an actual hole. Senior son warranted a clip round the ear and my marbles were confiscated. Luckily the hole was at the far end of the rug and Mum was able to hide it under a chest of drawers. When she wasn't around, we used to drag it from under the chest, bring out my replenished stash of marbles and resume normal service.

Having a rug with a hole in it must have been pure hell for Mum. She took house-proud to the highest level, about Everest level in fact. We were never allowed to have shoes on in the house. All footwear had to be left inside the doorway. And even if we were clad in our slippers we had to try to avoid stepping on floors and carpets too much. Just a micro-dot of mud or soil brought out the vacuum cleaner.

We learned to 'hover' when we were indoors, sitting with our feet up while Mum cleaned like an over diligent minesweeper. When I first started visiting friends' homes I'd hover in their houses, too, much to their mums' bewilderment.

I could only imagine what agony Mum must have been going through the day we arrived home and found a pigeon had infiltrated our pantry. It had made a right old mess. A bag of flour had gone over and there was bird crap and flour dust all over the place. A couple of broken jars and their contents were on the floor. Mum made a grab at the errant bird but only succeeded in turning it into a mini-whirlwind. Between them they scattered a box of dried peas, adding to the carnage. Dad feared that his neatly-built shelves were at risk so he tried to ensnare the bird with a saucepan. All he succeeded in doing was knocking over a jar of pickled onions. I tried to do my bit, snatching and diving at the pigeon, but with no success. Mum finally collared the frightened bird. I pleaded with her not to wring its neck. She marched up the yard and released it to flutter up to the rafters of one of the stables. It wouldn't be house-breaking again. Mum came back and played merry hell with Dad and me for leaving floury footprints all around the kitchen and living-room. All my brother was worried about was whether the bottle of cod liver oil had survived.

It was quite a trial sharing a bedroom with my brother. For some reason, I guess it had to do with Dad's line of work, he was always afraid of animals coming into his bedroom. The usual cry was 'Mummy there's a moo cow.'

It turned into bedlam one night. I'd dropped off to sleep when John suddenly started screaming blue murder. Not a moo cow this time but a cat. I shot over to quieten him when suddenly a screeching moggie leapt at me from his bed. The darned thing must have crept in unnoticed and was aggrieved at a warm and comfy spot for the night being denied it.

The cat certainly wasn't ours. Mum refused point-blank to allow us to have a cat or a dog. She wasn't having her house messed up by any animal. That included pigeons.

For a fortnight I did have my bedroom to myself again. I caught impetigo, coming out in myriad itchy blisters and blotches that turned crusty and sore and had to have this purple lotion put on them. After the initial discomfort I was quite happy with my impetigo. It got me off school for a while and I fancied I looked not unlike Geronimo when I studied myself in the mirror.

When John did start school I didn't have a lot of contact with him during the day, but I was still expected to be his guardian after school and at weekends. That often led to trouble.

On one occasion John was a real pain in the backside. We went for a walk with a friend down to the River Soar, right after Sunday School at the chapel. The river was an area supposed to be only visited with adults but it had a magnetic effect on us youngsters.

We were watching the barges and narrow boats chugging up and down and the water fowl skitting about the river when John decided he had to go. Not just a little go but a big jobbie. 'But we've got no paper for you to wipe on, you'll have to wait,' I bleated. He couldn't wait. It was probably the apples we'd scrumped before Sunday School. He was at least old enough to get his trousers down. I was in a right panic. I ran off to get paper. I saw a man and woman doubled up on a narrow boat and asked them for help. They produced a toilet roll, still almost helpless with laughter at the sight of brother with bum in the air waiting for brother.

Well John had made a right mess. All over his trousers. I had to go back and get a carrier bag from my saviours on the boat to put the trousers in. They also gave me an old towel to cover John's modesty. And that's how we turned up on our doorstep. A cowering elder brother and shivering towel-swathed sibling. John got plunged into our tin bath in the shed (see what I mean? Wouldn't want to follow on from him!) and I was sent to bed with no dinner – after a fair old clip around the ear. My punishment was not for John's misery, in fact I'm sure I heard Mum and Dad giggling for ages, but because I'd been down to the river and taken him with me.

One of my great loves was the cinema or, as we called it 'the pictures'. My theatre of dreams for years was Kegworth Picture House and its successor after a revamp, the Kim Cinema. This wonderful establishment stood on the Derby Road, just down Plummer Lane and up the road about 100 yards, very convenient. From the age of eight or nine I'd been allowed to go to the Saturday matinee on my own.

The matinees were a sort of organised bedlam. Only very brave or hard-up souls served as cinema managers, usherettes or ice cream ladies on a Saturday afternoon. Around 50 kids would flock to the picture house where there was a two-hour show that started with a cartoon, involving such stars as Bugs Bunny or Popeye. That was followed by some riotous comedy like an Abbot and Costello romp or perhaps something anarchic that went down really well, such as the Bowery Boys. Then came the highlight of the programme, the serial. We'd sit transfixed as Tarzan or Nyoka took on all sorts of unsavoury characters who were usually hell-bent on upsetting the jungle life in their search for riches. Cheetah, Tarzan's amazingly astute chimpanzee, was a particular favourite. I can hear Tarzan yodelling out as he swung from branch to branch, even now.

All the serials, such as Batman and Flash Gordon, would end on a cliff-hanger. You were certain your hero was a goner. That was of course to get you back at the cinema the next Saturday – when somehow the finale from the previous week had changed, so Batman or Flash avoided going to their doom. Charlie Chan, the inscrutable Chinese detective, was another favourite. Charlie always had a pearl of wisdom, usually imparted to 'honlable son': "Owner of face cannot always see nose", was one of Charlie's classics I remember to this day, "Curiosity responsible for cat needing nine lives" was another and, my particular favourite, "It is fool in hurry who drink tea with fork". We all tried to work out what Charlie boy was talking about. All was revealed the following week.

The cowboy serials were a particular delight. We would watch in sheer wonderment as the Lone Ranger and his pal

Tonto raced across the prairie at an unbelievable rate to escape the baddies. It never crossed our minds that the film had been speeded up. When the Lone Ranger warbled 'Hi oh Silver' at the end it brought the house down.

Occasionally there was our own Western saloon brawl, too, when the older and more rowdy of our fraternity got slung out by the cinema manager for a variety of offences: smoking under the seats, pinching smaller children's sherbet dabs, chucking bubble-gum down from the 'gods' and, the more brazen lot, grabbing at girls when the lights went out. This latter group were a little hapless. A: They didn't really know what they were trying to grab. B: It was too dark to see what they'd grabbed. C: They wouldn't know what do when they'd grabbed it.

I remember my cousin Robert coming to stay with us. He was a real tough hombre was Robert. We had our share of bullies at Kegworth and there was one particular nasty piece of work who was the self-styled king of the Saturday matinees. He was very loud and often spoiled the serials by shouting out what was going to happen next in the plot or just being a big-mouth in general. He got brought to book by Robert who marched up to this yobbo's seat and grabbed him by the scruff of the neck. Despite being shorter, Robert marched him outside and gave him a fearful seeing-to. He never bothered the stalls again.

Just to show how strong and resilient Robert was, when he was 15 he was run over and crushed by a double-decker bus in Nottingham town centre – and somehow survived. The accident ended his hopes of playing top-class rugby but he battled back from injuries that could have left him in a wheelchair for the rest of his life.

Then, of course, my brother had to come along with me to the 'flicks'. John became as avid a fan as me for the cinema but his first appearance in the stalls was quite an ordeal for me. Someone lobbed a lump of bubble-gum down from the balcony and when we came to leave I found John's hair had a huge, sticky, unyielding lump in it. Well, it became unyielding because of his howls of pain as I tried to free him from his lump. I couldn't take him home like that. We had to stop off at Nanan and Granddad Dabell's en route. Try as she might, Nanan couldn't get much of the gum out of John's hair. She used all her old wives' remedies: hot water, vinegar, even lard. But there was nothing else for it but to cut out the offending gum, which should have been patented as the forerunner of Super Glue. She did her best to camouflage her work but she couldn't disguise a rather large hole in John's locks. John had got it in the head and I got it in the neck. Perhaps I shouldn't have had mild satisfaction when, to John's dismay, we had to make a trip to see Bill Orme to get some uniformity to his hair.

Our wireless in the corner of the dining-room was another great source of entertainment. A good deal of the time Radio Luxembourg (208 – the Station of the Stars) was on. Thinking back, Radio Luxembourg was a slick forerunner to all the stations we have nowadays. In the '50s it was Hughie Green and Carroll Levis running all the talent contests which have now been superseded by such shows as 'The X-Factor'. Hughie's 'Opportunity Knocks' was a great favourite with our family and neighbours, although I much preferred 'People Are Funny': members of the public carrying out ridiculous tasks. Come to think of it, there wasn't much difference between these unfortunate souls and some of the so-called talent that was knocking on the door of opportunity.

And talking of opportunity, one of my vivid recollections of Radio Luxembourg was the endless advertising by one Horace Batchelor.

Horace tried to convince everyone that winning the football pools was a doddle if they followed his 'Infra-Draw' method. Punters were urged to send our money to Keynsham, Bristol and just to make sure we didn't get it wrong he spelt it out like a school teacher: "K-E-Y-N-S-H-A-M". I don't think he worried Littlewoods unduly but he had more air time on Radio Luxembourg than Bing Crosby.

On Sunday evenings I would join in on the 'Ovaltineys' club song with gusto ("We are the Ovaltineys, little girls and boys...") when the music request programme came on, even though I much preferred Horlicks to Ovaltine. Later on, Uncle Mac replaced this show in my heart. John and I used to sit quiet as mice on Saturday mornings in front of the wireless, listening to old Mac playing music requests. He had one of the most soothing voices you have ever heard. Looking back, he would have made a wonderful cinema matinee manager.

Uncle Mac played lots of our favourite tunes, although 'The Runaway Train' was definitely not one of them. It got played every Saturday morning without fail. "The Runaway Train came over the hill and she blew... (cue urgent whistle)..."

Would these sadistic kids never get fed up with it? John and I always wanted to hear 'Riders in the Sky', a ditty about ghost cowboys herding stock forever in heaven, by Frankie Laine, but it only got an airing once in a blue moon. We were always going to send in a request for it but I don't think we ever did. I'll never forget Uncle Mac's immortal pay-off: "Goodbye children (satisfied little pregnant pause) ... everywhere". "Hmm. Goodbye Uncle Mac. Send that blinking Runaway Train to the sidings."

Now I think back, I missed a trick. There used to be a radio programme called 'Smash Hits'. You sent in your request but it wasn't like any other request. For this show you picked out a record you hated. The disc jockey read out your particular dislike for the number, played it, then smashed it on air. I'm sure it was all sound-effects but it did give the participants a great deal of satisfaction. I distinctly remember the song 'Naughty Lady of Shady Lane' getting smashed. Uncle Eric protested at that. It was his favourite song of the day. It would have been very satisfying blowing the whistle on that darned 'Runaway Train'.

One record that Mum wanted smashing was not even by a human. My brother and I loved the 'Singing Dogs', a medley of songs sung by, well, dogs. We pleaded with Mum and Dad to buy it, especially as it had 'Jingle Bells' on it, a treat for Christmas. Now I don't know how the dog handler (one Carl

Weissman I have found through research) did it: 'Yap, yap, yap; yap, yap, yap; wuff, wuff, wuff, growl, growl...' went the first verse. We loved it. We played it time and time again, astounded at how the conductor got the dogs to come in on time. We imagined these doggies sitting obediently, barking when the conductor's baton pointed at them. The canines' role was a bit more convincing than the bark on 'How much is that doggie in the window?' which was obviously humanoid. But it was probably about as genuine as a ventriloquist's dummy talking on radio.

Another one my mum got fed up with was: 'I tawt I taw a puddy tat, a cweepin' up on me...' another novelty song of the time, about a cat stalking a canary. No, Mum didn't care for woofers or tweeters.

Chapter 5

LOBBY LUD? NOT ME

We had some great holidays when I was a kid, mainly staying in Anne the caravan, driving there in whatever car 'Uncle' Len Elliott lent Dad. A car was the height of luxury for the family. Dad had to get by with a bicycle or 'Shanks's Pony' for the rest of the year.

Mum decided she wanted to learn to drive on our 1954 jaunt to 'Skeggy'. It's rarely a good ploy for a husband to teach a wife to drive. And this was especially the case with a headstrong woman like my mum. This particular holiday was close to calamity when Mum nearly drove Len's Standard Ensign into a fen while negotiating the bridge at the entrance to the caravan site. It was the first time she had been behind the wheel of any vehicle and Dad had given in to her requests to have a go at driving. After that little escapade Dad never let Mum drive again. They had a right old barney. It was all Dad's fault, of course. John and I cowered in the back of the car, at least relieved that Dad's panicked grab of the wheel had saved us from a ducking in the dyke.

That same year I decided, now being ten years old, I needed to be a little independent and, having mastered the basics of swimming, was trusted to gang up with a group of slightly older youngsters at Skegness swimming pool. Mum and Dad went off for a look around the shops with my brother. At an appointed time I waited for my family to pick me up to go back to the caravan. I stood there, shivering for an age. No sign of them. In fear, I decided I'd missed them and struck out for the caravan site, about four miles from Skegness, just in my woolly swimming trunks.

Apparently Dad had found a bookmakers and the last race, on which he was on the winner, had run late. They were held up further while they had another fall-out. Both of them were distraught when they couldn't find me, particularly Dad. They scoured the pool, pier and beach but Norm was nowhere to be found. Mum tracked down a friendly policeman on his beat near the pier. "Have you seen a little boy who looks like me?" she put to the constable. Amazingly, he knew exactly who she meant. He told my parents the last time he saw me I was heading up the road to Ingoldmills. When they picked me up I was blue.

They always say that every cloud has a silver lining, though. Dad had a terrible conscience about me being left stranded. The next day he bought me my first real cricket bat. For a year or so I'd relied on a solid, one-piece, job which my granddad Dabell had carved from an oak branch for my uncles. It was a much practised art to even lift it, but you couldn't half whack a ball with it. Now I had a sprung, willow job. It hardly left my side for the next couple of years.

About this time there was this big advertisement in one of the daily newspapers: "Spot Lobby Lud and challenge him to win a golden prize of £10", it read.

Well, £10 was a small fortune then. Mum and Dad didn't need much persuading to give this a go when they found out Lobby Lud was going to be in Skegness on one of the days of our holiday. You had to be holding a copy of the newspaper and challenge Mr Lud with the words: "You are Lobby Lud and I claim my £10 prize".

So on the day in question in Skegness we scoured the promenade and arcade looking for Lobby Lud. Mum and Dad weren't sure whether they would know him if they saw him but I knew I would.

Mum and Dad soon tired of staring at blokes, worried that they might be accused of something, but I wouldn't give up. Suddenly I spotted this chap who just had to be the mysterious Lud. He was even walking along with a copy of the newspaper in question in his hand. I pulled at Mum's arm and implored her to challenge him. She wasn't convinced. I took over, running up to him, stopping him in his tracks and confronting him with the magic words: "You are Lobby Lud and I claim my £10 prize". The man jumped, visibly startled. "No I'm not. I'm Arthur Bagguley", he replied. Mum grabbed me by the arm, apologised profusely to the Lud lookalike and frogmarched me away.

I was sure I'd spotted Lobby at least five times that day, but each time I got dragged away before I could put in my challenge.

The rest of the six-week school summer holiday of 1954 was like most of those before it for me. I was really lucky to have a multitude of friends, even if they did come under a strict regime whenever they entered through our door. And with the building of the M1 motorway and the upgrading of the aerodrome to an airport still many years away, Kegworth and its countryside was an absolute joy for us boys to grow up in. We would roam for miles and miles, not doing anything in particular, talking boys' talk, which usually involved football or something that had been on at the pictures that week. We did a lot of digging and scrabbling about in ploughed fields, unearthing all kinds of things, horse brasses, bits of farm implements, things like that. We never did find the cache of Roman coins we were looking for though. The nearest I came to finding anything really old was a 1563 silver piece. It was a singleton. My friends and I nearly dug up a whole field trying to find more but without any luck. I announced to Mum that I was going to be an archaeologist when I grew up. She was really satisfied. She'd thought I'd said architect.

Swimming was another holiday pastime. Loughborough baths were not an option because of needing finance for a bus to the town and for the sessions in the pool. So we kids would often force ourselves on the owner of a large house next to the river Soar which was down a dusty old road from Kegworth called Lock Lane. The owner, a Mr Rayer, had his own swimming pool, with water sluiced in from the river. It was open house at Mr Rayer's all through summer. He was such a patient man. We'd tramp down the lane with our costumes rolled up in a towel, never in any doubt that we'd be soon splashing around in his pool. It didn't matter if he was gardening, cleaning his windows or cooking in his kitchen, he'd invariably drop everything and open up his summer house for us to get changed for a swim.

There was fun to be had close to home, though. The large yard just up from our house served as a football pitch for me and a whole host of friends, with a goal painted on the boundary wall between the yard and my friend Martin Sibson's home. Whenever a ball got kicked over the wall, though, I had a problem. Mrs Sibson, a real virago of a woman, didn't seem to like kids, although I'm sure she just about tolerated Martin and his elder sister, Carol. There was no chance of our ball being thrown back over the wall. The wall was much too high to climb over so it involved a nervous trip around to the High Street and a request to retrieve the ball. It was all right if just Martin or Carol or Martin's dad was around. They would allow me to nip up and get the errant football. If Mrs Sibson was on the prowl, though, no chance. So to avoid being rebuffed and the match in the yard in danger of coming to a premature end, I often used to sneak through Sibson's gate and, despite being terrified of being spotted, grab the ball and run for it.

Eventually, Mrs Sibson suspected I was sneaking in and out quite frequently and put a stop to it in no uncertain manner. The Sibsons bought a dog. They called it Shirley. Now any animal called Shirley must surely be a loving family pet with a waggy tail and docile demeanour. This one was a ferocious, snarling, black-eyed devil of a dog, an Alsatian with attitude. It was tied up but had plenty of play on its chain to get within a few inches of anyone brave or daft enough to try to skirt its area of attack. I would freeze as Shirley lunged at me in fury when I'd edged inside the premises, hoping against hope that her collar and chain held. I just know that Shirley's main aim in life was to tear out Norman Dabell's throat.

Once we were playing cricket in the yard when Uncle Alec, my granddad Elliott's cousin, came to visit. He got bored with all the chat going on between the grown-ups in the house so came out and asked if he could join in. He attacked the ball with gusto, sending it crashing through Aunty Hilda's kitchen window. Hilda was the Lane's infamous harridan. She was apparently carving a cucumber at the time and nearly sliced off a thumb when our ball smashed her window. The match ended and Alec had to fork out two pounds for a glazier.

After the summer holidays I moved to Bessy Mawby's class, the third-top tier of the school. I really liked her. She had style did Bessy. She had a new car, a great big Vauxhall, at the same time every year. The best thing about her, though, was her understanding of my big problem at that time, earache.

My ears and sinuses had troubled me from an early age. I have had numerous ear, nose and throat operations all my life. My first came in autumn 1954 when I had my tonsils and adenoids removed at Nottingham General Hospital. The horrible liquorice-like smell of the mask they put over my face to administer ether still fills my nostrils to this day when I recall the operation. That nagging pain in the throat remains stark in my memory and the awful moaning of the poor lad in the bed next to me. He was 13 and had calmed my fears before the op. Now there he was suffering so badly. I forgot my pain when the huge scoops of ice cream arrived to cool my tonsils. The operation did nothing for me, apart from the legacy of a loud snore in later life. It certainly didn't reduce my torment with earache. As winter took hold it would often come on while I was at school and Bessy could recognise the signs. She'd give me hot milk and put drops in my ears while Mum was called to take me home.

We had a day of sheer delight as the winter term of 1954 ended – no lessons, just making decorations and singing carols. Davy Crockett was all the rage by then and among our

Christmas gifts John and I were bought imitation coonskin caps. John lived in his, even went to sleep with it on. I put on a show of embarrassment when donning mine, as, rather sniffily, I felt I should at ten years old. But secretly I thought I looked every bit the western trailblazer when quietly admiring myself in the mirror.

Somebody bought Mum and Dad a bottle of 'egg flip' for Christmas and Mum celebrated another successful delicious Christmas dinner of succulently cooked cockerel, with a couple of glasses of the creamy liquor. She didn't realise its potency. She was no drinker. The game of 'blow football' we played on Christmas afternoon descended into total disarray when a giggling Mum, with the tail of my borrowed Davy Crockett hat continually slipping over her nose, kept blowing the ball off the table and stopping the match while we looked for it under the furniture. Then we had to use the reserve ball because she trod on the first one.

As the snow hit us in early 1955 it was again time to get the sledge out that Dad had built. By now I had a brake man: brother John was reluctant but eventually he warmed to the task. We were both pretty fearless. He would hang on to the back of the sledge for dear life with his death-defying brother shouting out instructions and warnings as we hurtled down Kegworth's 'Cresta Run'. This was a terrifying descent on paths and over roads from the top of the new council house estate to the bottom.

Mum, though, had started to suspect I was behind John's scuffed shoes, caused by him acting as a brake. I found him a new job. He made an ideal goalpost. I could keep an eye on him because he would stand obediently throughout the match, honoured to be given such an important, erm, post. It also kept him off the field of play where there was the danger of him being floored by the melee of players that hurtled around the pitch.

Winter was when Mum seemed more determined than ever to stuff me with hot food, despite my reluctance to eat it. Mum's always been one for eating correctly. She did her best when I was a kid to try to enhance my feeble, skinny frame by resisting what would now be called junk food. Chips were banned in our house, despite Dad occasionally locating the fryer and placing it optimistically on the stove.

I used to come home from school for my lunch, usually taken with either a customer from my mum's corset fitting business or friend or relative. I was terrible with food, though. It was largely to do with stealing around to my grandmother's house. I couldn't resist her mouth-watering sandwiches, made with lovely soft bread with crunchy crusts, oozing with fresh butter and her wonderful jams made from plums, black and red currants or damsons, all gleaned from my uncles' orchard. Tucking into her treats meant I rarely wanted to face what Mum considered the wholesome and nourishing food she served up.

On one particular day, Mum had cooked liver. Liver! I hated the stuff. I whinged and whined, pushing the two pieces of liver around my plate, avoiding it as if it were laced with arsenic. Her patience thinning, Mum told me I was going nowhere until I'd cleared my plate. That would mean I'd miss afternoon arithmetic, hardly a threat. Aunt Nancy, our guest on this day, unwisely said, "Oh leave him Sheila; he obviously doesn't want it," looking over sympathetically at the wretch about to retch.

After all the meals she had battled with me over the years and all my rejections, Mum suddenly snapped. With staring eyes and a very worrying growl, she picked up the two pieces of liver and slapped me around the ears with them. "Why don't you want good food when it's put in front of you?" Her terrified elder son dived under the table. One look at Aunt Nancy's blanched features and Norm scuttling for the kitchen door seemed to break the spell that had hold of Mum, though. She dissolved into tears of frustration, blubbering about me facing an early death from malnutrition, TB or any disease she could think of that might be brought about by not eating my liver.

It proved something of a watershed. From then on I had to eat school dinners, even if I was only a stone's throw from home. It didn't get much better for me, however. I couldn't stand the stuff they served up at school either. Frequently on the pain of punishment, like standing in the corner of the dining hall with my school mates catcalling me when they got the chance, I left most of my meals on the plate. When I could get away I made for Nanan's jam doorsteps.

I ate everything but the right food in those days. Take the times we used to 'house sit' for Dad's employer Len Elliott and his wife Beatty. Len always used to leave us a huge box of liquorice allsorts to make the stay a little pleasanter for we kids. John and I would absorb the whole box, something like 2-3lbs of liquorice allsorts, during the stay. No wonder I've always been very regular. What with apples, pears, plums, black and redcurrants, damsons and gooseberries and Len's liquorice allsorts, it's no real wonder.

I really had the team spirit as a youngster and I had become a very keen 'Wolf Cub'. In fact I eventually made 'Seconder' of my little 'Tawny Owl' group of six green-clad neckerchief-and-woggle adventurers. Our annual Wolf Cubs 'Bob-a-Job' week in the spring was always one I looked forward to, perhaps rather masochistically. This was a week when you carried a card with little squares on it to be filled in by householders for whom you did some casual work. For this you would be paid a shilling, hence the bob a job. At the end of the week, the Cub with the most bobs on his card was feted long and loud by his pack.

I would often team up with Paul 'Tucker' Tuckley, a bespectacled dead-ringer for the 'Milky Bar Kid' but with a nefarious streak in him. We would take on any task going – some of them sheer hard labour imposed by unscrupulous lazy slave-drivers. We would run errands to the shops, dig and weed gardens, wash cars, vacuum clean, walk dogs, that kind of thing.

Paul and I were hard and willing workers but sometimes a little accident-prone. I remember dislodging a ladder while were gardening for one lady and watching in horror as it crashed down into a large cucumber frame, smashing the glass pane cover into pieces, terminating the growth of several of her husband's prized cucumbers and marrows. Bless her, the lady still signed our card and gave us a bob each. She did, however, suggest we might bob past her house next year.

There would be an outcry from the health and safety wallahs nowadays. Ten-year-olds cleaning windows with rickety stepladders would be a no-go. Wielding fairly sharp tools would be off-limits, too, I guess.

Paul and I were given a job of tidying up some lawn borders at this otherwise rather neat house. We set to with gusto. After our first forays, though, we decided the edge wasn't straight. So we dug out more earth to make it level. Still not straight. No good doing a poor job or we might not get our bobs. We had numerous goes at carving a straight line but we were never satisfied with the result. When we finally, exhausted by now, called a halt to our digging we looked out on a border that was nearly as big as this bloke's lawn, we'd hacked so much out of it. And it still looked like a dog's hind-leg. When the chap came to inspect our work he went mad, barking at us about how he'd now have to either seed or turf over our efforts. The miserable wretch not only refused to pay us but left us in fear by threatening to report us to 'Akela', our wolf pack leader.

We had other means of raising money, not philanthropic either. One of Tucker's schemes to get us well-heeled was the beer-bottle-return scam. We often used to play at the back of the Flying Horse pub, not far away from where Paul's parents ran a fruiterers/greengrocers and little coffee bar and he knew there were crates of empty beer bottles at the back of the pub. We would shin over the pub back wall, gather up a few bottles then take them back and get a penny for a half-pint bottle, tuppence for a pint.

Another of Paul's schemes lay in his own backyard. After fruit was delivered to his mum and dad's shop there were always several orange boxes lying around. When they reached a reasonable total a chap on a contract would come along and load them up in a van. That was after Paul and I had skimmed off the pick of the bunch when his parents were busy in the shop or coffee bar. We did a roaring trade selling orange boxes at a shilling a go to rabbit hutch builders, for instance.

One of our favourite scams was 'Red Apple' (you knock on the door and run like hell), played by most of the village lads at that time. Tucker and I were pretty adept at it, both being fairly fleet of foot and with the 'Knowledge', knowing exactly where to find all the bolt-holes in Kegworth to deny pursuers. The roof of the old school-hall in Dragwell, was our favourite, if slightly dangerous, sanctuary. We never played Red Apple in the summer. In the winter it took a little while for victims to tear themselves away from the fire.

Chapter 6

LOST IN MUSIC

At Easter time I was down to sing in a concert. Mum was my escort when we turned up at the Baptist Chapel in Kegworth. My tummy was full of butterflies but I was determined to do well. "It's rather strange that Mr Maltby (our choirmaster) isn't here," said Mum when there was no sign of my music mentor at the chapel. "Not like him to be late. I bet you were expecting to do a bit of rehearsing."

Soon the concert was in full swing. A kindly man in a tuxedo jacket came over, asked me my name and what I would be singing. He seemed satisfied with my answers. I was told I would be on at the end of the concert.

My turn on the stage arrived. I had no idea how I was going to sing without Mr Maltby. But before I had chance to worry any further the grinning tux hit the ivories. He took a little while to bond with me as I at first faltered badly, looking out at a sea of unfamiliar faces. But we both rallied. I drew polite applause at the end of my number.

Afterwards, the concert organiser came over to me. "That was really good," he exaggerated, "but no-one seems to know anything about you. Are you sure you are at the right place? You do know there is a concert being held this afternoon at the chapel just down the road?"

At the other chapel, Denis Maltby had waited in vain for his protégé. By the time Mum and I got there his concert was just about over. I had been put down as a no-show and never did get to sing at the right venue.

Regrettably for me, my dulcet tones had been noted by a music teacher, one Fiddler Brown. No, he wasn't that way inclined. He got the name Fiddler because the violin was his weapon of choice when nurturing young voices like mine.

Desperate because of missing football with my friends I was sent to singing practice with Fiddler, an almost stone-deaf octogenarian whose favourite punishment when you hit a bum note was a whack around the ear with his bow. Mum was left fearing I'd developed dandruff early in life but the white flecks on my collar came from the resin shed by Fiddler's bow as it caressed my lugholes frequently. I didn't dare tell Mum. She'd have given us both a clip around the ear – me for not singing properly and him for child abuse.

Well he was finally satisfied with my efforts and entered me for a concert at nearby Castle Donington, a sort of East Midlands Song Contest. I can tell you now I picked up nil points for presentation but ten out of ten for effort.

My proud Mum and her friend Josie from next door sat in the audience as Norm and Fiddler went through their paces. "This is going to be something special," Mum predicted to the awestruck Josie, whose kids wouldn't dream of getting up on stage in front of about 100 people. "Norman's been practising hard for weeks now; he's got such a sweet voice. There's ten bob for the winner."

Of course Fiddler accompanied me on the violin. I'm sure he forgot to turn his hearing-aid on. The performance was a Dabell debacle. After a nervous start I accelerated well in front of Fiddler's hideous screeching and scraping and tried to slow down to meet him. Seeing the panic in my eyes, he must have guessed he was lagging and speeded up, easily overtaking me. I then hit the throttle to go gamely after him but failed miserably. The second quatrain of our piece ended in some disarray. I looked out at my mother and our next-door neighbour down in the stalls for sympathy and rescue, but none was forthcoming, mainly because the pair were doubled up, helpless in their seats. No time to feel betrayed. Fiddler was off again. His bow produced an even more terrifying noise on its way to our crescendo, this time some seconds after me. What with Fiddler's screeching violin and my panic-stricken warbling, it brought the house down. If I'd been up there telling jokes it couldn't have been more triumphant. They were not laughing with me, though. It was sheer humiliation and ended my professional singing career right there and then.

During the year I'd moved up to the penultimate class at Kegworth School which was run by Mrs Bradshaw, a huge Dreadnought of a woman who everyone referred to as 'Fatty'. She put the fear of God into us youngsters. Our class brought her down to size, though.

That early summer two school trips took place. The first one was to Liverpool. The idea was to show us physically the Lancashire port we had been taught about. It was exciting enough just to travel up on the train and our constant chattering and escorted trips to the lavatory must have been wearing for Fatty. She had to be in several places at once, too, to make sure none of her charges pulled the communication cord. There was no open carriageway in those days and the kids travelled in three separate compartments with a 'trusty' pupil expected to keep a semblance of order.

We arrived in Liverpool without the train needing to make any emergency stops and after a little lecture at the docks we all boarded the overhead railway. It was a wonderfully exciting experience looking down at the big ships in the port.

After our trip around the docks it was time to allow us to let off a little steam when we were taken to New Brighton, the Liverpool holiday resort that was tremendously popular in those days. Mum and Dad and Nanan and Granddad Dabell had provided pocket money so I was one of the lucky ones to be allowed to go on the paddle boats. Remarkably I was not the paddler who was missing when Fatty counted heads following our little trips on the boating lake. I can't remember now who the miscreant was. I was happy it wasn't me. The prodigal paddler was discovered fast asleep in his boat, no doubt worn out by his efforts. Fatty didn't hesitate to dust pants in days when corporal punishment was dealt out by irritated school teachers.

Later on in the year the whole school visited Hampton Court. It was a great day out. Fatty wasn't shredded this time because she had assistance from two student teachers. It took all three of them to locate one errant schoolboy who was discovered whimpering under a hedge he'd tried to force his way through when lost in the maze. Come to think of it, I'm sure it was the lad who went missing on the New Brighton boating lake.

Soon my most formative time at Kegworth County Primary School was upon me as I moved from Fatty Bradshaw's flock into the top class.

Polo Smart – he earned the sobriquet because of his habit of constantly sucking on that little mint with the hole – was our teacher here. Polo was a tall, slim man – well skinny really – who had a lot of strings to his bow. He taught everything from English to arithmetic, history to science and art (more of that later). He was a thoughtful cove who was rarely seen in class without his hands in his pockets. Older pupils reckoned he was an expert at 'pocket billiards'. I had no idea what they were talking about but it seemed funny.

At first I got on well with Polo. I was an enthusiastic listener in all his lessons and I loved his spelling 'Bees' for instance. But then I found myself in his bad books.

I was a pretty useful high-jumper and expected to do well when the North Leicestershire Inter-Primary Schools Sports took place in the early summer of 1955. Polo was my high-jump coach and put me through my paces as a hard taskmaster in the month leading up to the sports meeting which took place at Shepshed, a small town near Loughborough. I was quite keen on high-jumping and practised hard at home, balancing a cane on any sort of platforms that came to hand. Clearing the bar and landing correctly was pretty well a must because there was no sand pit to jump into like there was at school. The landing area was solid dirt and debris in my uncles' backyard. I'm sure this enhanced my jumping. However, there was no Fosbury Flop in those days. You would have broken your back in the sandpit on the school playing-field, let alone my uncles' back yard, doing the Fosbury Flop. I used the 'Straddle' method to beat the bar and as I became more proficient in later years, the 'Western Roll'.

We all packed into the bus for Shepshed, Polo quite confident his protégé was going to acquit himself well.

Now Shepshed was the home of my Great Aunt Nan, one of my favourite people. She used to come over on the bus from Shepshed every Saturday to do her bit cleaning and cooking for my great uncles. We could hardly wait for Aunt Nan to get off the bus. She always visited the sweet-shop before coming to Kegworth and her large Gladstone bag always bulged with goodies.

The high-jump competition at the sports meeting was not due until the afternoon so I decided to go and seek out Aunt Nan, having been encouraged to do so by my nanan. I was quite proud of myself when I knocked on a door and Aunt Nan answered. She really was thrilled to see me standing there. I suppose that was because the only time she normally saw me was at the head of a sizeable gaggle waiting for her to unpack her bag on a Saturday morning.

I explained why I was there and Aunt Nan sprang into action, whisking me into the kitchen. I'd only pecked at my packed lunch, so when Aunt Nan said she had a nice pudding boiling and I must have a portion, there were no protests from me. It was a wonderful treacle duff and I got a mammoth lump.

When I set off back for the sports field it was as if I had a diver's boot lodged in my colon. There was still an hour to go before I had to perform. "Where have you been Dabell? You should be practising." The words of my coach Polo. I got down to it right away – literally.

My leaden stomach proved a huge obstacle to getting airborne. I had a torrid time practising, crashing into the bar on heights I would normally sail over. By the time my name was announced I had also lost confidence. I was hopeless. I didn't even make third place. Polo was livid. He must have gone through two packets of Polos in his frustration.

Polo soon got his revenge.

The class had a painting lesson and I was quite proud of my efforts. We were told to put our names and addresses on the bottom in case any of our efforts were chosen for a North Leicestershire Exhibition at Kegworth Library. I saw Polo pluck my painting out of the bunch and hold it up. "Now what do we have here? 'Ducks on a Pond'. It's by Norman Dabell, 1 Plum." I'd run out of space at the bottom of my painting and carried my address over onto the back. From then on I was called 'Plum' Dabell, a nickname that stuck with me for years in Kegworth. My unfortunate brother was accordingly called 'Little Plum'.

One weekend, worms became my bêtes noires again. Len Elliott lent us his Standard Vanguard and Dad took us on a weekend to Hunstanton. We had often looked across the Wash at the Norfolk resort from Skegness. I wished it had stayed the hazy little vision we had seen so many times. Worms! Hunstanton beach was covered with worms. I suppose they would have been lugworms. I refused to walk over them down to the sea. I never did get a dip.

Amazingly, though, not long after Hunstanton, I summoned up enough courage to hold and stroke a snake.

One Sunday we were taken to Long Eaton Methodist Chapel to listen to a talk by George Cansdale, he of the warm voice and love of animals. I was spell-bound by Mr Cansdale's lecture, accompanied by a slideshow of all his travels. The real big moment came, though, when he produced two creatures for us all to see hands-on. Now a bush baby anyone can handle.

Everyone wanted to cuddle the lovely little bundle of fur with beguiling eyes. When Mr Cansdale pulled out a python it was a different matter. I nearly vomited as he brought it nearer and nearer our row. But even in those days I was imbued with a sense of bravado, along with a dislike of being labelled a scaredy-cat. My brother had quickly run a hand over the python before recoiling to the back of his seat. I had to show I had the bottle to do better than that. Somehow holding back my fear I held it and stroked it, relieved and, I must say, intrigued, to find it wasn't at all slimy like my enemies the worms. Apparently my face was as white as a sheet. But Mum wasn't half proud of me. She knew what it had taken for me to pluck up the courage to touch that snake. It didn't, though, lessen my abhorrence of earthworms. In fact I seem to remember waking everyone up that night suffering a nightmare about a very large worm eating my arm – but looking up at me with beguiling eyes.

When it came time for our week-long summer holiday, we had a change of venue. Instead of Skegness we were heading for Rhyl in Wales. I knew where we would be going because my uncle Eric told me that Randolph Turpin, one of his boxing heroes, lived there. Mum and Dad had decided, on the recommendation of my Uncle Douglas, a fervent Welshman, we should try Rhyl.

It was a calamity. All the family got raging sunburn, so bad that John and I couldn't bear to have anything touch our skin. The whole family suffered. We limped back to Kegworth feeling very sorry for ourselves.

When we arrived home it was Wakes week. The Wakes, a travelling fair with all the bells and whistles, would set up in a field above Slack and Parr's, just across the Derby Road from the bottom of Plummer Lane. Everybody loved the dodgem cars but my favourite was the cake-walk, which nearly ripped your kneecaps out as it spewed you along on juddering conveyor-belts. There were chairo-planes, fast revolving swings that catapulted you out further and further as the roundabout gathered speed. Eventually you were almost horizontal, stomach heaving and eyes screwed shut with the g-force. There was the 'Caterpillar'. This was a mind-boggling ride based on a small big-dipper but with the added novelty of a huge cape coming down to cover its customers when the ride reached its top speed. The cape's appearance would be accompanied by a shrill hooter which had the girls in hysterics. This was not the least because they were having to fend off amorous farm labourers and Slack and Parr mechanics, seizing their chance under cover for an illicit quick grope. Candyfloss, toffee apples, hot dogs, somehow staying where they had been crammed, added to the jollity.

This time there was to be no fun of the fair for John and me, however. We were grounded because of our sunburn. The thought of all this fun we were missing, though, caused my brother and me more agony than sore bodies. We listened enviously at the shrieks of delight, the pop songs of the day bellowing out, the whirligig-type music, the growls of numerous generators, drifting up the lane and in through our bedroom window.

I couldn't bear it. I had a shilling I'd been given by doting grandparents pitying my peeling back. This princely sum could buy approximately one ride, a few goes at trying to win a goldfish and either a toffee apple or a candyfloss. There was plenty of scope too, to perhaps double my money on the penny slot-machines first if I felt like throwing caution to the winds.

We had, though, been given explicit instructions not to move from bed, where we lay embalmed in calamine lotion. The call of the wild Wakes proved too much. Promising to bring back my brother a toffee apple if he didn't alert the guards, I gingerly, wincing with sunburn, pulled on my shirt and shorts and crept downstairs. I quietly eased myself out of the back door and sneaked past the sitting room, where Mum and Dad were listening to the radio and nursing their sunburn, too. I made off down Plummer Lane to the fairground.

All was going well. I did make a profit on the slot-machines and my sunburn was almost forgotten after a go on the cake-walk. I knew I didn't dare stay out too long because

Mum was bound to check up on us in the bedroom but it was hard to drag myself away. I had bought the toffee apple and had just a penny left to buy three quoits – rubber rings – to try to win a goldfish. The idea was to throw the ring over a hook to reap your reward of a little fish contained in a small plastic bag of water. There was only a one in a thousand chance of your aim being good enough to perform the winning move. The hooks were some ten or twelve feet away and craftily positioned so that it would take the guile of an expert dart thrower to home in successfully. It hadn't crossed my mind how I would be able to explain a goldfish in a plastic bag even if I did somehow beat the odds and actually slotted a quoit over its target. Undeterred, I was on my second throw, face screwed in utmost concentration, hand steady and eye fixed on target when suddenly an inimitable angry voice behind me completely froze me in chuck mode. Quoitus interruptus. Mum had discovered my empty bed. The game was up. My bottom, one of the only two parts of me that had not seen sunlight in Rhyl, soon became as hot as my shoulders.

Straight after Wakes Week it was always Kegworth Carnival, held yearly at Hallstone Meadow, near the roaring weir of the River Soar. It made for a wonderful extravaganza. There were such thrilling sideshows as the 'Wall of Death', motorcyclists zooming several yards off the ground around circular walls. Then there was the 'Rotor', where you were pressed up against a spinning wall by centrifugal force as the floor slid away – even your hair stuck to the wall.

On their way to the carnival site, huge leviathan traction engines, billowing out smoke, driven by industrious mechanics in grubby overalls pulling levers and frantically winding wheels, were the star attraction of the carnival. They would feature in a huge parade through Kegworth. Before them would come the marching bands: girl pipers in kilts, for instance. Then it would be kids and adults in fancy-dress, followed by a procession of colourful floats, lorries and carts dressed out in special themes. The Red Lion Pub regulars appeared several years running as, loosely speaking, Jayne

Mansfield lookalikes. Even then I worried about men cross-dressing. They didn't care what anyone thought by the time they were into their sixth pint on the float, big busts and bright red lipstick and all. The more flighty ladies of the village used to have a ball too. They were nearly always St Trinian's schoolgirls, showing rather more leg than was usual at that time, sporting racy underwear, garters and fishnet stockings. That always ensured a good following of local stags through the carnival gates. Commanding most attention of the floats was the lorry pulling along the reigning Kegworth Carnival Queen and her attendants. It used to be quite a competition, did the voting for Carnival Queen. Village vendettas still resurface periodically to this day, begun initially by one girl being chosen over another to be queen. I can still see the girls now, giving that royal wave as they passed through the village. I remember a lot of their names. I wonder what they look like now? My uncle Eric went out with a good few of them. He was quite a Don Juan in those days.

While the carnival was a memorable day in the earlier part of the summer then everyone also looked forward to Kingston Show, which took place around August Bank Holiday weekend. The Dabell family would walk the two miles or so to the grounds of Lord Belper's Kingston Hall. It was one of the biggest agricultural shows in the country, with most of the top show-jumpers coming to Kingston to ride. Dad sometimes used to take the show-jumping horses, so we would all pile into his wagon and get free entry. I think he once did some work for Pat Smythe, one of the top names in show-jumping in the 1950s. I don't think she was very nice to him. He was always willing her to fall off her horse.

Chapter 7

POLO'S NOT ALWAYS SWEET

Moving up to the Scouts from the Cubs during winter 1955 proved impossible. It was all about reciting the Scouts' oath. I'd always thought the Cubs' motto had been a bit silly. The Akela used to bark "Dyb, dyb, dyb" (do your best) and a couple of dozen enthusiastic little lads would squeak back, "Akela we'll dob, dob, dob" (do our best). The thing was, though, you could hardly forget that motto, especially as everyone joined in.

When it came for me to trot out the oath on the day of my elevation to Scout, though, it was all much more complex. With the commissioner for the area inducting us, I got stage fright, couldn't remember the oath properly. With my mind going blank, when ordered to say the oath, I froze. I just stood there, mouth agape, lips wobbling, looking a right chump. There was no way in if you couldn't say the oath. I was told to return to my Cub squad and that I'd have chance to have another go at the oath which was something about doing your duty to God and either the Queen or the team, couldn't quite remember which. I never did try to recite that oath again though. I'd taken to playing football in earnest.

I didn't think I could take any more of my old football boots, though. They were crippling me. I'd done my best to bash down the nails that had come up but to no avail. The nails stabbed into my feet and turned the inside of my boots into a blood bath. I'd hobble gamely on, trying to ignore the pain. Mum, worrying I might get gangrene, persuaded Dad that they should buy me some new boots.

I was bought a really brilliant pair. They were 'Tom Finney' boots, marketed by England and Preston North End's star, wonderful sleek black jobs. I imagined myself emulating Tom. He was one of my heroes. (Little did I know that I would one day be made a cup of tea by the revered winger at his hallowed Deepdale before I covered a football match there as a sports reporter. That's another story.)

The new boots did the job, lifting my game to new heights. Polo Smart, my long-suffering mentor at Kegworth School, was also the school's footie coach. You wouldn't have thought Polo (who looked just like Arsène Wenger) would have taken any chances with me again after the high-jump humiliation but when we were going through trials for the school football team, he seemed to see great potential in me. It might have been further revenge, however. He decided to put me in goal. Everyone else was loath to play there. I was keen to play for the school, however, so last line of defence I became.

I didn't make the best of starts in the school's first match of the season, allowing a ball to go through my legs into the goal. Even though we won, I thought that was that. Polo persevered with me though.

It was Polo who had provided my choice of Leicester City as the football club I would follow – an interest, nay obsession, that I have to this day. Polo would wax lyrical about Leicester when we played and practised and, sometimes in lighter moments, in class. I hung off his every word and decided I, too, would be a Leicester fan, rather than opting for the Nottingham clubs, Forest or County, or Derby.

I became a Leicester City fanatic by the time I was 11, catching the local coach from Kegworth market place with a dozen or more grown-ups on a Saturday, including Polo, for my fortnightly trip to Filbert Street. Once there I would go off on my own to watch, entranced, every kick and move of the game before meeting up with the adults, who sometimes had to sit patiently until I emerged from the throng leaving the ground.

When I got back home I would recount the details and incidents from start to end to anyone who'd listen.

One person who wanted to listen was my uncle Ron. Plummer Lane was a little commune for the Dabells and Ron, Dad's eldest brother, and Auntie Hilda lived up the path from my grandparents. Ron was very henpecked. He was not allowed to go to football matches. He used to hide next to his shed, pretending he was gardening so that Aunt Hilda would not suspect he was not hard at work, and listen avidly to my match report. I always got a thrupenny bit for my trouble (I don't know how he managed that because I think Hilda used to relieve him of his wages on pay day) but I would willingly have done it for nothing. My knack of memorising sporting details was, thus, honed early and has definitely been a great boon in my sports journalistic career.

As end of term approached I was chosen to play a leading role in our primary school Christmas production of 'The Pied Piper of Hamelin' by Robert Browning (no happy little Puss in Boots or Jack and the Beanstalk pantomime for us; we were at a tough school). I was to be one of the town fathers that did the dirty on the eponymous musician. I always had the words in my head perfectly – until it came to recite them. There was no problem with the acting, just freezing on my lines or getting them back to front.

My efforts only caused hoots of derision amongst my fellow thespians – so I had to go. My understudy got the job. I was given a new role: one of the rats. It was a non-speaking role. All I had to do was run about the stage a bit, waggle my whiskers and then fall into a mock-up river.

Mum and next-door-neighbour Josie came along to the show. I'd been too ashamed to tell Mum I'd got the sack. They spent the evening waiting in vain to applaud me. It was no surprise they didn't spot me. I was wearing this huge rat's head.

You can't keep a good man down, though. I was persuaded to go solo by the chapel choirmaster for the Christmas Eve carol service. I don't know why I agreed to do it. I was always so stressed out before my solos. The carol service was no exception. Nerves had got a hold. I was going to have to stand up and sing in front of a huge crowd in the chapel. What if I forgot the words? I spent some time practising in my bedroom. I couldn't eat, but that was normal. I wasn't a great eater anyway. Mum decided I needed cheering as well as feeding up. She brought out the chocolate log she'd, as usual, baked for me for Christmas. No matter how I felt I couldn't let that chance go by.

As the service started my stomach was churning. Our choirmaster, Denis Maltby, was such a kind man, though. He gave me a big beam of encouragement from his organ below me as I stood up. My nerves receded a little as I began my solo – "Once in Royal David's City" – and I soon rose to the occasion. Unfortunately, the chocolate log rose to the occasion too. I'd just got past the point where I'd needed to go up an octave or two, "With the poor and mean and lowly", when up came the log. I had to take an almighty gulp. Denis looked at me in panic. Down went the log again. I breathed out and continued "Lived on earth our Saviour Holy". I got through the rest of the carol without any more interference from below. When I received decent applause all my nerves disappeared. I could easily do it all again I felt. Mum was really proud of me. She didn't know how close I'd come to decorating our organist with her chocolate log.

At Christmas my wonderful new football boots were joined by my very own football, a real leather lace job which served me well for a number of years. Its life, though, was nearly cut short by the village bully called Tommy. He used to roam around Kegworth looking for trouble. Not with kids his own age but like Paul Tuckley and me who were at least five years younger than him. We were always falling foul of him, having sweets or marbles taken off us by way of an arm lock or a punch in the stomach.

Then Tommy made the mistake of trying to harm my football. Tucker and I were just setting up a goal down at the recreational field just below the school when the dreaded Tommy suddenly burst up through the hedge from the ditch behind us and pounced on my ball. He demanded something or other or he'd burst it. Normally we would have just given in but this time we weren't standing for it. We were enraged. We ran and grabbed him. We wrestled the wretch to the ground. Paul had got a length of chain in his pocket with a lock that he'd normally use for his bike. Revenge for all the cowardly acts he'd perpetrated on us over the years gave us strength. We dragged him over to one of the stanchions that held up the swings, wrapped the chain around his wrists a couple of times and manacled him to the bar. Then we grabbed the football and ran off, leaving an apoplectic Tommy bellowing at the top of his voice that he was going to kill us when he got free. We went home. Apparently somebody found him about an hour later, lying whimpering by the swings, wrists red-raw from trying to extricate himself. He had to be freed by hacksaw. We never had any trouble from him again.

Because of spending so little time at infant level, it had a knock-on effect and I was well ahead of normal primary schedule. Subsequently I had to spend a little extra time in Polo's class before taking the eleven-plus examination to try to win a scholarship.

It inevitably turned lessons into a bit of a bore at times. My concentration was never at its best towards the end of my time at primary school. I much preferred pulling Carol Sketchley's pigtails or sneaking a bite out of the chocolate cake Mum had packed up for me for my break. Flicking saliva-soaked blotting paper with a whippy ruler was something else at which I gained a great level of competence. I didn't dare do those things while class was taking place, rather when we were supposed to be working on our own while, I think, Polo nipped out for a fag.

Polo, though, used to sneak up to catch me out. The door would suddenly shoot open just as I was in mid-act of some felony, designed to cheer up my classmates, for instance the time I'd stood up to conduct the orchestra that was playing on the loudspeaker in the classroom. When Polo swooped in, there was Plum, rather stupidly with his back to the door, wafting his arms about like Sir Malcolm Sargent. When my classmates stopped laughing and buried their heads in their desks I knew I was in trouble. I was ordered to stand out in the corridor, sent on my way with a cuff around my ear. That became a regular punishment. In the end, it seemed, Polo only had to look at my face and think of some excuse to send me out of class.

It was the devil's own job to avoid the headmaster if he happened to have left the sanctuary of his study for once. If he saw pupils standing outside the classroom and felt the crime was bad enough, he'd add to it with a good dusting with a slipper or, if the transgression was major, the cane.

I became quite a furtive child, nearly always prepared for the worst. While serving my time outside the classroom I would sometimes slip away to the toilets (not allowed unless it was break time without explicit permission) when I knew the headmaster, a burly individual from the old school of zero-tolerance discipline called Roberts, was on the prowl.

I was once stranded, however, with no chance of avoiding old man Roberts. I had to think on my feet. As his stentorian voice announced his imminent arrival around the corridor corner, I picked up a milk crate filled with empty bottles after morning break, lying outside the classroom. I could only hold on to it with great difficulty and Roberts took pity on me as I struggled up the corridor with it. He strode into Polo's class and ordered another kid out to help me carry the crate, advising Mr Smart that it needed two to do the job if one of the hauliers was as skinny as me. Polo was totally nonplussed. He didn't grass on me, though. Good old Polo.

Kegworth School had had a pretty good football season, challenging strongly for the North Leicestershire League. In the event, we finished runners-up behind the much bigger and stronger Shelthorpe school. We also made it to the 1955/56 season Pollard Cup final, again against Shelthorpe. I choked like a good 'un.

I'd been brilliant in the lead up to the final, saving a crucial penalty in the quarter-finals and pulling off a couple of spectacular saves in the semis against another much stronger and bigger school.

When it came to the final about hundred spectators watched the game. It started brightly enough but as things began to go wrong for me – a missed cross and a dropped save – I went to pieces. We went from 0-0 at half-time to losing 5-0. I was awful, even being responsible for a penalty. The defeat was all down to me. My uncles, Eric, who was home on leave, and Alf, the second eldest of the four brothers, after whom I got my second name, had come proudly along to watch their nephew. They slunk away ashamed well before the finish.

Polo was so mystified with my performance he could hardly speak to me in school the Monday after that Saturday final. "What was up with you?" he rapped at me. "Every time I looked at our goal you were either biting your nails or picking the ball out of the net." All I could do was whisper, "I don't know." The jitters were to grab me on countless occasions when playing in goal over the years – one minute brilliant, the next a bag of jelly.

Give Polo his due, though. He still thought I was a pretty good keeper and put forward my name to play in goal for the rest of the league against the champions. I played a blinder. There weren't many spectators that I knew at Shelthorpe.

Even though I spent a lot of time standing outside the classroom, I was on top of my game as the eleven-plus exams came along. Plum Dabell wasn't expected to pass but I was determined to succeed to show all those people who thought I hadn't got a hope (not, incidentally, Polo Smart) of going anywhere but to Castle Donington's secondary modern school. I passed, and, apparently, with flying colours.

With the eleven-plus successfully accomplished the question of where I would further my education was argued long and hard by Mum and Dad. I had a choice of Loughborough Grammar School or Loughborough College. Dad was all for sending me to Castle Donington Secondary Modern, his old alma mater. It wouldn't cost the earth.

Mum wouldn't have any of that. She favoured the grammar school and so did I, as most of my friends who'd passed the exam were going there. Mum raided her lifelong savings to buy everything I was going to need, including a charcoal grey suit for the winter and spring, and dark blue blazer for summer, shirts, ties, caps, socks, new shoes, gym gear and sports gear. It must have taken up all her savings.

Dad did have some input into my education, though. He decided that if I were to go to what he called 'School for Snobs' then I should at least learn a little bit about his interests. He had a passion for animals and farms, despite the torment cattle-lorry driving gave him. His plan was to have enough money to set up a proper smallholding, not just dabble with livestock his family wouldn't allow to be killed. He was determined that I should have similar interests, so he decided that I should spend a week of the summer holidays before I started at Loughborough Grammar School on my Great Uncle Tom Cran's farm in Northamptonshire.

I can see Dad's satisfied smile as he dropped me off with my little suitcase at the top of the lane leading down to the farm. Little did he know that in two days he would be picking me up in shame.

I was desperately homesick and disliked intensely being away from my friends, from cricket, from Kegworth. Although I knew my relatives it was all very strange. Dodging cow-pats in the yard was not my kind of fun. I did strike up a friendship with my cousin Sheila, though.

On my first day at the farm I invented haystack bum-sledging. This involved hauling yourself up the huge hayricks in the barns and then scooting down them on your bottom into a bed of hay. It was similar to the fun we'd had in previous summers when a whole gang of us used to make for the 'Stoney Holes', an old quarry in the north of the village. There we'd plunge down a gulley in the quarry on pieces of zinc panels. My hay chute was far less dangerous. That was until I gave a nervous Sheila a helping shove when she was teetering on the edge of the rick. With a squeal she took off and descended quite fast in a blur of flailing arms and legs. Unfortunately she got deflected in her flight and landed, not on the cushion of hay I'd laid out but on more firma terra. She bruised her coccyx quite badly. Sheila was banned from playing with me.

I thus had to amuse myself as best I could on my own. I soon got bored watching the cows being milked. I wandered off into the orchard next to the farm and discovered a lovely little tinkling brook. Soon, though, I got tired of spotting sticklebacks and decided I'd build a dam. It was rather a good one, too, even if I said so myself. I went off to supper very satisfied with my efforts.

I was awoken at the crack of dawn the next day by a terrible commotion. Outside the house it was all hands to the pump – literally. My dam was very effective indeed. I'd turned the water course and the stream had found a new route. The farmyard was flooded. Dad was asked to come and collect me as soon as possible.

During the summer as I waited with great expectation to join my new school, I entered into the world of commerce. I took a job as a general help and delivery boy for Kegworth Co-op. A bike with a heavily loaded grocery pannier above a small front wheel half the size of a normal wheel, needed a muscular young Adonis to control it. Stick insects like me had to suffer frequent crashes. I often had to own up to butter packs that had suffered GBH, numerically disadvantaged dozen-egg trays, smashed jam jars… that bike was lethal.

It wasn't just the delivery rounds on the bike that caused chaos at the Co-op, though. My first day was a bit of a trial inside the store. A lovely chap called Harold Large was put in charge of me and instructed me on using a chute to send potatoes down from the store-room in the attics above, to bags down below. "Right Norman, you go on up to the store room and drag a sack of potatoes over to the chute and wait for me to call up. When I've got the delivery bag ready down below, I'll shout to you and then you let the spuds go. Whatever you do don't let them go until I'm ready to collect them underneath and only let them drop slowly."

With very little muscle in my puny arms it took all my might to pull over a two stone bag of potatoes to the top of the chute. I undid the bag and wrestled it into position, waiting on tenterhooks for the call from below. Suddenly the sheer weight of the sack proved too much for me to hold and it whipped out of my clutches. Down hurtled dozens of potatoes at a rate of knots. I heard a muffled shriek above the pounding of potatoes making their break for freedom. I raced down the steps and found hapless Harold sprawled out, surrounded by spuds. He had not quite made the chute end with his bag and a frantic dive to rescue the situation had only resulted in him being assaulted by the King Edwards.

Well, despite that particular mishap and the broken eggs I was still paid ten shillings at the end of the week. Having heard about my misdemeanours, my mum did not believe I could have earned that much. She marched me around to the Co-op office to make sure my salary had not been some mistake. It was rather humiliating.

I can still remember our Co-op dividend number from the 1950s. It was 10800. And I remember the curious system of payment by customers. Everything was cash, of course. Your bill was totted up and then the shop assistant put your money into a brass cup above the counter, switched it closed and then pulled a lever down to send it hurtling along a line to a telephone-box type cash office that would nowadays be christened the Tardis. Your money was taken, change, if any, and receipt, were placed in the cup and it was swished back to the shop assistant and waiting customer. That was all before the work study bods moved in. It was a particular delight on a busy day at the Co-op watching the brass cups skimming along their lines all round the store like crazed metallic mosquitoes. You never saw the cashier, locked away in her box. I was sure we had a trained octopus working for us until one day I actually spotted the unfortunate employee, a middle-aged woman, staggering out of her office at the end of the work day, hair plastered with perspiration and eyes that looked like one cherry and one apple rotating on a fruit machine.

Thursdays were a great adventure at the Co-op. That was the day deliveries of pre-ordered groceries (the forerunner of internet shopping) were done by lorry, with an affable chap called Les driving. I used to sit on the back of the lorry and do the delivering. Once, Les hit a bump on a farm track and actually spilled me off the lorry to lie in a heap on the road (placed there by an incontinent cow). It was only when Les drew up to the farm he realised he'd lost his running mate.

Les spent a lot of time studying horse racing form in the *Sporting Life* and smoking while on his rounds and that made him apt to be a bit absent-minded. He would park the lorry when we came to a delivery address and get out his tin of Old Holborn. He'd roll himself a fag while reading the runners and riders at Kempton Park while I did the delivery.

After a final delivery of the day once, he'd thought I was aboard when he drove off but I was left stranded at a farmhouse way out in the country. I was only rescued after the farmer phoned the Co-op to tell of my plight and Les had to come and fetch me.

Conscious of how much of a struggle it was to afford everything that was needed to start me at my new school, I decided I had to do my bit on a regular basis. I took on the job of newspaper delivery boy at seven shillings a week. I would rise with Dad at about 5.30am and bike down to Station Road and collect my newspapers, then start my round at 6am.

I saved most of my wages, foregoing my daily fixes of Crunchies or peppermint creams. I needed a new bike. My old Phillips was now too small for me and it was a Herculean task to ride it with a heavy paper bag over my shoulders. It was almost impossible on Fridays when I had to also deliver all the bulky weekly magazines, like *Farmer's Weekly*, *Angling Times*, *Radio Times* and *TV Times*.

Seeing my predicament, Mum and Dad broke the bank to buy my new bike. It was a beautiful metallic blue Raleigh with proper gears.

The bike was something of a little reward. We had had a telephone installed by Len Elliott (Kegworth 410), so that Dad's boss could get in touch with him if an urgent job came up when Dad was at home. Dad hated the phone and one of my household duties was to answer it. Sometimes it went off when I was alone. Bearing in mind that telephones were not so common in houses in those days, I dreaded the sound of the bell, worried that I might get instructions wrong.

When I was over the fear of the phone though, soon I was making calls myself. That often led to confusion.

Mum: "Call your brother at Hudsons; his tea's nearly ready."

Me: "Is that you John?"

"Yes." (Wary voice on the other end.)

"Well it's time for you to come home."

"Come home?" (Perplexed voice on the other end.)

"Yes, come home."

"But I am home." (Even more perplexed voice.) Hastily replaced receiver.

I had found the number in the telephone directory and thought I'd called the house where my brother was playing with a friend. I had the surname right but the number wrong. By a chilling coincidence the person on the other end of my call was also called John.

Several years later I found myself good friends with this same John. I couldn't resist it. I revealed to him one day: "The family's really spooked. We keep getting these mysterious calls telling us we have to 'come home'. It's frightening my mum." Soon there was a rumour going round that Kegworth telephone exchange was haunted.

Chapter 8

MAKING UP THE NUMBERS

I was full of trepidation in August 1956. It was as if my carefree boyhood days were over as I was escorted to Barton's bus station by Mum to catch the double-decker school bus which was to take me to Loughborough Grammar School. I clambered on board, very self-conscious in my charcoal grey jacket and grey short trousers, new, well-polished shoes, with a new satchel on my back.

Kitting me out at Coleman's school outfitters and buying a complete set of encyclopaedias (down to a smooth-talking books salesman on the doorstep) had broken the bank. So Dad had finally relented and allowed Mum to take a job as a waitress at the Oxford Café in Long Eaton. It was the only way my parents could get by as I started at my new school.

My first day at the school in the picturesque Burton Walks was a huge trial for me. I was all right on the school bus because many of my friends who'd also passed the eleven-plus were on board. But at the school we were separated. I was put into '3a', the form considered the top strata of first-year boys. I felt really uncomfortable. Most of my form were non-scholarship boys from seriously wealthy families whose parents were paying for their further education.

Our first task was to copy down our timetable for the week, forming squares for each lesson. Horror of horrors, I found out the school week wasn't over on Friday. We had lessons on Saturday mornings. Why hadn't somebody told me about this before I decided on grammar school? This was supposed to be offset by having Wednesday afternoons off. As my time at LGS wore on, though, school became a six-day week.

Maths, taught by a gentle soul with a quiet voice called Mr Trowbridge, was my first lesson at LGS. It didn't go well. It wasn't just because I didn't really understand what Mr Trowbridge was talking about but what he was saying at all. I was right at the back of the form and just couldn't hear him properly. I would scribble things down in my 'rough book' but when I tried to read it back to do my maths 'prep' (what I'd always called homework), it all looked like mumbo-jumbo to me. My week would start with double-maths and eventually that would leave me a bag of nerves.

Maths was followed by French, a totally opposite experience to maths. Our French master was a rather wild-looking chap with the almost onomatopoeic name of Tivvy. He conducted his lesson at a high decibel rate, ranting loudly at our first hesitating attempts at pronunciation.

In the afternoon of my first day we had a music lesson with an enthusiastic fellow called Mr Shields, who was to become affectionately known as 'Reggie'. He was absolutely dedicated to his job and, as he did on our first music lesson, always went on after the bell had rung. I liked Reggie. He didn't whisper and he didn't shout. And he was very patient with a lad who didn't know a crochet from a quaver but who could sing pretty well.

On the evening after my first day at grammar school, I went through the proceedings with Mum, who had changed her waitress shifts to make sure she was always there when I came home from school. I was still in a daze as I told her about lessons and so was she. It was mostly mumbo-jumbo to her too.

My first attempt at prep was something of a flop and it would lead to more expense for my parents. I had neatly written everything in pencil. The next morning when my work was marked, it was returned with the epic phrase: "3/10 see me". When I did see him, I was swiftly informed that pencil was only for my 'rough book'.

I then had to revert to the old stylus-like pen, which looked like it came from a 17th century monastery, that I had used at primary school. I now blotched at grammar school.

When I told Mum about my problem she was keen to make sure I looked the part at the school she had chosen. She bought me a magnificent Parker fountain pen from Kegworth post office, which must have cost her a good portion of her weekly wage. I have it to this day.

I really struggled at maths, desperately trying to understand algebra and geometry which was all Greek to me. It never did really sink in. I was not going to be a great mathematician. In fact the only way I seemed to be able to get a maths question right was to look in the back of my prep book – where the answers were. I thought it was strange that you should be able to cheat so easily. However, I hardly ever got the important bit in between right: showing how I had arrived at the answer.

English, though, I could do.

My early mentor at Loughborough Grammar School was 'Mooks'. Clara Mulcahy, my first English tutor and my form mistress, was a ferocious-looking little Scots lady, with sharp features and gimlet eyes. But I worshipped her. It is Mooks I have to thank for my love of English grammar.

One teacher I feared, though – everyone did – was Mr Squires. Old 'Squibs', a dead ringer for Chalky White in the Giles cartoons, looked about 102 but he was a real hard taskmaster with a fiery temper which he worked up in no time. Get an answer wrong or make a mistake in a translation, and a piece of chalk would be on its way at the force and successful strike-rate of an Exocet missile. That was when he was the other side of the room. If he happened to be near you when your answer fell short of his expectation or you just didn't understand his often impenetrable growl, he would whack his walking stick down on your desk. If you weren't as versatile as Chopin your fingers could be in great danger. I was greatly relieved when they retired Squibs, dragged him off muttering passages from *Civis Romanus* to the loony bin, I suspected.

My mind was often in a bit of a whirl as I came to grips with a hectic syllabus and, possessing a zany sense of humour, my cause wasn't helped by the group of masters that took them. A couple would have made wonderful 'Spitting Image' dolls. Our geography master, a passionate Welshman, had a huge, glowing, whisky nose, of which Rudolph would have been proud. It would grow brighter in the afternoon when, we all surmised, he'd paid a visit to the pub. Our history master's nickname was 'Neddy'. He had quite a small face but enormous ears and could have had a permanent job playing in the cast of *A Midsummer Night's Dream*. For chemistry it was Wally 'Fumes' Brown. He earned his sobriquet through producing a variety of the most evil and noxious substances in the lab during lessons. Physics was with an earnest master called 'Buddy' Murray. He was a lovely man – when you could see him. He was a very short chap. I think the buddy nickname signified that he hadn't quite fully grown. Biology was taught by a master so directly opposite Buddy that you sensed there was a reason why they never appeared together. His name was 'Tiny' Jules. He was all of six feet six.

Despite coming from a humble home I quickly made friends with my better-off form-mates at school. One of the boys who became a good pal for a time was the only son of a bank manager in the days when that job almost qualified you as a royal. Richard Hayes, a nerdy swot, and me, Kegworth oik and sports mad, were like chalk and cheese, apart from our love of 'The Goon Show' and being the possessors of stick insect frames.

Hayes invited me to stay at his home one weekend. I decided he was a bit strange for when I arrived at his home I found he had been allowed to dig up a formerly pristine back garden and produce a hole of which pit-workers at Gotham

Gypsum Works would have been proud. I can't remember the exact reason for his excavation. I don't think Hayes was paranoid enough to fear a blitz in Long Eaton so had decided to dig his own air raid shelter. No, I think he was a budding archaeologist. I had ambitions in that line myself when I decided on my work career. But this was just a bloody great hole. There was nothing in it at all. A mammoth waste of time, I thought, when he should have been out kicking a ball about.

After an inspection of the hole we were called in to dinner. It was liver! I left nearly all my meal, much to the disgust of Mrs Hayes. She was definitely not amused when I went out to a nearby shop after dinner and bought a box of Maltesers. I offered her one. There was no placating her, though. I was taken aside by Hayes and told how much I had hurt his mum's feelings.

Fully chastened I readily agreed when Hayes suggested we might go and look in his prized hole again. We didn't even scrape any earth to try to find anything, just crouched there. I was afraid a worm might appear. So I announced I was going back up top. Getting out of the hole was really a two-man job. A whole load of earth got displaced as I heaved myself out. Next thing I knew, a white-faced Hayes was scrambling for his life as the hole imploded.

Hayes was incandescent. Two months' hard labour had caved in on him. He blubbered off into the house to his parents. I was unceremoniously bundled on to the bus. "That's what you get for mixing with the hoi-polloi," said a chuckling Dad.

While we had double maths on Monday at school, we had double games on a Friday for last two periods. I loved playing games but not the mad scramble that came after rugby practice. The LGS rugby pitches were a mile or so away from the school, so you had to hurtle back to the changing rooms where you suffered the mandatory cold shower that was supposed to build boys' moral fibre. Woe betide you if you were caught trying to funk out of this torture. It was mayhem. Many was the time I had to hare down Burton Walks half-clothed in a frantic dash for the school bus.

Rugby Union wasn't a sport much favoured by me. Being, let's say, not on the robust side, I suffered plenty of mauling in the mauls after it was decreed I should be a forward because I was quite tall for my age. I wanted to be a scrum-half where I could collect the ball and hurl it out to the backs, using my diving skills as a goalkeeper.

It wasn't being trampled into the mud or the derisory comments about my lack of talent for scrimmaging that caused me woe with rugby, however.

Mum had decided that there was no need to buy me a bag for sports clothing. Her corset bag was big enough to house my games gear. I died a thousand deaths when I got on the school bus with it. Somebody noticed the 'Banbury Corset Company' motif on it. Soon, the whole bus knew about it. Soon the whole school knew about it. I had to stick with it, though. Mum and Dad had spent enough on me. In the end the bag toughened me up as I frequently squared up to lads who took the mocking too far.

I still don't know to this day whether my brother played a part in an episode that could have caused me more rugger grief. John insisted it was he who swapped the footwear in my bag. I'm of a mind that I got confused in the early morning gloom when I was hastily packing my rugby gear before shooting off to do my newspaper round. When I opened my bag in the changing-room I had one rugby boot and one of Mum's black high-heeled shoes. I wondered what on earth I was going to do. Our rugby coach, one Tom Docherty, was a bit of a Tartar. I was fearful he'd make me play with one boot and one high-heeled shoe. Luckily for me, he never discovered my mishap. After my team-mates had been unmerciful in their ragging, we united against the common enemy. We found a spare boot, lost for years in the dust under the lockers. While it hurt like hell because it was a size too small and also had several nails coming through, it was better than having to suffer the Doc's treatment.

I hadn't realised we wouldn't be playing football at grammar school or maybe I would have favoured Loughborough College for my secondary education. However, many of us got around that problem. After a morning dissecting verbs in French lessons or frogs in biology, we couldn't wait for lunchtimes. Then we would play football with a tennis ball on the large asphalt hockey pitch which adjoined the school cricket and athletics field. We were so keen to play we'd often skip lunch to join in a kick about that was at least a 20-a-side affair. Kids would hurtle up and down the tarmac, trying to 'net' inside a goalmouth that had been chalked on an end wall or between two satchels at the other end. I was still wearing short trousers because Mum and Dad couldn't afford to promote me to long ones. I shrugged off the numerous spills on the tarmac that led to asphalt burns and grazes on my knees.

My involvement in the fun, though, was brought to an abrupt end one day when one over-enthusiastic opponent kicked my left thumb instead of the ball. I was taken to Loughborough Hospital and then Mum had to come all the way from Kegworth to meet me in the emergency accident department when it was discovered I'd broken the thumb in two places. That was pure misery for me. No more football anywhere for a long spell, home or at school on the tarmac. And I found out I was allergic to the plaster they encased me in. My whole left hand swelled up and my skin broke out in little bumps that made it look like a plucked pullet's.

In the summer when enthusiasm for tarmac football waned during the cricket season, I would on occasional 'flush' days, wander up to Lydia Abel's Tuck Shop. I wasn't quite as fond of confectionary as sport but, after inevitably only pecking at my food in the canteen, I looked forward to three or four minutes at Mrs Abel's shop deciding what treat I'd spend my meagre pennies on.

I was walking back to school, chewing heartily on a bubble-gum substantial enough to have provided the tread for a motorcycle wheel. Suddenly I felt something hard in the bubble-gum. On investigation I found that quite a large part of one of my molars had broken off. There was nothing for it. I had to go to a dentist.

Mum came to meet me on a Saturday afternoon in Loughborough to take me to a surgery. Before going in she assured me that everything would be all right and it wasn't going to hurt very much, just be a little uncomfortable. I had great faith in her. She hadn't pulled any punches when I had my tonsils and adenoids out. That had hurt a bit, as she had said it would, but it hadn't been the end of the world. Well, the next hour will remain lodged avidly in my memory forever. The dentist, a Mr Smales, who looked more like an undertaker, liked to be referred to as 'Uncle Ken' by his younger patients. He located my damaged tooth and decided it had to come out, saying that he was sure it was just a milk tooth. Uncle Ken was not a dental surgeon, so I think his anaesthetics were fairly rudimentary. The only part of the following procedure I do not recall is where he gave me a painkilling injection. I cannot remember feeling any of the deadening of the gums and jaw that should come before dentistry. I can remember what at the time I identified horrifyingly seemed like a pair of pliers being wielded above my face. Uncle Ken set to with zeal. It was agony. The tooth wouldn't budge even if the dentist did. He yanked and growled concurrently; I whimpered consecutively. Mum, listening outside, was about ready to break the door down. Finally, my tooth gave way and my head jerked back with the sort of whiplash that nowadays would put you in a neck brace. While Uncle Ken gazed first in triumph and then embarrassment at a tooth with roots on it like a prize vegetable, I leapt out of the chair, bleeding profusely from a large hole full of gruesome debris and in great pain. I fled to Mum in the waiting-room. She was full of sympathy. She knew I had been through an awful ordeal. If I had a mouthful it was nothing to what Uncle Ken received.

Having both Mum and Dad working must have been paying dividends because they bought a wonderful present for us all on hire purchase from the Co-op. Our ancient wireless which had served faithfully for a number of years, had finally crackled its last. It had given such treats as 'Workers Playtime', 'Music While You Work' and 'Housewives' Choice'. But now we could listen to records, too. We now had a radiogram.

Mum and Dad listened to records by Dean Martin, Al Martino and Rosemary Clooney. John and I could listen to our favourite radio programme, 'Journey into Space'. I also enjoyed 'Top of the Form', when two schools were pitted against each other. I couldn't wait for Loughborough Grammar School to get chosen but it never did while I was a pupil.

A great ritual came at 6.45pm on weekdays. Before Dad tucked into his dinner the familiar strains of 'Candlewick Green', 'tum-tee-tum-tee-tum-tee-tum-tum-tee-tiddly-tum', would fill the air at One Plummer Lane – warning us all that 'The Archers' was about to start. Everything stopped while we listened to Dan and Doris bitching about the weather or the cows drying up, and haughty son Phil pontificating on politics and the price of pigs. I rarely understood what Walter Gabriel was talking about. He would rasp out his lines (usually preceded by his catchphrase of "Allo me old pal me old beauty") like a sea-lion soprano on 40 a day, augmenting the usual static we suffered on the radio. The Archers was right up Dad's street. But he felt he knew far better how to handle livestock than the show. And he wasn't averse to letting the cast of 'The Archers' know about it. Most nights were spent with Dad giving the radiogram a good old tongue-lashing. He couldn't stand "Phil Archer's blasted whiny voice" for love nor money, but I suspect it was just his old class-war inspiring him. Only once did we get through an 'Archers' programme without a murmur from Dad. It came fairly early on in the long-running serial, the night when Grace Archer died trying to save her horses from a stable fire. Dad loved horses. Mostly he called them names when they didn't win for him but he loved them nonetheless. And the thought of a couple of them perishing in the flames affected him. After the familiar closing bars at the end of the programme he was finally moved to say something. Not about the death of Grace but "the poor horses".

Sunday was best, though, when we were all together at home, either dreaming of Mum's exquisite roast to come or basking in the afterglow of apple crumble. 'Two-Way Family Favourites', with Cliff Michelmore and Jean Metcalfe, began the proceedings. If somebody from Kegworth had a song played it was big news at Lottie Stockton's and the Co-op all week. Programmes such as 'Educating Archie' (now, how did that work? A ventriloquist on RADIO!), 'Life with the Lyons', 'Meet the Huggetts, 'A Life of Bliss' (George Cole's pre-Arthur Daley days) and 'Hancock's Half Hour' followed to give us wonderful entertainment. On Sunday evenings it was 'Down Your Way'. We always hoped Franklin Engelmann would visit Kegworth. Don't think he ever did. If he did, we were out.

Reception some nights on the radiogram could be absolutely awful but we didn't let it spoil our enjoyment. Sunday nights were a great highlight for Dad and me. We never missed 'The Goon Show'. We hung on to every line from eccentric geniuses Spike Milligan, Peter Sellers and Harry Secombe. Mum was totally bemused by it all.

She was definitely not impressed when I bought her a record of the 'Ying Tong Song' by the Goons instead of 'Legend of the Glass Mountain' by Mantovani and his Orchestra, which she had requested for her birthday. She refused to give the 'Ying Tong Song' even one play. I'd paid two bob for it, too. I had to sell it on at a great loss, then go in search of this 'Legend' thing.

Sometimes the reception on the radiogram was so bad that for small breaks we lost it altogether. It was bad enough when it happened just as Bluebottle or Eccles were sparring but for it to go during the horse racing or football results was a mini-catastrophe. It must have been agony for Dad. "Newcastle United... crackle, crackle, silence... and Hove Albion... crackle, silence." "Four-fifteen at Newmarket, first... silence, crackle, crackle, double crackle... silence." From Dad: "Blasted radio".

Chapter 9

NEW BALLS PLEASE

Around my birthday time in 1956 Mum and Dad bought a budgerigar. We had to decide on a name for it. Because it was my birthday I was given first go. I suggested "Arthur Rowley", a perfectly reasonable name I thought, one of my heroes of Leicester City. They decided to call the budgie 'Binky'. I thought it was a stupid name for a bird. Arthur Rowley would have been far more manly for a start.

Binky really liked me but he had a funny way of showing it. Perhaps he was secretly aggrieved that I didn't push harder on the naming front. He'd be allowed out of his cage at night when we were all together at home. His favourite trick was to steal up on me, via the back of my chair and my pullover to take a hold on the back of my neck. As I tried to brush him off he'd then transfer to one of my ear lobes and give it a fearful nip.

He was brilliant, though, Binky, if perhaps a little confused sometimes. He could mimic Mum's voice to a tee. She would shout my brother and me down for breakfast from the bottom of the stairs and Binky perfected her bellow. "Jawman," he would shriek in the mornings as soon as Mum moved away from the oven. He absolutely refused to say "Arthur Rowley", however, no matter how much I repeated it to him, preferring to screech out "Spin a wheel Binky," as if in defiance, whenever I moved up to his cage to chat to him.

At Christmas time I was wary of eating too many sweets. I didn't want to end up at the dentist again. My brother ensured I didn't eat too much chocolate. He bought me an impressive box of Cadbury's Milk Tray. Somehow, though, he managed to ease out the whole of the bottom layer before presenting me with what looked like an unopened gift. He always protested it was the shopkeeper that had diddled us.

Being good at English, history, French and geography, particularly map drawing, didn't seem to impress the school authorities when assessment time came up after the Christmas holidays. Perhaps it was my ineptitude at maths, I don't know. I was told I would be joining 3C in the new year.

When I began the new term of 1957 I found my new form mates in 3C were a tad more relaxed than in 3A. I made friends immediately with a lad from Bunny, near Gotham, called Christopher Dicken. Dicken, for we rarely used first names at school, would become my best pal at LGS.

Johnny Lello was my new form master and the house master for those in the 'C' streams. We all looked up to Johnny. He treated us like young men instead of boys and encouraged a little banter in the form-room during lessons. I already had a love of puns and Johnny encouraged me fervently in this aspect of my English grammar. I've never lost the love of puns and I don't think a day goes by when I don't use one.

I can remember Johnny writing in my report card at the end of term, that I was a "permanently cheerful child, ebullient and volatile". Mum and Dad checked in the dictionary and then seemed cautiously pleased. They were happy with the 'cheerful' and 'ebullient' part of the report but mystified by 'volatile'. I knew what Johnny was talking about. He'd given Dicken and me six of the best with the slipper after he caught us throwing water bombs at each other in the toilets.

I can't remember now whether it was just a scholarship boys thing but one day we were told we were to take elocution lessons. I'm sure this was to rid us of colloquial accents which were not exactly encouraged by the headmaster, a Mr Garstang, another one with a rather onomatopoeic name. Speaking in a 'Kegguth' brogue was frowned on. I enjoyed elocution immensely. I couldn't think of anything better than reciting passages like Blake's 'Tiger, tiger, burning bright...' or, my particular favourite, 'Not a drum was heard, not a funeral note...' from 'The burial of Sir John Moore after Corruna', by Wolfe. I loved bringing some soul into the pieces. And, whether I appreciated it or not, my diction improved 100 per cent.

We used to make up our own versions of some of the works we read out. I'm not sure John Masefield would have enthused at my interpretation of his little ditty 'Sea Fever', though. During a break in one of our sessions, I launched into: "I must go down to the seas again, to the lonely sea and the sky. For I've left a pair of socks out and I'm flippin' sure they're dry." Our elocution master, who had quietly slunk into the room, gave me a clip round the ear for my amendment.

While I tried to work hard at school I would often find my brain a little scrambled. I put this down to my newspaper round. Getting up at the crack of dawn and delivering a bagful of newspapers before gulping down a breakfast and running for the school bus was probably not the best preparation for a school day. Hundreds of kids, though, used to go through this.

One day I nearly missed the morning school bus because of my paper round. It was a Friday. My customers also had to have their magazines, some of them stuffed with free gifts. It meant a gargantuan load in my bag. I tried every way I could to balance the huge weight but it was an uneven battle. As I started my round I had to keep stopping as the bag dropped off my shoulder and swung into my handlebars.

As I took a corner by the small brook at the bottom of the council estate, my bag betrayed me again, slipping right into my front wheel. I was catapulted over the handlebars into the brook. Thankfully, the bike and bag didn't follow me. But I was drenched – and smelly.

I knocked on the door of one of my customers. A lady in a dressing-gown, although staying at arm's length when she got a whiff of the brook, gave me permission to leave my bike at her bungalow. I sloshed along for the rest of my round on foot, with the bag threatening to throttle me.

When I got home Mum nearly had a fit when she saw the state of me but I was more worried about missing my bus and getting into trouble at school. I made it to school on time, which was just as well. Loughborough Grammar School had a policy of discouraging its boys from doing paper rounds. I wouldn't have been able to use that as an excuse.

After the Easter holidays my form became 4C. There was a change in some of my masters and some of my subjects. I no longer did Latin, instead switching to Greek and Roman mythology. I was getting on much better at the lower status so perhaps the headmaster had been right.

There was particular excitement in 1957. Before the Second World War, Kegworth Carnival had always had an ox-roast as one of its main attractions. A 10 hundredweight (454 kilos) ox would be roasted and carved up to provide hundreds of giant sandwiches, a real money-spinner for the carnival. However, that tradition had died. So the carnival committee decided to revive it. The trouble was, oxen were very expensive. One Norman Brown, a local bus driver who was the Mr Fixit for Kegworth Carnival, went on a television show called 'State Your Case' to try to win the money to pay for the beast. By then, my uncles, the deaf and dumb ones, had bought a television. About 20 of us crowded around it to watch Norm state his case for the money to pay for the ox against opponents who felt they, too, were deserving causes. Good old Norm. He won the £100 to pay for the ox. He was quite a village celebrity then for years. Whenever anyone got on his bus he'd get a pat on the back and 'Good old Norman'. My granddad Dabell's friend Harry Ridgard did the roasting and carving of the ox. He slipped me a slice of ox but I was more into candyfloss and toffee apples really.

Our old bully friend Tommy also featured in this particular Kegworth Carnival. Tommy had taken a job as a stable boy, mainly mucking out horses. This, of course, made him an expert horseman. He just had to show off his new skills at the carnival and paid for a ride on a pony, one of those you paid a bob to have a quiet stroll on around the field. We all thought the ponies had been sedated, they were so lethargic. Nobody, normally, could persuade them to even canter. Well Tommy, who was about 16 or 17 at this time, must have done something to this one. Perhaps he'd decided to show it who was master and dug his heels into its flanks. Anyway, it had got up a fair head of steam. Tommy screamed in panic when the pony careered towards the exit of the field. Tommy tried to dismount. Not even Buffalo Bill or Roy Rogers would have tried this manoeuvre. Feet out of stirrups, Tommy finished up half-facing the back of the crazed beast as it tore along. It looked as though he was heading (literally) for disaster. Then my dad came to his rescue, lunging at the reins and dragging the pony to a halt and calming it down. As he helped the quivering Tommy down he offered him words of advice: "Try the donkeys next time Tommy."

Amazingly, Tommy went on to become a jockey! You had to give him ten out ten for trying. Another of his escapades came a few years later. He had failed his driving test several times but that didn't deter him taking to the roads. For years everyone shook their heads in wonderment as they recalled Tommy coasting around the new roundabout built on the A6 just outside Kegworth – going the wrong way. Despite cars and lorries hooting at him and taking avoiding action, Tommy wove round and round the roundabout, unable to fathom how to get off it, but mouthing obscenities and shaking fists at perceived persecutors. Eventually traffic had to grind to a standstill to allow Kegworth's own Flying Dutchman to take an exit, on the wrong side of the road. I don't know whether Tommy ever did pass his test.

That summer I decided I had to augment my pocket money, so I joined up with the gang of kids who would walk the three miles to the farms just outside Kegworth that grew potatoes. It was before machinery that dug up and gathered in the crops of potatoes, so the farmers relied on temporary labour. We would be loaded up onto trailers behind tractors and be transported to fields to dig up the potatoes, clean them off, mostly with our hands, and then put them into sack bags. We then helped load the bags onto the trailers and they would be taken away to the farmers' barns for collection by buyers. It was back-breaking work from very early morning to early evening.

We called it 'spud-bashing' and actually looked forward to the 'season'. The farmers were on to a good thing because they paid us seven shillings and sixpence (37p) a day for our toils. When you were paid your dues for five days' work at the end of the week, though, you felt like a millionaire.

There was a certain amount of revision work to do during the summer holidays but spud-bashing, also helping to stook straw (two shillings a stint), sport and long hikes up Broad Hill to Whatton Brook, always took precedence over revising. A gang of us would wander up to the brook to see if we could spot a kingfisher. Or we might sit under Tom Moore's Tree, where the local poet Thomas Moore composed his famous odes. There we would discuss such matters as Cyril Washbrook making it back into the England test team or which of us had now got pubic hairs. My swotting was saved until a few days before going back to school, done frantically and not very well.

The summer of 1957 was also a memorable one for cricket for me. I was bought an even better cricket bat and a cricket ball, having become cricket-mad. We honed our cricketing skills in a paddock owned by my friend Brian Dakin's dad, with a proper marked out pitch, stumps, the lot. Dakin's paddock was a field of dreams for us youngsters, budding Peter Mays, Colin Cowdreys, Fred Trumans, or Godfrey Evanses.

I had a couple of excursions with school chums to Trent Bridge that summer to watch Notts play, although I was a Leicestershire man. However, the highlight of the year was watching England host the West Indies at Trent Bridge, a fantastic treat. Not only did I actually watch my English heroes but saw, live, the Caribbean cavaliers I'd heard about in the calypso song of the day, 'Those good friends of mine, Ramadhin and Valentine'. Seeing the three 'Ws', Worrell, Walcott and Weekes, playing was a great thrill. I'd gone there to see England win, though. I didn't lose a moment's focus even when Tom Graveney and Cowdrey spent the whole of one day amassing runs. It was only slightly disappointing that the test petered out into a draw. I'd be able to recount every ball to my schoolmates when the new term started.

I used to watch Kegworth 'Town' (village, really; the population was only circa 2,000) Cricket Club, of course, on Saturday afternoons, dreaming of the day I'd be old enough to play for them. It came sooner than I expected. One day Kegworth's captain, George Green, asked me to step in because he was a man short. The match was about to start and the cricket-obsessed kid watching from the boundary was positively the last resort.

Our opponents won the toss and batted first. I was hidden away in the field and didn't see a lot of action. My first official innings, however, is imprinted on my memory. Our opposition's score had proved out of Kegworth's reach. When it was my turn to bat, at No. 11 of course, we were in great danger of losing. I don't remember how much we were behind, only that it was a lot. I waddled to the wicket wearing pads that came up to my waist, determinedly clutching a man's bat. I tried to concentrate but I had butterflies big time. We had about an over to play out for the draw and save the match. I felt really proud walking out, but when I got to the crease pride was replaced by fear. The opposition might have outwardly seemed sympathetic to this callow kid, Kegworth's last hope, but pretty well the whole away team, apart from the bowler, crowded around me at the crease. I made a feeble paddle at the first delivery I faced. Even though I sensed the bowler was holding back a little I was still wafting at mid-air by the time I heard the 'thwack' of the wicket-keeper's gloves behind me. "Must concentrate; don't want to let Kegworth down". Somehow I fended off two or three deliveries, playing forward-defensives, all just short of lurking fingers. The vultures moved in even closer, almost touching me. I looked back at the pavilion where the team were watching with bated breath. My nervy glance was greeted with thumbs up and encouraging shouts to stick at it. That just made me more nervous – consequently bringing on a complete rush of blood. With as much of a flourish as was possible for a lad of about seven stone, I went on the attack. I gave the ball an almighty wallop. It didn't go that far of course, being just a slip of a lad, but it was travelling at a modicum of speed when it found the man fielding at extra silly, rather foolhardy, silly mid-off. He went down groaning, clutching his crotch. His team-mates were first so shocked at the kid suddenly opening his shoulders, they froze. Then they fell about laughing at their pained team-mate. All their great will to win dissipated. Suddenly my batting partner at the wicket was racing up and ruffling my hair. I realised then it was match drawn. The men in the pavilion and the two tea ladies were splitting their sides as I stumbled towards them in a daze. Then everybody wanted to slap me on the back.

After that, I had to have more cricket gear. Pads and gloves were added to my kit. Feeling that my school cricket garb of white shorts and shirt didn't exactly look the part, I raided the jumble sale again, this time coming up with a pair of yellowing flannels whose bottoms came well over my feet.

Mum and Dad worked like stink to enable me to keep up with the rest of the boys of my age. When I went back to school it was in a new pair of grey suit trousers – long grey trousers. I had reached that formative part of a lad's life when he at last discards those short trousers. It had been long overdue. Just about every lad in my year had long trousers. It was another expense for Mum.

It got better. My birthday present was a pair of jeans. They were more like dungarees than jeans and had to be turned up about six inches on the bottoms and to my chagrin Mum put creases in the front of them, but I was very proud of them.

If Dad had had his way I might have had a horse for my birthday. I'd been allowed to have a go on a friend's pony a couple of times and Dad knew I was keen to learn to ride. So that I didn't need to beg rides from the friend, whose family he described as "idle rich", he was going to "see a man about a horse" at market. The horse, which somehow he planned to buy, was to be kept in the old stables in my uncles' yard.

Mum wouldn't hear of it though. She took the pragmatic approach, pointing out how much it would cost to feed a pony and maintain it. Dad caved in. Mum suggested I could have riding lessons on Saturdays, for which they'd buy me some jodhpurs. It all went by the board though. Jodhpurs were too expensive. So I was bought my first pair of jeans.

I couldn't face being the odd man out without jodhpurs, so I scrubbed the riding lessons and opted for sessions at Loughborough Baths on the Saturday mornings instead, to hone my swimming skills. I soon became a very strong swimmer and even passed my life-saving certificates at quite an early age, a great boon when it came to my Naval career a few years later. You can bet your riding boots I'd have suffered a few spills on a horse.

.

Chapter 10

TRAGEDY STRIKES ON NEW YEAR'S DAY

Christmas saw the arrival of our very first television set. Dad had a windfall, winning £20 on the football pools, just about enough to pay for a second-hand television. I remember the TV clearly. It said Ekco on it. Often it did. And often it was reduced to a lot of spots or wavy lines. It was a big moment in my life, though. Up until then I had had to rely on sneaking a look through Auntie Hilda's window until she would spot me and angrily whisk her curtains closed. Or I would squeeze on to the sofa with Nanan Dabell and Aunt Mag at my uncles' home. My favourite programme was Armand and Michaela Denis on their safaris. I loved any wildlife programme, even if I had to imagine hard the real colours of the animals, who all appeared as either black, white or grey. I did have a clear idea of what a zebra looked like, however.

Tragically, my dad never got to watch the television for long. As we moved into a new year, he was killed on his motorcycle in a road accident.

It was a terrible time for all of us, of course, and the day it happened is as vivid and dreadful in my memory now as it was then.

It was January 1 1958. Dad wouldn't even have gone to work on New Year's Day in the modern world. It was not a bank holiday in those days. He had, with regret, left his old employer Len Elliott to work for better pay in Derbyshire and now, unable to walk to work, travelled by way of his new BSA Bantam. It was a bleak, dark morning with driving sleet and rain and Dad collided with the back of a stationary bread lorry, killing him instantly. My poor old Uncle Eric was biking to work soon afterwards and came across the accident. I'll never forget his cries as he rapped on our front door. I was upstairs and heard him frantically asking to check Dad's log book to confirm what he already knew, his way of breaking the awful news. It must have been terrible for Eric. My Nanan's anguished scream as she ran down the lane to Mum can still pierce my mind when I think back. I threw myself on my bed and cried and cried for hours, until I had no tears left. It gouged a huge scar on my emotions. I didn't shed another single tear for 10 years before tragedy struck our family again.

Dad was only just over a week away from his 34th birthday when he died. I had not long turned 13 and my brother was seven, going on eight. Mum was inconsolable. She couldn't bear to listen to the radiogram. Nor could I. Dad had left for work as I got up to fetch my newspapers. I can still hear him now quietly whistling his favourite song of the moment: Jane Morgan and 'The Day that the Rains Came'. The radio was not switched on for weeks. And I couldn't bear to listen to a 'Goon Show'.

My brother was too young to take it all in fully. It nearly broke Mum's heart when on the evening of the accident she asked John why he had left his shoes by the door. "They're there for when I go out with Dad in the lorry tomorrow morning," he said. Mum had to sit him down and gently try and impress on him that he wasn't going to be taking any more trips with Dad.

Life was bleak. John and I needed some levity in our lives. But our pals stayed away from us just when we needed some friendship. They didn't know what to say to us. Our relations and Mum and Dad's friends came round to comfort us all. When John's teacher came in to find out how he was coping, it finally all sank in with my brother. He just went into a shell then and hardly spoke for days.

Recognising I needed a bit of a lift, I was persuaded to go to Filbert Street with my adult minders to see the mighty Manchester United play Leicester. It didn't take my mind off matters but at least I had football to console me. Unfortunately United gave us a right drubbing, 4-0. But I was thrilled to watch such schoolboy heroes as Duncan Edwards, Tommy Taylor and my own particular favourite, Harry Gregg, a quiet Ulsterman who spoke like my granddad Elliott.

It was thus a crushing blow when the news came of the disaster in the snows of Munich when many of the 'Busby Babes' perished, among them the imperious Duncan Edwards. The numerous bulletins from Germany and Manchester, and reports about the stricken players in hospital, chilled the heart even at my tender age. It just seemed to add to all our woes at home and it is all imprinted on my memory forever.

As 1958 wore on it all became a real struggle for Mum. She tried to raise our spirits by taking John and me on holiday to Llandudno. Her mind wasn't really on the job but I unwittingly provided her with a little light respite, I like to think.

I'd taken my beloved football with me on holiday and, at the end of our stay, while Mum paid the landlady's bill, couldn't resist playing with it. It was taking a while for Mum to return so I got John to go in goal – the fireplace – and tapped a few shots at him. He was on form and saved my first couple of attempts so I slammed the ball a little harder. He couldn't stop this one. The ball rattled into the fireplace front. It caved in. It was only a facade covered by a paper brickwork design. Mum came back while I was frantically trying to cover up my handiwork. I expected her to go ballistic. But she was more worried about the cost of any repair. She'd spent up, apart from the bus and train fares home, so couldn't afford to pay for any damage. We were ordered to keep quiet and then Mum did her best to cover up my felony, using sticky plasters to help stick the facade back in place. We were scooted outside with our bags. Mum shook the landlady's hand and thanked her for a nice stay. The landlady ruffled my hair and said how well behaved we had been. Butter would not have melted in any of our mouths. The three of us made off smartly down the road. When we finally sat down in the train compartment for our journey home, Mum finally let rip at me. When we got home, though, I overheard her giggling fit to burst as she related my Arthur Rowley exploit to our next-door-neighbour.

That was about the only instance Mum laughed at that time. It must have been so difficult trying to make ends meet, bringing two boisterous kids to book and vainly attempting to blot out her woe. I was now the man of the house and I'm not sure I did too good a job of it. I did try to help and I had my share of duties. In fact I felt quite grown up when I was entrusted with catching the bus to Long Eaton on Saturday to shop, mainly for the weekly meat supply. Mum had become friendly with the butchers near the Oxford Café where she worked. We used to get a real good deal from Mr Barker and his staff because I think they all fancied Mum on the quiet. Every month I had a haircut in Long Eaton on the Saturday of shopping day. I was advised to have my haircut before calling at Barkers. A dog had once followed me into the barbers and was only just thwarted from pouncing on my shopping bag.

We soldiered on. It was a torrid time. We tried to lighten up our lives with the television. My brother was really into westerns by then. I certainly didn't demur at watching such programmes as 'Rawhide' and 'Wyatt Earp' (we thought we were the only two people in the world, my brother and I, to call him 'Quiet Burp'). I might have sniffed at the idea but I hadn't really grown out of cowboys, no matter how sophisticated I tried to be.

Eventually the strain of everything became too much for Mum. She needed to get away from Kegworth before she had a full-blown nervous breakdown or something even worse. She was suffering badly from anaemia, not eating, and she just wasn't looking after herself properly. Once she'd collapsed and frightened the life out of me. Luckily I'd been able to get help. But she couldn't go on. John and I were in danger of losing a mum as well if she wasn't careful.

Auntie Blanche's clotted cream was called for.

Blanche wasn't really an aunt any more. She had been married to my uncle Bob, the oldest of Mum's three brothers. Bob had been the flagship of Mum's family, the hero to two brothers and three sisters, an accomplished diarist, short-story writer and poet and a great sportsman, He died of tuberculosis during World War II, in which he served in the Royal Navy. Even though Blanche married again to 'Uncle' Ken, she was more than part of the Elliott family still.

Mum was invited down to Plymouth to recuperate at Auntie Blanche's. My brother went with her. I moved in with my paternal grandparents where I was ensconced in Uncle Eric's bedroom. He had married Auntie Brenda by then. I was with Nanan and Granddad Dabell during the week and stayed at my maternal grandparents in Gotham, Nottinghamshire, for part of weekends.

Although I missed my mum and my brother, who was enrolled at a Plymouth school, I quickly accepted my lot. It proved another formative time for me because, unfortunately or otherwise in the long scheme of life, I had too much freedom. I didn't quite turn wild but I did take advantage of the rather lax regime at Nanan and Granddad Dabell's home. Concentration on lessons proved almost impossible. My mind would wander everywhere rather than on the subject in progress. How many runs would Willie Watson score today? How many are there in that flock of sparrows squabbling outside the window? That was apart from English, of course, and history.

Maths, especially geometry and trigonometry, confounded me. I managed adequately at physics, chemistry and biology. In fact I got on really well with my science master, 'Buddy' Murray. French and geography I was reasonably competent at but not startling. None of this added up to a brilliant scholar.

I took quite a keen interest in Religious Instruction, undoubtedly inspired from the past by Daddy Stafford's teachings at Sunday school. However, even here I came a cropper.

Our R.I. teacher was one Connie 'Top-hat' Topping. She was a pleasant lady, a real blue-stocking, who treated me as one of her favourites. That was until we were given a project as homework to find a passage in the Bible that we considered interesting and then we would be told to read out the passage to the class at the next R.I. lesson. Well football practice inevitably took precedence over poring through the Bible of course. I completely forgot about the project. In our R.I. session a couple of days later, Top Hat went to each pupil to read their passages. It threw me into a right old tizz. I would have to improvise. When it came to my turn I just flipped open my Bible and started reading from Acts 9 – largely dealing with Saul's conversion to Paul. I read authoritatively, unabashed at lack of pre-knowledge of the piece, but then came to the part that said: "It is hard for thee to kick against the pricks". I had not seen that one coming. How could I? I had never read the passage before. As my voice tailed off in dismay, there was a tittering all around the form. I was ordered to stop reading by Top Hat, who was red-faced with fury. I was accused of deliberately choosing a passage that had an ambiguous phrase in it that was bound to cause a disruption to the lesson. I was really stymied then. I couldn't tell Top Hat I'd just turned to the passage by chance because that would then prove I had not done my homework. I just had to take her chastisement on the chin. No more was I one of her favourites. And the result was detention.

You could often get detention at Loughborough Grammar School for the slightest misdemeanour. For instance, I got banged up for one Saturday afternoon for telling my great school friend Chris Dicken a 'dirty' joke that was overheard by one of the masters. I don't know which one squealed on me. I was just summoned to our house master Johnny Lello and told to explain myself. When I repeated the joke, Johnny couldn't resist a giggle but said: "I don't know where you've heard this Dabell but there's nothing I can do. I've been told to punish you. So what's it to be? Six with the slipper or Saturday detention?" I opted for the detention. Nice chap though Johnny was, I couldn't see him 'sparing the rod'.

I'd been told the joke by my Aunt Nancy. She was a bit of a rebel and definitely very emancipated. I guess she'd thought it was about time I should listen to adult humour. My first rude joke: "There was this café that had a board outside which read: 'We pride ourselves on our extensive menu. Whatever you fancy we are sure we will be able to suit your needs.' People tried their hardest to come up with meals the restaurant couldn't serve but the café always won. Then this bloke came in and said: 'I'll have elephant's balls on toast'. The waitress went away and then returned with a long face. She said: 'I'm sorry sir but we've run out of bread'." Aunt Nancy told me several risqué jokes and stories subsequently. I made sure I didn't repeat any of them at school again, though.

Apart from an obsession with sport there were other distractions from schoolwork now. I discovered girls. They were not, after all, meant to act as the stumps for cricket. And after being given a sex education by one of the older boys at school, I began to notice that girls, who up to then were just tolerated, could be quite appealing. And they had quite interesting bits.

Chris Dicken, my great mate, had discovered the opposite sex a little earlier than me. We were rather unsuccessful Romeos, though. I had a sneaky suspicion he rather fancied himself far more than anybody else. He spent most of his time combing his hair and checking out his appearance, oblivious to the fact that Wendy, studying at the adjacent Loughborough High School for Girls, was breaking her heart for him. Even when Wendy turned stalker, switching school buses and going five miles out of her way home just to breathe the same air as him, Chris ignored her. He was bent on chasing a girl two years older than him who showed him even less attention than he was giving the girl who worshipped the ground he walked on.

It proved an unhappy time for me because I had scant success making my romantic debut. The object of my desire was called Jillian, who was also at the High School. But there was a great obstacle to my first foray into romance – my painful shyness (the chipped tooth didn't help). I could not pluck up the courage to tell her I fancied her. I think she might have guessed because on the few occasions we bumped into each other she would flash beautiful green eyes under a mass of black curls at me, either teasing me or (I fantasised) inviting the crimson-faced Dabell to do something about it. I would blush and fart and flee more often than not. I certainly never gathered the courage to really talk to her. In fact I became a bit of a stalker, too, hanging around waiting for her to appear near the High School, looking on doe-eyed from afar most of the time. I did take the trouble to find out her address and sent her a Valentine card but stuck to the rules and didn't include my name on it. A conspiratorial look when she next flashed past me got me nowhere. Dejectedly, I realised she hadn't a clue who had sent her the card. And I decided she'd probably received loads anyway.

So, after much anguish, one afternoon I also decided to implement the changing of bus routes ploy to break the ice with the young temptress. Her route was different to mine but had a similar terminus in Kegworth on a much longer run home. I thought I could just about swing it as long as the driver didn't check my bus pass. The covert assignation did not come about. I had a real struggle making the girl's bus after rugby ran late and scrambled up the steps almost as it pulled away. I looked around for my dearest heart but could see her nowhere. I found out later that she had been coerced into accompanying Chris Dicken's pining young paramour for moral support on his bus service.

I couldn't decide whether I felt relief at not having, after all, to make that first move or disappointment at my plan going awry. My thoughts were interrupted by the driver asking to see my bus pass. Fortunately he didn't insist on the sixpence fare, when I pleaded ignorance, i.e. getting on the wrong bus. That was a huge relief. It would have been quite an operation in order for me to pay. Some time before, Mum had sewn sixpence into my trouser pocket – not to be used except for dire emergency. My fear of mater was such that I hadn't even dared touch it when she was hundreds of miles away in Plymouth. If I'd had to resort to emergency measures, it wouldn't have just been my romantic notions that were punctured. I would also have had to make a hole in my pocket in front of all the passengers.

My scheme turned into a real debacle anyway. I asked to be dropped off so that I could catch my rightful, and quicker, service to Kegworth. But by the time I'd run back my regular school bus had just gone. I had a long, miserable, walk in the rain down to the bus stop in town, on the way ripping out the stitches in my trousers and releasing my tanner. I hoped Nanan could give me another sixpence and stitch me up again when I got home. Romance, I felt, was overblown.

I never did find enough courage to proposition my first serious love. You could imagine how I felt when a couple of years later, by which time I had joined the Royal Navy, I received a letter from her, taking me to task for being such a shrinking violet. Things never did work out for us, though. Just as our letters were starting to get to the mildly passionate stage and I looked forward to finally arranging a tryst while I was on leave, she told me her family were moving from Loughborough to open up a fish and chip shop in Watford. That was the last I heard of her until I spotted her name on 'Friends Reunited' over 40 years later. I decided to leave well alone and didn't contact her for old times' sake.

I found a new object of desire when I went down to Plymouth to stay with Mum at the home of my Auntie Blanche during the summer holiday.

My uncle Norman (aka Bill) lived not far from Plymouth in Looe, Cornwall. While I was on my summer break we went over to meet him and my Aunt Daphne. And my cousin Gina. Gina, about two years older than me, was a wonderful vision to an impressionable lad approaching 14. She had shimmering auburn hair. I worshipped the ground she walked on. If a psychiatrist got hold of me he would say Gina has been the reason for my lifelong love of redheads. She hardly knew I existed that week. She did allow me to listen to her new record, 'At the Hop'. She played it over and over again, to the chagrin of everyone – but me. I felt no monotony. I was busy being transfixed by this copper-topped vision bopping to Danny and the Juniors.

Back in Plymouth I soon got her out of my mind, though. Blanche and Ken lived near a station and there were Western Region trains to spot. Also, Plymouth Hoe and its lido was within easy reach. Then there were visits around Devonport Dockyard, where Uncle Ken worked, to see the ships. We also had several boat trips and a couple of beach jaunts. On one of the boat trips I scooped up a sailor's hat which was bobbing about in the waves. I was quite fascinated by it, by its symmetry, the gold tally band around its brim, before I was ordered to throw it back into the water. Strangely, that hat had quite an effect on me. I wondered what it would be like to wear one and serve in the Royal Navy.

While I was down in Plymouth my cousin, well not really my cousin, Jacqueline was often my escort. We got on like a house on fire, purely platonic this time, though. Jackie was a great sport. And then there was Auntie Blanche's Devon Cream. She skimmed it off herself. It was magnificent. I ate so many jam and cream scones I must have put on half a stone while I was down in Devon.

It was no surprise, considering all the treats provided copiously by Auntie Blanche, that I developed toothache. I kept it quiet at first, terrified of another visit to a dentist. Eventually I had to give in and report sick to Mum, though. She understood full well why I was so worried about the prospect of another dental nightmare. This time, however, I was taken to a proper dental surgeon, a former Naval one who had set up practice in Plymouth. Despite all my fears, this time it went like a dream – literally. For the second time in my life I went under the gas. I never felt a thing and had no post-surgery pain either.

The trip to the dentist couldn't spoil an idyllic holiday but it all had to end. I had to return to Kegworth and go back to school.

Chapter 11

MAKING A PIG'S EAR OF IT

Before autumn term started I had chance to catch up with my big pal John Sketchley, on what had been going on in Kegworth during my absence. 'Sketch', well into his time at Loughborough Grammar School, was a couple of years older than me, so I held him in some esteem. And he was the brother of the girl whose pigtails I used to pull at Kegworth Primary School, Carol. I had by now realised that pulling her pigtails was not for persecution but because I had a huge crush on her. So calling on John and having a cup of tea with the family while we talked cricket and football was also an excuse to see Carol, who had started at Loughborough High School at the same time as I had at Loughborough Grammar School. Alas, Carol was not interested in me. The lad she fancied, her brother John's peer at school, didn't know she was on this planet. I think he fancied Carol's best friend, who was going out with someone else. It was a real little web of amorous intrigue, of which there seemed to be no winners. Every girl John fancied, too, gave him the big blank.

Sketch was my role model, so when he suggested we could make five shillings apiece doing some work at a fete. I was all for it. "I'll be running the quoit stall and the bran tub (lucky dip)," Sketch informed me. "I've got you a job on the 'bowling for a pig' stall." I felt I'd got the better of the deal. I'd been rather put off quoits since getting that clip around the ears from Mum at Kegworth Wakes.

Skittling for a pig was held on a makeshift alley on the fete field, with bales of hay around the end to stop the bowls and skittles flying all over the place. All the macho men from the village, trying to impress their girlfriends, just had to have a go. They got three goes for a shilling. The best score at the end of the day won, well, a pig. My duty was to collect up the skittles, re-spot them and make sure the bowlers had enough bowls, sending them back up the alley.

My first customer was a farmer I knew well. He was one of the Kegworth cricket team, a massive fellow with big shoulders who could clear the pavilion with ease. He was deadly and knocked over all the skittles with his first bowl. That meant I had to jump down from my bale and scurry around collecting all the pins. An octopus would have made a great job of it. I was like an uncoordinated juggler on Speed as I tried to pick up more than one skittle in each hand. The skittles were quite heavy for a lad with skinny arms. They seemed to have a life of their own, wriggling like frightened rabbits, disappearing over my shoulder, assaulting my chin or dropping on my foot.

Again this farmer achieved a wipe-out, knocking over all the pins. Again I had to jump down and scramble for skittles like a demented litter-picker. Even though the farmer left three pins standing with his final effort, by the time I had tidied up the target I was exhausted. Then I had to roll up the bowls. They were very heavy. Two didn't make it; they barely made halfway. "You're going to have to do better than this or I'll have to get somebody else doing the job," I was warned by a watching fete official.

The chance of losing five bob sharpened the mind. Fortunately most of the ensuing bowlers were not half as deadly as my first customer. And I found that cuddling the pins to me as I collected them, then dropping them one by one near their spots, enabled me to speed up the process no end.

I was beginning to think I'd cracked it as we came towards the end of the afternoon. Then a trio of noisy fellows turned up at the alley. They had obviously given the ale a good lash. One of them put his shilling in the tin and let rip at the pins. A complete miss. The hoots of derision from his pals stung and fired him up. Dropping down his trouser bracers to give himself more freedom, he wound himself up and hurled down his second bowl. Another complete miss. My grinning face at the other end did not make his dwindling humour any better. With a look of great determination, he tried again. This time he exerted so much power he fell over. His bowl ricocheted off an end bale and knocked over one pin. "Don't think you'll be in the running for the pig," I gloated as I rolled back the bowls. This twit had been a doddle, I thought, as I bent down to replace the one disturbed pin. "Watch out," someone screamed from the other end of the alley. I sprang up like a startled meerkat. My inebriated friend at the other end had decided to have a fourth go – at me. Fortunately his aim had not improved. I, though, did manage a 'strike' on the pins as I leapt out of the way. It didn't qualify me for the pig. The porker went to my farmer friend. Just what he wanted. He had a sty full of them.

Martin Sibson, who lived the other side of the wall from my uncles' yard, and I were great pals, even though that still didn't rest all that well with his harridan of a mother. She was mellowing a little though. Occasionally, when Ada was in less than ogress-like spirits, I was actually allowed into the Sibson yard to meet up with Martin. Only once was I allowed in the house, for a birthday party, the quickest I'd ever attended. But I used to help him collect eggs from the coops in the orchard or feed the pigs in their huge pigsty. I loved it, especially when litters of piglets came along.

Relations, though, were seriously affected by one incident, involving a powerful airgun Martin had been allowed to use. He had been taking the odd potshot or two at the numerous pigeons that roosted in the rafters of my uncles' stables. They had been racing pigeons at one time but had gone feral. My uncles were really upset when they found several half-dead pigeons staggering around badly injured, some with an eye shot out. They wanted me to do something about it.

I promised I would confront Martin and, risking the two viragos, Shirley and Ada, I paid him a visit. I suggested pointing the gun at a target down in his orchard would be better than popping off at pigeons. I asked if I could have a go and, after some cajoling, he reluctantly let me. We picked out a distant target. I let rip with several shots. Martin was amused at my waywardness at first but then became nervous as he reckoned he could hear the tinkling of glass each time I shot. When we checked the target not a pellet had found it. However, an empty hen coop had had its glass windows shot out. Martin daren't tell his father he had allowed someone else to fire the gun and took the rap. He was never allowed to use the gun again.

I endured some pretty hectic weeks while Mum was convalescing in Devon but football and cricket continued to rule my life. On the days I actually managed to catch the official school bus home I couldn't wait to get off it to play or train. The youth club and Young Conservatives (only because they had the best table-tennis facilities) were also high on my priority list. This meant my prep suffered badly. Nanan and Granddad Dabell were not exactly hard taskmasters in standing over me until it was written up and I used to kid myself I'd get it done after supper. But then I was tired and didn't want to do anything but go to bed and drop off while reading one of Uncle Eric's sports magazines. Invariably it meant doing the homework first thing the next morning. With a paper round, it proved almost impossible, of course. Unless it was English or History, which I did always find time to do the previous night because I loved the subjects, invariably I was scribbling away at my homework on the school bus. Often I'd crib from my pals. For maths, I always used to look at the answer and work backwards to make it look good on paper. This had never been a successful ploy. Reverse maths was even harder than the regular version.

Well, my rather cavalier approach to school caused me plenty of aggro and several stays in detention on Saturday afternoons. On one occasion I was accompanied in detention by an unfortunate friend who had allowed me to copy his homework. As I had also included his mistakes it gave the game away. Willing homework helpers soon became scarce.

Even without my various diversions in Kegworth, I had an exhausting schedule. I had the paper round starting at dawn before scrambling for the school bus. Wednesday afternoons were supposed to be time off but I spent most of them either playing some kind of sport or doing enforced prep. We had lessons on Saturday mornings and then there was sometimes more sport to play for the school in the afternoon (or detention). Fridays I stayed on late at school for Combined Cadet Force. I also stayed late two nights a week as a member of historical and film societies.

My state of frazzle was noticed. Something had to give. When the school found out I had twice funked rugby to play football they put a stop to that. My days trying to gain a full-time place for Kegworth Rovers second team were over. And the headmaster had always frowned on pupils doing paper rounds. Not the image Loughborough Grammar School wanted. I just could not afford to give up my paper round, though. For instance, it paid for my trips to watch Leicester City on Saturdays when I could get away. I had to carry on the round illicitly but I inevitably got found out and this did not sit well with the headmaster.

No matter what I did at that time I'd find myself in trouble. There was the day the cook at LGS canteen made a mess of lunches. I don't know whether she had accidentally used soap instead of margarine when making pastry for a meat pie or had failed to clean off soap suds from the dish, but the taste was gross. We were almost blowing bubbles. Mrs Benskin, the head canteen lady, though, was an absolute Tartar. She refused to believe anything was wrong with the pie, despite protests from pupils. Incredibly we were ordered to eat it. I refused and ditched the monstrosity in the leftovers dustbin. A furious Mrs

Benskin reported me to the master on lunch duty. Another black mark for Dabell, although, give him his due, the master did try out the pie and spat it out. I think that saved me from a beating but the word was going round that Dabell was a rebel.

I was a rebel without a cause, though. So I decided I had to enhance my looks and James Dean seemed a fitting role model. My hair had always been enthusiastic but delinquent. I decided to invest in a pot of Brylcreem. I plastered my hair back from my forehead. My uncle Eric was a great follower of fashion. He urged me not to stop there and get my hair styled. He gave me the money to do it. I went to my Long Eaton barber but found he didn't do a 'James Dean cut'. He could do a 'Tony Curtis' though. This was slicked sides, a 'Boston' straight cut at the back and quiff on the front. I was delighted with it. The transformation was nothing short of stunning. I went from callow youth, with hair of which Ken Dodd would have been proud, to modern young man. I saved up my paper money and bought a new pair of black shoes that had a little more flair than the usual boring versions. When my geography teacher asked me if I was trying to look like a Teddy Boy I was ecstatic. It was another black mark for Dabell, though. I was holding on to my place at Loughborough Grammar School by a thread at times. That thread would eventually be broken.

If Mondays to Saturday afternoons were turmoil then I found my peaceful haven and a whole team of new friends on Saturday nights and Sundays in the little Nottinghamshire village of Gotham, staying with my maternal grandparents. Gotham was the home of the fabled 'Wise Men' and the Cuckoo Bush. On Saturday nights I would catch the South Notts local bus service to Nanan and Granddad Elliott's house five miles away, to where they had moved. There was no local service on Sundays so I had to come home to Kegworth via Loughborough, a tortuously long journey broken by an equally trying wait at the 'Rushes' bus station. That was in the winter months. As spring unfolded I decided to cycle to Gotham, either juggling my large weekend bag around my handlebars or slinging it over my shoulder. Remarkably, I had only one serious mishap. The road from Kegworth to Gotham is hardly a busy one even now and in those days there was little traffic for me or my loved ones to worry about.

My calamitous spill came on a foggy Sunday night as I returned from Gotham. It was a real pea-souper and my lamp was pretty ineffectual but I'd got about a third of my journey complete when I came to the entrance of Kingston Hall, the home of Lord Belper. Here, in the enveloping, swirling fog I came a real cropper. Thoroughly confused, I mistook the broken lines of the estate entrance for the lines of the centre of the road, swerved in alarm to the left of them before, perhaps, an oncoming car hit me – and, understandably, taking into consideration my sudden positional change, crashed into the wall that surrounded Kingston Hall. My wheel was buckled badly enough to make cycling impossible. I limped into a worried Nanan and Granddad Dabell's an hour later than expected, both thighs badly bruised and sporting large wall burns on both elbows. I was too injured to play sport for weeks. It was a disaster. A pity my head hadn't taken the brunt of my fall. I would have been all right then.

The bike ride from Kegworth to Gotham and back did have its delights, however. I used to stop off around twilight at a favourite spot near Leake Lane where I knew there would always be a kingfisher to watch. I would be entranced by the gorgeous, shimmering, little cobalt blue and rusty red little bird as it dived into the stream then came up with bill full of wriggling sticklebacks or minnows.

Then there were the times when instead of going via Kingston I would take the longer route via Kegworth Station. I might have time to wait while the 'Royal Scot' went through on its way up north on the London Midland Scotland line. I had just about grown out of trainspotting by then but it was still in my blood.

Nanan and Granddad Elliott had moved from Leake Lane briefly and their home for the interim was in Gotham, close to where they had first set up home. It was a comfortable house with all mod cons, although without central heating. At first my bed would be made cosy at night before I turned in with an old copper bed-warmer in which dying coals from the fire were placed. I was happier with the hot-water bottle that replaced it. That could stay with me while I was in bed.

Nanan wasn't the greatest of cooks in my opinion. Yes, I loved her sausage meat and tomatoes on toast before going to matins at Gotham Church and yes, I looked forward to her warm pilchards on toast for supper. But her Sunday lunches were not my favourite. Nanan had been used to a Spartan existence when she was younger so there was no butter in the mashed spuds, for instance. She seemed to have only one recipe for pudding, too. It was 'college pudding', a wodge of dried mixed fruit flan which I had to fight to keep down. Nanan was very fierce and I was too terrified of her to not clean my plate.

My cousin Robert Plant, son of my mum's older sister Jessie and my uncle George, the bully-basher earlier in my story, was my mentor for years. He introduced me to his friends in Gotham and to all kinds of music from rock and roll to classical. While I was doing my weekend stints between Kegworth and Gotham I was under Robert's wing. We sang in the church choir, along with a whole cadre of my relatives.

I remember some absolute debacles singing in the choir. Our lady organist was reputed to be quite fond of sherry and allegedly boosted her playing at evensong and choir practise sometimes with a nip or two. But her mistiming on the keys was not helped by the old boy who was supposed to pump up the organ as she played. He would often drop asleep, causing her efforts to waver and occasionally draw a blank altogether, producing giggling from the choir stalls. It certainly brightened up religion for me at that time..

We didn't take the sermon and lesson reading very seriously. As soon as the Rev. Norman Copeland got up to speak it was the signal to get out the Spangles, the fruity boiled sweet. It must have been very frustrating for Rev. Copeland, having to periodically break off for coughing in the choir stalls as we tried to disguise the rustle of Spangles being unwrapped.

After matins came my highlight of the week. A gang of us, me, my cousin Robert, his sister Gill, my two other cousins in Gotham, Margaret and Lesley, and all my cousins' friends, would go on a long walk in the summer and discuss, perhaps, the latest pop music scene. It's hard to believe nowadays that a mere walk, perhaps to Strawberry Wood on the hill above Gotham, could offer such delight. We loved each other's company so much, though. Even my accounts of the previous day's match at Filbert Street ("we wuz robbed") were born with patience by the group. Some Sundays, especially in the winter, many of us would descend on a group member's house where snacks and drinks and a record player were produced. It wasn't always Elvis either. I discovered Tchaikovsky, Beethoven, Sibelius, Gustav Holst, and the composer who wrote my favourite 'Peer Gynt' Suite, Edvard Grieg, through the encouragement of cousin Robert and his friends.

One activity that Robert used to love was bell-ringing – campanology. Before a service began Robert, his dad (Uncle George), my granddad Elliott and several other strong-arms, used to peel off the bobs in the Gotham Church belfry with élan. I was invited to join them. However, when I nearly got hauled through the belfry trapdoor because my arms were too thin to combat my bell's upward force, I was relieved of my corner. Instead I was allowed to ring the little call-to-service bell. A five-year-old kid would have been able to pull on it.

Chapter 12

IT ALL ENDS BADLY

While mixing with older teenagers only helped my general knowledge and grasp of current affairs, I was still running into trouble at school. I excelled at cricket but my report card for the summer term was not a thing of beauty. Also, the headmaster was not impressed when he found out I was managing and arranging fixtures for two football teams I'd founded – Kegworth Imperial for the lads in the village and Loughborough Nomads for my schoolmates who preferred the round to the oval ball.

Of course, pupils were expected to spend a fair amount of time swotting. I abhorred the very thought. I got a warning from Norman Walter, the new headmaster: if I didn't shape up and climb from a ranking of 29th of 32 in my form, then my future at Loughborough Grammar School might be in doubt.

Mum insists that it was not anything to do with my bad school report that encouraged her to return home with my brother. But I did have to shape up better than I'd been doing now we were all back at home in One Plummer Lane.

It must have been so difficult for Mum coming home to all those memories. Very thoughtfully she sent me off to Gotham to the Plants for Christmas and New Year.

There were lots of activities at Gotham Church during the festive period. I loved singing Christmas carols and being with the old gang again. I also resumed my stint on the warning bell at church. Attired in my surplice and cassock, I looked pretty important. I felt bold enough to tip a wink in the direction of one pretty girl I'd fancied from afar. To my delight she gave me a huge smile and a wink back. This same young lady then turned up at the Christmas party Aunt Jessie and Uncle George put on for the youngsters later that night. When we were matched up at 'Postman's Knock' my confidence drained. I was trembling outside the door when it burst open and she grabbed me forcibly in a clinch. I reacted pathetically, freeing myself and bolting for the toilet. I didn't come out until she had gone back in to the party and reported what a wimp I'd been. She got her own back by pinning the tail of the donkey on me several times. I'm pretty sure she could see through the blackout mask. I had to decide whether the winking gambit was a good one or not. A: I wanted to tempt pretty young things. B: I was terrified when they were tempted.

I didn't want the festive season to end, though. I gradually plucked up a little courage on the opposite sex front and can report several little blushing moments under the mistletoe by the time I had to head back to Kegworth and begin a new term at school.

It was to prove a make or break year for me and sadly it was the latter. Loughborough Grammar School was pretty elitist and, looking back, I'm sure it took scholarship boys under sufferance. However, I don't think my less than unwavering dedication to schoolwork helped my cause in 1959.

I did apply myself much better with Mum in charge. Homework was done at the right time and sport put on hold until I'd done it. I took on a more involved role in our historical society and counted a couple of much older LGS intellectuals among my friends.

Trouble was always just around the corner, though. I made an enemy of the head prefect and school captain, one Peter Preston. Well, it wasn't enmity from me. He rather had it in for what he called the 'Kegworth Crowd' and seemed to seek me out as a special target. I reckon by the time he left school he had awarded me well into the thousands of lines. Some of his subjects for writing 200 lines, the maximum punishment at this level, ironically called 'minors', were devised, I'm sure to give me writer's cramp. They did help my spelling, however. 'I must not endanger other pedestrians in the Burton Walks or risk pneumonia by running for my school bus in a state of dishabille,' was one of his little gems, I recall. 'I must not come from Kegworth,' would have been more like it. I don't think it helped when he overheard us referring to him as 'The Mekon', the villainous little 'Treen' who swooped around on a powered seat causing trouble in the 'Dan Dare' strip in the 'Eagle' comic. Rigorous interrogation unfortunately pointed the finger towards me for inventing the sobriquet. Then there was the fake dog turd incident. Three of us form-mates out on lunch break in Loughborough decided to buy the disgusting looking novelty. But where to position it? 'I must not place imitation canine excrement outside the prefects' common room.'

Peter eventually became the editor of the *Guardian*. Having become a journalist myself and looking to widen my horizons from a small town newspaper, I wrote to Peter asking for a job. Needless to say I was unsuccessful. He remembered me with affection, he said (typical *Guardian* hyperbole), but the newspaper was not taking on staff at that time. I did subsequently meet Peter at Heathrow when we were both waiting for a plane, me to go to a golf tournament and him with a group of fellow editors. His pipe nearly fell out of his mouth when I told him who I was.

My occasional spats with Preston and a couple of other prefects didn't help my cause at school. Nor did the fact that I'd discovered a new sport. This was tennis and girls wearing skimpy tennis frocks down at Kegworth Tennis Club Hut. I much preferred serving to swotting in spare time. I was actually quite proficient at tennis but I have to confess that it was my great friend John Sketchley's sister who was the chief attraction to tennis. My fondness for Carol continued to be unrequited, though. It wasn't until I'd joined the Navy that the flame finally flickered and went out.

Not long after returning from the 1959 Christmas holiday I had a sense of doom. It came largely because Chris Dicken and I had misbehaved at an extra-curriculum activity at Loughborough's Victory cinema, during a performance by the actor Emlyn Williams. Mr Williams was reading Charles Dickens to a packed house of LGS pupils, most press-ganged into the trip. I was actually enjoying the show and well into the bearded Mr Williams' portrayals, especially his Fagin from *Oliver Twist*. Then Dicken pointed out the shadow from the footlights being created by the actor. Williams' bobbing and weaving silhouette was that of a demented nanny goat when launching into: "What a fine thing capital punishment is…" Dicken and I could not control our hysterics. A hissing schoolmaster commanded us to be silent. We were lucky to be given yellow cards and not red.

News of our misdemeanour of course reached the headmaster. While we both escaped the 'cod', a thrashing with the cane, it had more far-reaching repercussions. With my exam results still far from satisfactory in several subjects and now further proof that I was not exactly a model student, the powers that be at Loughborough Grammar School had more ammunition.

At the start of 1960 Mr Walter and the school governors were intent on losing a few pupils. Dicken's parents moved him to another school and, along with – surprise, surprise, two other scholarship under-achievers – I was earmarked for the sack.

Mum was sent for and told by Mr Walter I had to be removed from the school. Three of my teachers, Mooks, Buddy and Johnny Lello, stood my corner. They tried to dissuade the headmaster but got no joy. Arrangements were going to have to be made for me to leave Loughborough Grammar School forthwith. It was suggested that I should transfer, perhaps, to Loughborough College.

I had other ideas. After long discussions we decided I should take steps to join the Royal Navy. It seemed natural that one of the next generation of Elliotts should follow in the adored Uncle Bob's footsteps. That was to be me. Stories of Uncle Bob in the Navy, and that sailor's hat I'd tried to rescue the year before, had had a profound effect on me.

I passed the education test at the recruiting office in Green Lane, Derby, and Mum and I signed the document which committed me to the Royal Navy. I would begin my career at HMS Ganges, a shore training base in Suffolk. I think Mum was a bit confused when signing my life away for me, though. She misread the document. She was quite distraught at first when she found out we had committed me to at least 10 years' service. She thought it was a sort of initial term – one year!

School allowed me to stay on until a joining up day had been arranged with the RN, expected to be in the summer of 1960.

I was growing up fast and my wardrobe was extended to include two pairs of long trousers. I had hard-wearing trousers that had been part of my school uniform for some time. My very favourite clothing, though, was a lovely pair of light-grey worsted trousers, only to be used for really major occasions.

Well the everyday use pair would easily crease up and gradually they started to part company with my feet, through my natural growth and their frequent visits to the dry cleaners. Sketchley and I were to attend a very grown-up affair, a dance at Sutton Bonington, a nearby village. I pleaded and cajoled with mother to be allowed to wear my worsted trousers but to no avail. There was no way they were going to the ball. So the cunning Dabell took action.

Of course, before being allowed to catch the bus to the dance I had to have a full meal. As I drank a cup of tea the cup suddenly and mysteriously loosened itself from my grip – and flung its contents all over my trousers. I was soaked. "There's no way I can wear these trousers now Mum; I'll have to get changed into my best ones." Good idea but, as the Yanks say, no cigar. "You are not wearing your best trousers no matter what happens," was Mum's chilling decision. "But the bus goes in half an hour." "Well you'll have to miss it and miss the dance," part two of Mum's decision. I had been rumbled. There was nothing more I could do. I didn't even have time to dry out my trousers, which now, as well as being creased, at half-mast and slightly threadbare, smelt badly of PG Tips.

When I met Sketch at the bus stop he was aghast at my appearance. "You've got a great big stain on your trousers," said the erudite Sketchley. "I know; it's a long story," answered the wretched Plum. "Well sit on a seat away from me," was the unsympathetic response from Sketchley, "you pong to high heaven. And when we get to the dance we're splitting up. I'm never going to get a dance with anybody if they see you and your tea-stained trousers." I spent a thoroughly miserable evening trying to cover up my woe. I decided to give up cunning ideas for the moment. Mum was too good for me.

I should have realised that when I tried my first cigarette. We certainly couldn't countenance smoking down the bicycle sheds at school like the secondary-modern boys did. Smoking at LGS was punishable by six of the best. I had no great urge to smoke, but there was always the dare-factor. My uncle Eric still had some of his belongings in his old bedroom where I had stayed at my grandparents' home and amongst the magazines in his drawers I'd found an old packet of Player's Bachelor tipped cigarettes and a box of matches.

I sneaked off with my booty to my uncles' wash-house. There, with trembling fingers, I lit up. I immediately coughed myself silly. I always did have a barking cough. My lungs protested vehemently but I soldiered on, trying to avoid bringing up breakfast, too. I was into my third drag when I heard Mum coming down the path to my uncles' home. Her gait was unmistakable and she had fantastic radar. However, she didn't suspect for one moment what her eldest son, cowering by the big sink in my uncles' wash-house, was up to. Then she saw me smoking. Not smoking the Bachelor tipped.

Just smoking. In my panic I'd stuffed the fag in my pocket. It wasn't out and was smouldering away in my jacket.

It's remarkable what a smack around the ear at about the force of 'Henry Cooper's 'Ammer' does for your bravado, even if you are 15. I didn't smoke another cigarette until well after I had joined the Royal Navy, when they were virtually free. In fact I never really had any great enthusiasm for cigarettes. Perhaps that was because often when I lit one up, even when I was a couple of thousand miles away from her, I imagined Mum smacking me around the ears for being so stupid. I gave them up before I was 21.

John Sketchley was an enthusiastic dancer, just like me. Our big night was Saturday and the 'Nine-penny Hop' (nine-pence to get in and that also entitled you to snacks and fizzy pop or a cup of tea) at the old former school hall in Dragwell, Kegworth. Now this was no rock and roll extravaganza. The dances were Barn Dances where we would trip around doing the Gay Gordons, Strutters, Waltz, Polka, and, of course, Barn Dance. By this time I was poised to join the RN and I was at last allowed to wear my worsted trousers. A sports jacket and a pair of pointed shoes that were as near as I could get to winkle-pickers with Mum's approval, made up my ensemble. However, Sketch, whose hair resembled that of a young absent-minded professor, and I were fairly hopeless at getting very far with the opposite sex. All the girls would sit around on straight-backed chairs waiting to be asked to dance. As soon as they saw Sketch and me walking over, the section we were heading for would take to the floor like startled rooks. They opted to dance with each other until a realistic offer came along. We did have the occasional success, normally a blushing young thing that had the same problem as us in reverse. On being invited to dance, the neglected wallflowers would grab us in an arm-lock normally only on show on Saturday afternoon wrestling and whisk us gratefully on the floor. But gauche young men like us always lived in hope that we'd click with a beautiful blonde or, more accurately on my part, a ravishing redhead.

I remember John having a particular passion for the daughter of our biology master at Loughborough Grammar School. She was rather cute, an elfin-like leggy blonde. Sketch never got round to propositioning her. He was just as shy as me. We even rode out to Hathern, her home village near Loughborough, once, in the hope of John seeing her. Amazingly, we did actually come across her. We spent a tortuous hour, well for me it was, watching her play netball. That was all. John couldn't pluck up the courage to talk to her. This time I was the one disgusted. Perhaps it was because her dad, nickname 'Tiny' because he was six feet six, had expressly forbidden grammar school boys going anywhere near his daughter.

Eventually the Ninepenny Hop did become old hat. Jiving at Kegworth Youth Club became more de rigueur. The weekly dance at the village hall, too, was soon much more of a Mecca for young spirits. But I'll never forget that call from the master of ceremonies at Dragwell: "Take your partners now – for the Barn Dance."

A couple of weeks before I was due to join the Navy I had yet another cycling mishap. This time I came to grief on two wheels, two saddles, two handlebars and four pedals.

Having been advised he should try to prise himself out of his fireside chair, my granddad Dabell took up bicycle repairs and renovations. He was pretty good at transforming clapped-out old bikes into working machines. Then he'd sell them. His renovation pride and joy was a tandem that had come his way. Having made such a good job of it, though, he decided to keep it in the family. Uncle Eric was first to use it, taking his girlfriend Brenda out on it occasionally. When Eric bought a car, though, it was redundant – until I discovered it and wanted to try it out. Granddad gave it an overhaul and seal of approval. I invited John Sketchley to take a spin on it with me.

Sketch had often been the fall-guy on several of our escapades. For instance, he had nearly been shot by an unwitting farmer while we stalked an unreceptive young lady in a cornfield. An emergency canoe roll, which we had seen on television, had nearly drowned him. So he was loath to mount this tandem. I calmed his fears. "It's perfectly safe, my granddad is now an expert at bikes," I assured my dubious pal. "This is his best ever work. It's so good he won't sell it on." John wasn't convinced. "It doesn't look that safe to me. The bell fell off when I tried to ring it, for a start."

When he finally relented we began a tentative foray down Plummer Lane, with me, as the owner's grandson, insisting on taking front seat. We soon found out you should never backpedal autonomously and the backseat rider should never try to manipulate his handlebars. They do not move, even if your co-pilot has no confidence in his mate up front. John's chief concern was that I was the one in control of the brakes, so it was no good gripping his handlebars and hoping for something to happen.

Learning these nuances inevitably caused a few minor spills but soon we launched ourselves off into the countryside. We warmed to our task and I could tell Sketchley was at last enjoying himself, even though I'm sure he would have sooner been in charge.

Fields and hedgerows whizzed by. We soon found ourselves in the lanes around East and West Leake, not all that far from where I had lived as a baby and toddler. I thought back to my tricycle mishap of years before as we soared past the spinney and the now hardly used Lady Angela line in Leake Lane. "Here Sketch, did I ever tell you about the time I rode over the edge of a quarry in this wood?" I shouted, leaning behind me and nodding at the spinney. Sketchley bellowed back: "For goodness sake keep looking ahead at the road in front of us." His voice went from a command to a squeal as we waggled alarmingly when I took a hand off the handlebars to give him a thumbs-up.

Sketch and I were soon going like the clappers again. "Watch out old lad we're coming to a junction," I shouted behind me." We then put on a fearful wobble as I stuck out my hand to signify we were making a right turn.

Soon we were going like a train again, zooming down the hill which eventually runs, with several slaloming bends, into Gotham. Sketch was starting to get the wind up a little at our speed. "Don't worry, granddad's given it a complete overhaul; we'll be fine," I assured him over my shoulder. A muffled screech behind advised me to apply the brakes. There was a frantic pull on the back handlebars and then I heard a dull 'ding' as his bell hit the road. Then more alarming debris littered the road in our wake. Both sets of brakes had disintegrated.

Somehow I managed to guide the runaway tandem around one fairly gentle bend, with Sketchley's shoes burning rubber frantically on the tarmac. We were still going at a hell of a lick. There was no escape at the next bend. It was too sharp for me. We sailed over a strip of grass and plummeted into a hedge.

As I helped a groaning Sketch out of the hedge he bleated: "You're a flaming menace – and so is your granddad." Apart from a few bruises and scratches and several elderberry stains we were relatively unscathed, however. That's more than could be said of the tandem. A loudly grumbling Sketch and I had to push it five miles back to his house.

I kept telling my granddad we'd had a minor fault with it and we were going to put it right before returning it. However, it stayed there forlornly in Sketchley's yard until finally being picked up by a scrap metal merchant.

For the second time in about 13 years in the Leake Lane area my life had flashed past me. It took slightly longer this time.

Mum and Dad proudly showing me off...just before Dad went to war and
Mum nearly dropped me.

Aged around 18 months sitting on my doggie at Leake Lane.

Aboard my trike, which accompanied me in my plunge down the pit. I still bear the scars of my escapade. Cousin Margaret, the reason for my terror of worms, is alongside.

Mum and Dad. Our tin bath is behind them.

Dad and me in our Sunday-best.

A lazy summer's day in my great-uncles' orchard with Dad

My lovely nanan Ciss with my deaf and dumb great uncles, snapped at Skegness. Sadly I could find no picture of my granddad Joss, who was always camera-shy.

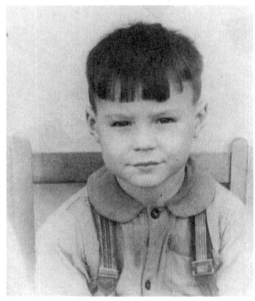

My first school picture.

Something has tickled my fancy; my brother John looks wary.

Brother John, Uncle Eric home on leave and the faithful 'cab-hoss' Joe.

Where is Lobby Lud? The family striding out in Skegness.

Frolicking in the surf with Mum at Skegness.

Wicksteed Park in 1954. My first crush Kathleen is the one on top of the fountain.

Kegworth County Primary School football team with our coach Polo doing a fair impression of Arsene Wenger. My 'Bob-a-Job' partner Paul Tuckley is the Milky Bar Kid lookalike top row, second right; my great pal Mick Snape holds the shield alongside me, the goalie. They wouldn't let me hold the trophy in case it slipped through my fingers.

My great boyhood friend John 'Sketch' Sketchley – subsequently to become a brilliant mathematician, but as unlucky with girls and tandems as me.

My maternal grandparents (Nanan and Granddad Elliott) with the uncle after whom I was named, Norman, and my pal Mick Snape.

Granddad Elliott on leave in 1917, pictured with my much revered Uncle Bob, Auntie Jessie and Nanan Elliott.

THE SAILORBOY

Chapter 13

BOXING CLEVER

It all came quite suddenly. I was expecting to join HMS Ganges, the training establishment at Shotley, Suffolk, around June time in 1960. However, a place came up early because a recruit had gone down with something, probably stage fright. A letter was sent to Mum inviting me to join the recruitment of May 3rd.

The big day came and Mum and brother accompanied me to Kegworth Station, where I was to meet up on the train with other East Midlands boys joining on the same day. I resembled a packhorse. I had a suitcase, a bag with food packed up by Mum that was nearly as big as the case, my beloved cricket bat and a tennis racquet. The train arrived and there was a tearful farewell from Mum and a proud handshake with my brother.

The carriages were alive with excited youths on their way to HMS Ganges. I met up with the recruiting officer and his entourage. He didn't seem quite as matey as he did when persuading Mum and me that a life before the mast was for me. In fact I quite recall a bit of a sneer on his face when he looked around at the motley crew that alighted at Liverpool Street Station in London on the way to Ipswich. We were quite a bunch, kids from all walks of life. There were all shapes and sizes. Some looked as though they had needed dragging onto the train. Some looked a bit tough and tried to make light of it all. Deep down, though, I think everyone was understandably apprehensive, callow 15-year-olds, switching their home environments for a life unknown. I had left Loughborough Grammar School the previous day. I could still feel the goodwill slaps on my back from my schoolmates and hear the whistles of the 'Sailor's Hornpipe' by some of my more ironic pals as I walked down the quadrangle for the last time.

For my foray into the unknown, I must have looked quite dapper compared to some of the boys, wearing a sheepskin jacket, my beloved worsted trousers and Italian-style shoes. That day would be my last as a follower of fashion for many a long month.

On the journey I struck up a conversation with one John Charles Wood from Tibshelf, Derbyshire. The diminutive but stocky 'Slinger' Wood and I would become inseparable 'shipmates' and partners in crime over the years.

By the time we had been mustered and collected from Ipswich Station, it was early evening. On arrival at HMS Ganges there was a lengthy process of allotting us 'mess decks' in the annex building of the training establishment. This was a separate compound with its own parade ground in the centre of a dozen living blocks, our home for about a month while we were sorted out into specific branches of the RN. It looked very austere. For a month we were to be dehumanised – well, at least de-civilianised.

First of all, though, there was, for me at any rate, quite a treat. Before we were sorted out into our respective blocks we were fed in a huge and, understandably, noisy canteen which rang with excited chatter from the boys of 31 Recruitment. Some, though, were sullen and tight-lipped, full of foreboding over what the immediate future had in store for them. I was a little fearful, it would be less than truthful of me to say otherwise. But Mum had instilled into me a sense of getting on with things, making the best of it all. How could I be too down, anyway? They served us up huge portions of eggs, beans – and chips, food to which I was totally unaccustomed but devoured with a will.

We were then introduced to our mess chief petty officer. I think we had hit the jackpot with CPO Brotherton, a kindly man with a lot of patience. We were not so lucky with our junior leader. Junior leaders were boys only a couple of years older than us who had already spent 18 months training and then been seconded to the annex to serve as mess deck mentors to the 'nozzers', the name given to raw recruits. Our junior leader was called 'Biff' Bailey, I'll never forget him. He was a sadistic bully who made our lives a misery the minute he got us on his own. Biff was a very apt name for him.

Having spent a restless night when the pangs of homesickness bit in, although not as badly for me as several boys in my mess who sobbed themselves to sleep, we were awoken by junior leader Bailey bashing a large, silvery receptacle, which I learned was called a 'spitkid'. This was in effect a huge, heavy ash-tray for cigarette ends and rubbish, which obviously also served in the past as a matelots' spittoon. We soon learned, though, it was anything but a receptacle for anything. It was a mess deck trophy to be polished until burnished enough to shave by. It was also, as I was soon to find out, an object of torture.

Well the evil Bailey had roused us at just before 5am. That wasn't a problem for me. I had been used to rising at that time before starting my paper round. A gaggle of bleary-eyed fresh recruits then took cursory ablutions before being herded into the canteen for breakfast. Even if it had been eggs, beans and chips again, I couldn't have eaten it. From what I remember, breakfast was uneaten in near silence. For the rest of the day I had some idea how Dad's cattle must have felt on the way to the abattoir.

For the next two days we were herded around like lambs to slaughter. The first part of the process I remember vividly. We were marched – well; they tried to march us; it was a rather chaotic tramp – to the camp barber. His name was, appropriately, 'Shotley'. He might easily have been called Crazy Horse or Geronimo. We were lucky to get out of his shop with our scalps. We all felt really miserable, reduced to a squad of toilet brushes by Shotley's manic clippers.

Then it was a medical and check by a dentist. I'm not sure why we were deprived of our locks first. It meant if someone failed the medical he would return home looking like a shorn sheep.

During the medical we were warned that there would be copious injections to come – smallpox, yellow fever, TB testing and so on. That really cheered us all up. The dentist wasn't much better. My teeth were pretty sound but years of sweets and chocolates had taken their toll. He told me I would need three fillings. I hadn't had any treatment since my trip to Plymouth. I remember one unfortunate lad, though, being told every one of his teeth had to come out! He was billeted in my mess. His teeth really were in a state. He didn't last the month out. He returned to the Black Country from where he hailed with his black teeth – and crew cut.

Worse was to come. My prized worsted trousers, jacket and Italian-style shoes were whisked away from me. So were my cricket bat and tennis racquet. My clothes were placed in a package to be sent to my home. The bat and racquet went into store until I went home on my first leave. There would be copious amounts of sports gear available over the next 15 months. Being parted from the cricket bat, though, brought me close to tears; but I held on.

My civilian garb had been replaced by a cotton 'white front' vest affair with blue piping around the neck that was as rigid as cardboard, worn under a light blue shirt and dark blue trousers, both stiff denim. We wore gaiters and unyielding black boots. A replica of the flat-top hat I'd found two years before, with a gold cap tally bearing the proud name 'HMS Ganges', made up the ensemble.

Soon we were issued with the main uniform: a full serge suit which was comprised of a tight-fitting collared tunic and bell-bottom trousers; more white fronts; sea jersey, a dark blue wool replacement for the white front for colder weather, itchy and, like the suit, smelling of mothballs; blue, stripe-edged collar that tied, out of sight, around the waist; black silk ribbon to go around the neck under the collar and down the front to be knotted at the bottom by a thin black cotton tie-up; a white rope lanyard, which went around the neck and ran down your tunic front above the silk. Boots were replaced by stout black shoes.

Deck slippers were issued for wear indoors. I loved these. They were rather snazzy black slip-ons. But I soon found out these were for polishing only, never to be worn. Much too stylish. Then there was the trench-coat style raincoat, made by Burberry. The 'Burbs' was, I soon found, one of a sailor's most treasured possessions. For the time in the annexe, however, it only came out for kit inspection. We were expected to utilise only our oilskin raincoats. With the uniform, we were issued with a bewildering array of kit, everything from kit bag and attaché case to shaving brush and Wilkinson razor. The shaving equipment was at that stage superfluous to requirement as I wasn't even sporting fluff on my chin. It didn't stop Biff Bailey ordering me to use it. Without copious use of toilet paper I might have bled to death on only my second night in the Navy.

All this kit had to show proof of ownership and woe upon the hapless recruit who lost any tiny part of it. When I had been at school, all my uniform and sports kit bore a woven tape with my name stitched on it in copperplate red silk. Would that HMS Ganges could have used the same ploy. No, we had to stitch our names on every piece of uniform and most of our kit, including towels and sheets, in red cotton. Everything had been stamped with your name on it. You then had to follow the marking in red cotton. Having never stitched a thing in my life, this was persecution far worse than homesickness. In fact, trying to make my name recognisable as 'N A Dabell' with extravagant 'homeward bounders', using as few stitches as possible, commanded a lot of my attention for hours. This included the sparse leisure time in the evening we were allowed, when most of the other boys wrote home or read, having finished their needlework.

Subsequently this kit would have to be laid out on a blanket near your bed. It was the first of myriad kit inspections, 'musters', where everything had to be spotless and in perfect order. The command: "Stand by your beds" barked at high decibel level, would strike fear into our hearts.

We were all dead beat, of course, by the time lights out came at around 8pm. On the third night we were awakened by a scream from one of the beds. The brutal Bailey, wearing a gas mask and shining a torch on the goggles, had shaken one wretched recruit and terrified him silly. Nearly everyone else lay cowering in their beds. Not so I and another foolhardy individual called Richard Carrington, a boy from Blackpool. We rather inadvisably urged the dreaded Bailey to leave us alone and let us get to sleep, knowing we'd be receiving a 5am call in a few hours' time. Bailey flew into a rage, ordering Carrington and me to get out of bed. Telling a junior instructor where to get off, even at this early stage of our Naval career, was considered a heinous offence. The spitkid was produced and Carrington and I had to take it turns holding out in front of us while 'bunny-hopping' around the mess, watched by the fearful eyes of our messmates, peeping from under blankets. Round and round we had to go bouncing on our haunches. The punishment lasted for an hour. Carrington and I were almost prostrate with exhaustion before Bailey allowed us back to bed.

In the morning Carrington and I could hardly stand with stiffness after a smirking Bailey gave us our alarm call. We felt it wasn't worth complaining to anyone. We would have only come in for more punishment. As it was we were earmarked for a month by Bailey for the dirtiest jobs in the mess, like cleaning up the bathroom area. Our messmates were less than sympathetic at the treatment we had meted out to us, either. Twice I got drenched by buckets of water emptied over the top of the toilet I was sitting in. My comrades neither liked the stand I'd made against Bailey because his behaviour went from bad to worse – nor what they judged a 'snotty' grammar school accent. It just hardened my resolve. I was determined not to lose my old Plum Dabell identity, nor any perceived plum in my voice for that matter.

I was soon to find out how tough I could become. First it was the seemingly endless array of 'jabs' that didn't hurt so much going in as the effects after, invariably a high temperature and headaches which you were expected to shrug off and get on with your introduction to the Navy. Then there was the follow-up visit to the dentist for two fillings. Then came parade ground drill. I'd done plenty of marching in the Combined Cadet Force at school, so that was no problem. Unlike some of my wretched fellow recruits, my arms swung and feet stepped correctly in unison. The assault course we were sent around was not a trial either, as I had negotiated something similar at Loughborough Grammar School in the CCF. I couldn't wait to put on muscle, though. I ached dreadfully at night. I also suffered from the onset of growing pains.

As well as all the disciplinary drills in the annex, designed to whip us into some kind of shape, there were assessment tests to carry out. First, though, there was officialdom to satisfy. We all had to officially become a set of digits which would come before our names. I understood we would all have to be numbered but it was what came before the numbers that left me responsible for making a major choice in my life without my mum being called upon to make it. Did I want to be a Devonport (Plymouth) or Portsmouth rating? My answer could have great bearing on my career I was informed. Whichever one I chose would be my 'home' port, where I would largely be based throughout my career – and once decided could not be altered.

Unlike the rest of the lads, who huddled in lengthy discussions, I made my mind up right away. Neither Naval port was particularly near to home but it wasn't logistics I was thinking about when I chose Devonport. It was my Auntie Blanche's cream teas.

So I became a 'Guz' rating as opposed to 'Pompey'. I was then officially D/056190 Dabell for the rest of my time in the Royal Navy.

There was even more important decision-making to come. And this time it wasn't jam and Devon cream that influenced me.

When we joined up we were all classed as 'Junior Seamen'. Now we had to decide which branch we would like to join. I liked the idea of being a radio operator. I wanted to join the Communications Branch.

Thence followed a quite involved aptitude test which took some time. First we were shown an alphabetical chart of the Morse code. I had a vague idea what it was from the Wolf Cubs, but the rows of dots and dashes took some explaining. We listened to each letter and its corresponding Morse code for what seemed an age. Then the chart was taken away and dits and dahs played over a loudspeaker. We had to write down each letter as we deduced it. I was considered proficient at the test and subsequently enrolled as a very junior radio operator, status pending, relying on how got on when I began tuition in the main establishment in a month's time.

Then we were given further education tests, these much stiffer than the one I had passed at the recruiting office in Derby. This was to assess us for GCE examinations we would be taking the following year.

It was not all work, though. To my delight, sporting acumen was also assessed. It was no surprise to me that I got good marks for the couple of cricket matches we played. That was despite not having my own bat. I was less than enthusiastic about gym exercising and my introduction to 'soft-ball', a sort of upgraded rounders and downgraded baseball. We were told that our days over in the main establishment of HMS Ganges would involve communications and educational lessons in the morning and evening – with most afternoons dedicated to sport. I was delirious at the prospect.

As the month-long stay in the annex drew to an end, however, there was one sport that caused more than a few anxious moments. Everyone had to take part in the annex 31 Recruitment boxing matches. They meant everyone. There wasn't a medical condition that could save anyone. Conscientious objection to the thought of having your nose punched was not allowed. Bouts of vomiting and diarrhoea at the prospect of stepping into the ring cut no ice. Boxing day was compulsory.

My only link with the noble art lay with all the boxing magazines of my uncle Eric's I'd read. I had been allowed to listen to Don Cockell and Dai Dower lose title fights over in America and I'd watched Jack Gardiner crown our carnival queen once. But that was it.

After a fitful night's sleep we were all herded into the annex gymnasium to stare nervously at its centrepiece, the ring. Each boy stepped onto weighing scales and we were sorted out into what we weighed rather than how tall we were. This was to produce a few odd matches. Then a list of bouts for the tournament's first day were announced. I was matched against a boy named Crowe.

It was a very fraught business watching the bouts before it was my turn. Matches were three one-minute rounds unless, as was occasionally the case, one boxer could not continue. There were no head-guards. There was little finesse. Each lad just tried to knock ten bells out of the other. Sometimes you could tell a boy had already studied the art of self-defence and that produced a very uneven contest. I don't mind admitting, I was a mound of jelly when my name and Crowe's were announced.

Physical training instructors checked our gloves and then the Chief PTI announced to the New Entry Divisional Officer: "Boxers ready sir." A whistle went and that was it. Having never worn a pair of boxing gloves in my life and never willingly attacked anyone before – I'd defended myself a couple of times – I just used animal instinct. Crowe could not have been better named. He had a huge beak. I just ran towards him and hit it as many times as I could. I regret to say, after several flurries of punches from me, Crowe's beak disintegrated. The bout was stopped with the poor lad's vest absolutely splattered with blood. I was euphoric. It was all over. I'd come through unscathed. Then I realised that only meant I'd got to fight in the next round.

My second match came in the afternoon, an opponent called Watson. I knew him very well. He was a real streetwise kid and had been really kind to me, telling me all the dodges to make life easier in the annex. I responded by launching at him like a raging bull as soon as the whistle went. I was no Jake LaMotta, however. The startled Watson ducked enough to allow my glove to go over his shoulder but he was helpless to stop my forehead smashing into his eye. The inadvertent Glasgow Kiss stopped the fight for a few moments while I was reprimanded and told that points would now be deducted from my score. The fight resumed. Watson's eye came up like a tomato. He could hardly see where he was going, let alone land a punch. I was loath to hit him in case I caught his bad eye, but reeled off a few body punches to show willing. Subsequently Watson was awarded the decision even though I can't remember one punch being landed on me. My explosive but illegal start had counted against me. I was told that if I was as handy with my fists as I was with my head then I could go far as a boxer. It proved a pyrrhic victory for Watson as he was unable to fight in the semi-finals because of his eye. There were no hard feelings from him, though. He was relieved he didn't have to step in the ring again. It took quite a while for his eye to go down. In a way I felt rather proud when those messmates who hadn't witnessed the afternoon's proceedings opined that I must have given Watson a hell of thump to cause a shiner like that. I had earned instant respect.

Chapter 14

HE WHO BARES WINS

Finally our stint at the annex was over. Before the Queen's Birthday Review at HMS Ganges, to celebrate our matriculation we were marched from the annex over to the main establishment. We were dressed in our best suits, by now having been fitted with the much less itchy and softer worsted No 1 outfit with a beautiful gold 'sparker's' badge on my right arm, the pair of wings with a lightning flash going through it that indicated I was a radio operator.

After inspection and march past we then met up with proud parents, who had travelled down to see the QBR and our passing out ceremony.

Mum and John had had some journey. They had caught a bus to Leicester and a train to London St Pancras. After a trip on the underground they then had to wait for four hours for the train from Liverpool Street to Ipswich. That involved an overnight journey. Mum remembers a kindly policeman finding them a carriage where my brother could get his feet up and a few hours' sleep. Mum was so apprehensive she didn't sleep a wink. Brother had been put in charge of a sandwich cake Mum had made for me and my friends. My brother would not let it out of his grasp. He was determined he should be the one who would present it to me.

After a bus trip to Ganges, Mum and bro., complete with a squashed sandwich cake, were greeted by the lieutenant who was to be my divisional officer and the petty officer telegraphist who would be my class PO, one Tony Cokes.

It was at this juncture that Mum became fully aware of the facts surrounding my joining up. I don't know what had been going on in her mind when she signed the form committing me to 12 years' service. I had been under no illusions what it all meant. Mum confessed to me later on in my career that she thought it was one year and that I could come out of the Navy after that time if I wasn't happy with my lot.

I wasn't exactly ecstatic with my lot – the annex had been pretty daunting – but I didn't suffer terrible homesickness like some and I was excited by the thought of getting to grips properly with my new life in the main part of HMS Ganges. I know we had to get up early and work late but in between we had afternoons of lovely sport or sailing on the rivers around Ganges, the Orwell and Stour.

My escapades in the boxing ring in the annex had not exactly given me a bloodlust but I was aware that I probably needed to put on some muscle on my arms and learn to defend myself properly. I had been able to look after myself when suffering some brief bullying but mostly through sheer bravado and bluff. I decided I was going to volunteer for the boxing training group when I got over to the main establishment of HMS Ganges. That was until I did some investigating and found out that potential boxers had to rise an hour before their colleagues, go down to the gym to get their faces disfigured – all before breakfast. Much as I wanted to elevate myself to an Adonis, the thought of getting my mouth whacked before breakfast did not appeal. I decided against boxing.

I was approached by a Royal Marine band sergeant, though, having let slip that I'd had a few sessions with Ruddington Silver Prize Band pre-joining up. The Ganges Bugle Band was looking for drummers. I fluffed my interview, however, not exactly endearing myself to the bandmaster who found me in the band shed pretending to be Gene Krupa. I wasn't what they were looking for. Good job for me really. I found out the bugle band got up even earlier than the boxers for their practice. And I soon discovered the racket they made when appearing on ceremonial occasions made them the object of great derision.

When we settled in our messes in the main establishment of HMS Ganges, all the juniors who had passed the test for communicators, 44 of us, were split into two classes, '223' for tactical operators and '232' for radio operators. We were all housed in Five Mess of Keppel Division. The tactical operators, under the wing of Chief Communications Yeoman (CCY) Alf Songhurst, were to be taught skills in semaphore, sending the Morse code by lamp and hoisting signal flags (bunting-tossing, we called it). We radio operators (sparkers) would learn to send and receive the Morse code by radio, send and receive voice messages, use teleprinters and, like the bunting-tossers, learn all about convoy communications. Both classes would be taught how to type on ancient cast iron typewriters. These lessons would be interspersed with school as we built up to GCE exams (the old General Certificate of Education that was replaced eventually by GCSEs).

Friendships were fashioned at this stage, a couple of which remain to this day. Denis Lloyd, a fellow goalkeeper, and the diminutive chancer I've mentioned called John (Slinger) Wood, struck up a camaraderie that has lasted into our 60s.

Before any lessons began in our first week in the main establishment both the classes from our mess were marched down to the swimming pool. I thought this was a rather nice way to begin our training – a pleasant dip. It did prove to be a baptism of fire.

When we got to the pool we were unaware what was to come as we were ordered to change into swimming costumes. We'd all thought it a bit strange that we had to carry our overalls with us but assumed they were just to change back into to avoid wetting our number eight uniform. However, when we were told to put on the overalls over our costumes, we were all a little nonplussed. It soon became clear what was going on though.

"Right you lot, up you go to below the main diving board," barked the PTI in charge, an unsmiling sadist, not for nothing, we found out later, called Basher. "You will then take it in turn to climb the diving board and jump off – in your overalls. You will then swim to the side of the pool – in your overalls. After this we will practise life-saving – in your overalls." "But I can't swim sir," bleated one hapless individual who had obviously fiddled his induction form. "Well you're soon going to learn laddie, aren't you?" growled Basher. One by one we jumped off the board and struggled to the side, our overalls billowing out like dark blue life rafts. The unfortunate lad who couldn't swim was grabbed by another PTI with a boat hook when he came spluttering and thrashing to the surface. He was terrified but Basher was unabashed as the kid was hauled out of the pool. He was consigned to swimming lessons in the shallow end, while we were taught how to rescue our opposite numbers in overalls that now weighed about 30lbs. This was the first of two swimming tests every sailor had to undergo in his career. The second part came about a year later when I had to jump off the side of a bow and swim underneath the ship, also in overalls.

That particular test didn't faze me one iota. I'd earned two swimming certificates well before Ganges and I'd been taught to life-save (not in overalls, however). The next one did.

The next day the two classes were told to 'muster' underneath the 143ft-high HMS Ganges mast. We were then ordered to climb it. One boy passed out. It wasn't the same one who couldn't swim. But this lad got the same short shrift. When he came to his senses following a couple of sharp slaps on the cheeks by the gunnery instructor who was soon to enhance our parade drill, he was told: "You might as well pull yourself together laddie because you *will* climb the mast. If you don't you will go no further at this establishment." I think the lad was ready to walk out the main gate there and then. However, a gentle arm around the shoulder from his class instructor, Chief Yeoman Songhurst, and a few encouraging words and he was ready, if resembling a strawberry jelly, to commit to the task.

He was not the only one terrified of the climb. I would say 90 per cent of us were trembling in our gym shoes as we made the ascent. It wasn't the rope ladder up to the first spar that troubled you, it wasn't the rungs that took you up to the second spar and it wasn't even the rungs that took you up to just under the top of the mast. It was getting around the 'devil's elbow' to progress to the middle of the mast. This entailed you scrambling around and over a large bulge that allowed you to ascend the mast. Imagine yourself hanging about 90ft above the ground with no safety harness and clawing at iron staves in order to haul yourself past this obstacle. There was a safety net underneath but that was hardly a comfort. Indeed, one of the Ganges legends told of a lad dropping off the devil's elbow and bouncing off the netting onto the nearby NAAFI roof. A broken neck had killed him. Good job we didn't know it when we were taking the test or I think the whole two classes would have fainted.

We all accomplished the feat, although I came close to needing clean underpants. I don't know what 'health and safety' would have made of it nowadays.

Remarkably, climbing the mast, well three-quarters of it, became quite a pastime for all of us on sunny weekends. We'd sit and eat a Crunchie or a Bounty on top of the devil's elbow and take in the Suffolk scenery and the rivers. However, we never had to scramble over the devil's elbow. You got to its platform via a trapdoor – which was locked when we did our test.

Life soon swung into a pattern at Ganges. The mess would be called to rise – abruptly – at around 5.30am by Tony Cokes: "Okay you ugly lot, hands off cocks and on socks." Ablutions would follow in a communal bathhouse after visits to the 'stalls'. I was a trifle delicate so that never rested very easily with me. I have had a loathing of communal toilets and bathrooms ever since. After sprucing up and donning working clothes we were then double-marched to the Central Mess

Galley (CMG), a huge refectory, for breakfast. Eventually we were trusted to get ourselves to breakfast unaided.

Before getting into this vast dining room we had to queue in the lobby, a huge cloakroom where your caps and rainwear could be deposited before eating. This meant an agonising slow shuffle forward to the entry to the dining room, made worse by the tantalising smells wafting from within. Sometimes you'd have to wait half an hour before you could sample the delights of streaky bacon (the camp officers had the lean slices), mushroom stalks (the officers had the heads), scrambled powdered eggs and anaemic tomatoes. Occasionally it would be a dish we lovingly called 'shit on a raft': evil-smelling and sinewy kidneys in gravy on teeth-breaking fried bread. We were no connoisseurs, though. Each morsel was absorbed with relish and seconds looked for if they were (rarely) on offer. When you returned to the lobby it was invariably to find your hat had been swapped for one in a worse condition than yours or 'frisbeed' to all parts of the cloakroom.

It could be a very frustrating start to the day but you soon got used to the routine and took everything in your stride. Well, nearly all of us. We had a lad in our mess called 'Titch' Howlett. He was given his sobriquet because he couldn't have been taller than 4ft 9ins and weighed about six stone. His clothes used to hang off him. He was pretty plucky because most days he'd make a run for the dining room entrance to skip waiting in line. He did it once too often though. He was grabbed by one chap and hung up on a coat-hook. When we came out of breakfast poor old Titch was still hanging there, howling, with his feet thrashing the air like some overturned insect.

Breakfast over, it was parade to show your uniform was clean and then to work, either school or signal school training before lunch, when you went through similar purgatory as you had at breakfast. A typical lunch menu would be meat that was frequently indistinguishable as pork, beef or mutton, powdered potato, broccoli and cauliflower stalks (the officers had the heads), bullet peas, gravy that you could slice, followed by a pudding so heavy with suet you felt as if you'd swallowed one of HMS Victory's cannonballs. No matter, we tucked in with gusto. We were burning off so many calories.

Mum would have been so proud of me. I developed an appetite. It didn't matter what was on offer at mealtimes. I ate everything. I even managed liver. There was no need this time to wear it around my ears.

I could never get enough to eat. On 'blank weeks' (we were paid fortnightly) when I didn't have enough for 'nutty' (confectionary), food from home was a Godsend. Every day when the mail was dished out, every lad lived in hope of the much-coveted 'parcel chit'. This meant you had had a parcel arrive at the Ganges post office. You could hardly wait for morning sessions to complete so you could go and fetch your prized booty. Mum kept me going in chocolate cakes all through my time at Ganges. It made me a very popular messmate. Everyone wanted to know me when I got a parcel chit. The mail was a lifeline with home and the thrill I'd get when I had a letter or parcel lived with me throughout my career. It kept me going through thick and thin. I was never so dismayed, though, as when a postie would look over at me at the end of mail call and say, "Sorry Dabs, nothing for you today."

Afternoons would be dedicated to sports and sailing (deadly if you fell overboard after a treacle duff). Early evening we resumed training before attacking supper (yes, similar routine at the CMG and similar fare). Late evening meant cleaning up the messdeck before an hour of leisure activity and ablutions. We were in bed by 2100 hours.

However, there was always plenty of chat from bed to bed before the mess settled down for the night. One night I was the victim of a scam by Slinger and another reprobate called Mick Clifford that I remember all too vividly.

Our mess was situated in a covered avenue of messes called, not that puzzlingly, 'Long Covered Way', not far from a machine that dispensed such highly sought after delights as Bounty, Mars and Crunchie bars. Having enough money to be able to use this machine was very rare. Normally we eyed the goodies wistfully for about 12 days, only able to afford to use it on payday and perhaps the day after.

"Come on then Yogi," – my new nickname, gained, I think, for my penchant for goodies like the scavenging bear of the times – "we dare you to climb over the roof after lights out and get a bar of nutty out of the machine," said the grinning Woods, Clifford adding: "We've got the sixpence – you have to go and get the goods." I couldn't resist.

Accepting the dare meant I would have to possibly run the gauntlet with the duty officer and petty officer who patrolled the premises like SS men. There was no way this act could be done conventionally via the front of the mess. First I would be spotted by our leading junior, a sort of trusty in our ranks who had higher status and slept in the front bed near the corridor leading out to Long Covered Way. Then I'd be bound to get my collar felt by one of the hawkeyed duty officers. There was only one way of doing it – clamber out of a mess window, scale the roof, drop down to the nutty machine and bring back a bar as proof of the feat. "OK, I'll do it," I acquiesced.

Our messdeck was a low-level building and, clad in Naval regulation stripey pyjamas, I clambered out of the window. Just as I'd scrambled onto the roof I heard the click of a latch. To my chagrin and horror, my so-called pals had closed the window.

Now the idea started to lose its appeal. I decided to abort. "Let me in you swine," I gesticulated to Wood and Clifford as I hung down to the window. I could see them, doubled up in devilish mirth. Their faces disappeared.

What to do? I did have the tanner and after all there was a Bounty or a Crunchie at stake. I heaved back up to the roof, scaled it, jumped down the other side and sprinted across to the machine. I put in the coin from a sweating palm and plucked out my bar of chocolate. What to do now? Back up to the roof

I suppose. Surely Wood and Clifford would put me out of my misery. I heard the window catch click. With relief filling my being and almost my pyjamas I swung down to the window. The treacherous Wood and Clifford leant out. However, any thoughts that I had that they were going to help me in were swiftly dashed. As I hung there they pulled off my pyjama bottoms and closed the window again.

There I hung, half naked – the important part of me naked. The giggling from Wood and Clifford and desperate cries from me had attracted an audience. The whole mess, including our leading junior Paddy Bates, was awake wondering what was going on. The spectre of Dabell at the window with private parts in full relief must have been less than a pretty sight. Finally Wood and Clifford gave in, realising that any more fuss was going to alert a duty petty officer and they'd be implicated if I got caught. They allowed me to swing in through the window.

The helpless titters of Wood and Clifford can haunt me to this day. It was difficult to attain reparation from the pair. Slinger was only a little chap and I would be classed as a cowardly bully if I gave him a seeing-to; Clifford was the best boxer of our recruitment. I eventually acceded to the fact that it was a great sting and I'd been stupid in not realising I was being set up. Anyway, I had the Crunchie bar. And I wasn't going to be sharing any of it.

Soon we were working hard on our careers as communicators which first involved learning the Morse code at speed and how to touch-type. An exercise either written or typed taking down Morse code was called a 'biffer'. Nobody ever explained why it was called this but 'biffer' it was throughout my career. I suppose it was onomatopoeia, the tapping sound made by a Morse key. More involved studies concerning voice technique on the radio, telecommunications, operating within convoys and the like, would come later.

We learned to touch-type in the most perplexing way. In the typing classroom we used a cast iron typewriter apiece, something like one of those old Imperials which weighed about three stone. They were virtually indestructible. None of the keys on the keyboard had any letters or figures on them. The only way you could negotiate the keys was by peering up on to the ceiling where the keyboard was laid out. You were given an exercise to type, moving from nursery rhymes as we became more proficient to perhaps an old movie script or a piece from a radio show. We had to type like metronomes in time to a march by John Philip Sousa – 'The Washington Post'. The record in the classroom would boom out until it was gauged you should be at the end of a line and then the music would stop and a stentorian voice would bark out: "Carriage return". It was pure havoc at first as you tried to get to the end of that line before the command rang out. Sometimes you'd get there too early so that would bring a welcome breather. However, that could lull you into a false sense of satisfaction and sure enough, you'd be belting along to catch up.

Eventually though we got the hang of it and that must have then been pretty soporific for the typing teacher. To someone listening outside the classroom it would have sounded like a carpenter hitting a nail ever so slowly in time to band music: tap, tap, tap, tap... "Carriage return". It wouldn't have been so bad if we could even just had a bit of Sousa variation but no, it was the old 'Washington Post' over and over again.

As we became fairly adept, typing training got a bit more lax. The instructor often left us alone for long periods, leaving us to tap on our own. He would then return when 'stand easy' blew out on the bugle on the Signal School tannoy. This denoted a 15-minute break for us all, normally spent absorbing a Bounty bar at speed before someone cadged a piece off you. Sousa would be switched off during this period.

One day, someone had the bright idea of smuggling in an LP and using the typing room record-player during the break. Our only record player in the mess had long given up the ghost, a bit like the iron that got fed up with doubling as a toaster. Elvis Presley was voted in as the record of choice.

During this 'stand easy' we were all swaying away when one of our number – he'd gone out for a Woodbine – came hurtling back into the classroom, warning us that our instructor was on his way back early. Elvis was frantically halted in full flow but there was no time to pluck the record off the machine before the instructor strode in. "What have you lot been up to? You all look guilty as sin," he growled, as we all melted into our seats in front of our typewriters. Over to the record player he went. We feared the worst. However, without as much as a glance at the vinyl he switched on the machine. The Elvis LP owner blurted: "But, but sir…" It was too late. On came Elvis to dumbfound the instructor. He was quick on his feet, though. "Right, if that's the kind of music you want to type to, so be it," gloated the instructor. We found it awfully difficult to tap away in time to 'Blue Suede Shoes', but we had to do it. We didn't even have the benefit of "carriage return". "If anyone has just one mistake in their typing piece then he'll do some doubling up and down the Signal School steps," snarled the instructor. Needless to say, not one piece was error-free. We all finished up running up and down 'Faith, Hope and Charity', the name of the three lots of steps that led down to the foreshore of Shotley harbour. I went off Elvis for a long time.

Our schooling was not dissimilar to Loughborough Grammar School. However, history was replaced by 'Naval history' and general science was augmented by two separate subjects: magnetism and electricity, useful especially for wireless operators; and mechanics, probably more useful for the seamen. We also studied navigation separately from geography. I got on far better at school at Ganges than I was ever going to at LGS and passed everything at either GCE or Education Test One – apart from maths, well geometry really, which I still couldn't fully grasp.

There were various methods to provide character-building for us young recruits. Most of this was carried out on either the lower track or on the rivers Orwell and Stour. Our 'division', called Keppel, would be pitted against the other divisions at sports on the lower track. I enjoyed this in the summer but slogging around the steeplechase circuit in early November was no joke. I remember doing my best but stamina was often a problem for me. I was even leading one steeplechase when my scrawny legs just gave up on me. Unfortunately for me this happened just as I came to the water jump. With my poor old legs wilting badly I hit the top of the water jump with a good old clatter and went neck and crop into the water. It was about three feet in depth. I was dragged out coughing and spluttering, nearly the first person on record to drown in a water jump.

Sailing on the rivers below HMS Ganges was a delight in the summer. What could be more efficacious and exhilarating than cruising along, full-sail, with a cloudless sky above you? It was not so idyllic in the winter. When your whole body is in shock at being hit by freezing spray and your hands are rigid with cold when 'going about', your misery knows no bounds. It was considered moral fibre-building, though, and it had to be done. It was remarkable just how many heavy colds got reported to the sick bay on winter sailing days. That wasn't much better than the ordeal on the Orwell, however. You'd have your head jammed over a tin basin of menthol crystals and a towel draped over you – to sweat out the cold. A sick bay attendant would hold your head down to make sure you didn't rise from your basin, even if you felt you were choking to death. The effect of the crystals was something similar to tear gas. It soon cured malingerers.

Chapter 15

UP THE CREEK

Ultimate character-building came when our class was sent on 'expeditions'. These 'expeds' saw the class embark on various exercises, either tramping to a destination in the wilds of Suffolk using map-reading and compass skills when on foot and basic navigation when on the river.

Our first exped saw us loaded into a lorry and then dropped off in the Suffolk countryside. The plan was to find a camping spot and stay the night at it, then the next morning find your way back to Ganges on foot. We all paired off with our tents and groundsheets, pots and pans and exped rations. Of course it was Slinger and I against the world. We were almost doubled up with the equipment we had to carry, me a human stick insect and Slinger not five feet tall. Quickly we lost contact with the rest of the gang after we had been booted off the lorry. However, eventually we came to a spot where we reckoned a camp site could be.

There wasn't a sign of anybody around and it was starting to get dusk. "Let's put the tent here," said the adventurer Dabell, choosing a spot up on a mound and under trees. "Don't think that would be the best place," advised Slinger, having taken on the air of some kind of midget Baden-Powell. "There'll be loads of insects in the trees and, besides, something might fall on us." I gave in and we pitched our tent at the bottom of the rise instead. I casually say "pitched the tent" but of course it wasn't as easy as that. Neither of us were expert campers. I'd had only limited experience as a cub scout and Slinger wouldn't have known what a tent peg was if it rose up in his soup. Tempers got frayed several times as we frequently saw our new home-to-be flop flat. A strong breeze didn't help the proceedings and threatened to send our planned refuge back to Ganges. Eventually it was erected, although it did look very lopsided and fragile. It was just as well. It started chucking down.

The day had been exhausting, though, and after a few nervous comments about whether the tent would stand a really bad storm, it wasn't long before we were both sound asleep in sleeping bags on our ground sheets. I was awakened in pitch dark by whimpering from the tent entrance, near where Slinger had opted to sleep (as protector of our tin opener). "I'm soaked," moaned the wretched Wood. "Water's come into the tent." When I squeezed my head out of my sleeping bag I knew it was not just Slinger in trouble. I was lying in about two inches of water, too.

We had no idea what to do but decided that we had to stay put until it got light. Slinger had tried crawling out of the tent and found himself up to well past his elbows. A torch we had been given had met a watery end and didn't work. There we sat, huddled together in inches of water, waiting for dawn.

When first light came the extent of our woes became evident. The stream below where we had camped had burst its banks. We were marooned. There we stayed, with only tinned corned beef left that was edible. Our bread had floated away. It even took an age to locate the tin opener in the bog that was now our tent floor. "You and your blasted insects Slinger. I'd sooner be covered in bites and dry."

Thankfully the rain gradually eased but it was not a happy duo that slopped its way to the meeting point that morning, hauling dripping equipment in soaking clothes. We came in for much derision. Our expedition mates had spent a warm dry night after sitting around a camp fire, drinking pop. They'd given up looking for us when it started raining.

I rather hoped there wouldn't be too many more expeds but sure enough, another one was devised a couple of months later. This time we were given options. We could either go off on another hiking expedition or take a cutter along the River Stour and up Manningtree Creek. Several of us opted for the cutter, a fairly substantial sailing boat, the next size up from a whaler. It sounded as though it would be great fun.

About a dozen of us set off in great style from the jetty just below the Faith, Hope and Charity steps down from Ganges. We sailed with faith and hope but weren't deluded enough to expect any charity.

The idea was to sail up to Manningtree and then put ashore. Visions of Bounty bars and dandelion and burdock from a shop near Manningtree harbour danced before my eyes.

Would we had got that far. Almost inevitably a squall blew up before we had gone a mile. There was precious little cover in the cutter apart from a smallish tarpaulin sheet. I didn't even get chance to get under cover because I'd volunteered to be bowman. That was the second most important job after the coxswain of the boat. I was now wishing I'd not wanted to be that important for this trip.

Basic navigation hadn't included a check on tides and obstacles along the creek. After all we were only in a cutter, not the Queen Mary. Big mistake. After about two hours sailing and with Manningtree just about in sight, there was an almighty crunch which shuddered the boat, followed by a chilling scraping noise. "Land Ho," the bowman (me) shouted out, rather sarcastically. We'd run aground on a small sandbank. "You bloody menace Yogi, you were supposed to be lookout," barked the coxswain, Paddy Bates, our class leader. "Right, everybody overboard to make the cutter lighter and I'll try and steer us off." Over the side into about two feet of water we went. Well, we pushed and heaved, but the cutter would not budge. With the tidal flow of the Stour, as time went by we became stuck even faster. The cutter eventually swayed but it proved to be falsely optimistic of us to think we might have been free. The boat merely leaned over. We were marooned. Not exactly up the creek without a paddle because we had emergency oars. But they don't work all that well in six inches of water.

There we had to stay, cold, drenched and miserable, trying to huddle under a tarpaulin. And before long, hungry. "Right, let's see what provisions we've got," said Paddy. Not very much was the answer. As it was just supposed to be a day trip, we had been provided with only lunch rations, which we perennially starving lot had demolished within half an hour of setting off. All we had left was a tin of salmon and a loaf of bread. There was no Jesus on board.

We were stuck there for hours. My name was mud rather than sand. "Why didn't you keep your bloody eyes open, Yogi?" Eventually, joy of joys, we felt the cutter starting to sway again and we swung upright. With the tide changing, soon we were free. We'd been stuck for about six hours. The oars were brought into action as well as the sail. We might still make breakfast.

Needless to say, when Keppel 232 class decided on its rowing crew for the annual Ganges water sports day, Dabell was not picked. It wasn't just because of my puny arms. I was considered a Jonah, shudderingly remembered for a night on a sandbank and a tin of salmon. There was no way anyone was going to run the risk of me catching a crab.

Time at Ganges sped along. It was hard but fulfilling work learning to be a communicator and readying ourselves for examinations at the end of our 15-month stint at the establishment. To offset the studies there was plenty of lovely sport, at which I proved to be fairly accomplished. This brought real advantages, like getting extra trips away from the establishment in cricket, football and rugby teams. I'm not too sure about the rugby match we played against the local approved school, though. The opposition took great delight in venting their ire at being locked up and literally walked all over us. Cricket, though immensely enjoyable, had a downside, too, when a misjudged hook earned me my first broken nose.

Leave was allowed on Saturday afternoons to Ipswich and Felixstowe and on Sundays after parade and church, normally a day for parents to take offspring for tea and sticky buns locally in Shotley. Ever the dreamer, I had amorous hopes – like two of my classmates, who had girlfriends in Ipswich – of meeting a dreamboat. I'd grown tired of visits to the roller-skating and ice rinks. Because of my shyness I never got very far with the girls, until one day I somehow got talking to a young lady on the bus to Felixstowe. I have to say she was a little bit forward and did all the running. Perhaps I should have heeded the warning signals being relayed to me by several mates on the bus. Enveloped in bliss that a girl had actually taken interest in me, I ignored all the hissed comments and agreed to her suggestion of accompanying her to Felixstowe Fair. I didn't have a lot of money with me, we recruits were always broke because we were only paid 7/6d a fortnight out of our princely salary of two pounds ten shillings; the rest went into a Post Office savings book. But I had enough to take her on the dodgems and buy her a candyfloss. I was rewarded with a little cuddle as she squealed with mock fear when we crashed our way around on the dodgem cars.

My money was soon spent. And so was my love life. With empty pockets I reluctantly caught an early bus to Shotley. My new squeeze said she had some relatives to visit and bade me farewell. I was thoroughly miserable when I arrived back at Ganges, especially as I got it in the neck from the duty regulating chief petty officer (nickname Gessler after William Tell's infamous persecutor) for having white fluff on my suit jacket. It had come off my young lady's cardigan when we cuddled on the dodgems.

When I made my way to the CMG later that night, miserable that an afternoon that had promised much had come to nothing, I ran into a few lads who had caught the last bus back to Ganges from Felixstowe. One of them had white fluff all over his jacket. He, too, had been taken for a ride.

One week we were warned that there would be a major exercise taking place at Ganges – how we would be involved if there were a nuclear attack on Britain. It conjured up all sorts of ideas in the young minds of our gang in 232 mess. We imagined devastated buildings being mocked up; nurses running about all over the place; discovering secret bunkers in the Ganges grounds which had been set aside as nuclear shelters.

I finished up handing out rock buns.

It was indeed a major exercise, with endless commands posted on noticeboards about where we should muster in the event of a nuclear attack. (By the Russians of course. The Cold War was in full swing.) Then we were told we would have to carry out a variety of duties to assist the public, who we had to assume would be, well, running about like chickens with no heads.

My post was the huge indoor parade ground where we had had our passing out parade when we arrived in the main barracks. There were chief petty officers and petty officers barking out orders all over the place. On a noticeboard it told each rating where they had to carry out emergency duties in the building. My duty was to hand out rock buns and little bottles of milk to the refugees from the nuclear attack. Just what they wanted. No gas masks or protective gear. Just a rock bun and a swig of milk. The duty did have its rewards, although I can hardly stare a rock bun in the face nowadays. I must have eaten at least a dozen during the exercise.

About this time in 1961 my mum got married again and I was delighted that the ceremony had been timed to coincide with my leave. Mum's new husband was a great bloke called Ray, an aircraft engineer who had served in the Royal Navy Fleet Air Arm. Ray was just right for our chaotic family. He had survived his first ship being sunk within just a few weeks of going to sea and when he rejoined the fleet another ship got sunk underneath him. Ray had been a bachelor all his life until he met Mum. I remembered him tearing around Kegworth in his Morgan JAP. He was a lovely, cuddly, man.

I had plenty to talk about while home on leave. Ray nearly split his sides when hearing about my exploits, remembering back to when he was a 'matelot'. Mum adored her new husband. I was so happy for her. My brother seemed settled. We were a family again.

On the second week of leave, conscious of the fact that most of my pals in the mess had girlfriends at home I decided I must take the plunge myself.

It was a terrific act of bravery by me because I was desperately shy with girls. It wasn't so much the act of talking to them, rather the thought of being shunned. The little episode with the girl in Felixstowe didn't help and nor did that dratted chipped tooth. However, I'd found out that the girl who lived next door to my maternal grandparents – they had moved back down to their old home in Leake Lane – was quite sweet on me.

Patsy, a petite, dark-haired girl, was like me, very shy. We'd swapped smiles now and then whenever I'd gone down to see my nanan and granddad. But I'd never actually spoken to her. Urged on by my grandparents, though, I somehow summoned up the courage to knock on Patsy's door, with the idea of asking her out. When her mum answered I very nearly copped out, undecided whether to flee or ask if Nanan could borrow some self-raising flour. All-of-a-tremble, I was ushered into the dining-room and invited to have a cup of tea with Patsy. It seemed the whole family knew why I was there. It took a huge amount of courage to ask Patsy to go to the pictures with me at the weekend. I was elated when she agreed.

A couple of days later I rode to Leake Lane on my bicycle, parked it at my grandparents' house and Patsy and I caught the bus into Loughborough. I can't remember the film because I was on my nerve ends trying to make sure she enjoyed what was my first real grown-up date. She assured me she had when we arrived back at Leake Lane. I shook hands, as per protocol in those days and suggested we might do it again. I was delighted when she agreed. It would, though, have to be when

I was next on leave as I was due to return to Ganges two days later.

I was so shy in those days that I was too embarrassed to tell Mum and Ray about my date. They had thought I had gone to Gotham to be with my cousins. In conversation, though, it somehow came out that I had taken Patsy on a date. I can remember now admitting it guiltily, as if I had committed a felony. Mum and Ray were thrilled, though, and made quite a fuss of me. I then felt as if I had surmounted one of life's great hurdles.

Patsy and I wrote to each other for months and we swapped photographs. I was really proud to exaggerate a little and show off my 'girlfriend' to the lads. That date was to be the only one, however. Patsy took a job at Boots the Chemist in Loughborough and obviously overcame her shyness because her letters dried up. Then her family moved. I never saw her again.

Just before returning off leave, Ray decided we should all have ice creams when we heard the van's chimes outside. Ray and I went out to fetch them to find a terrific shemozzle going on. Two ice cream sellers were brawling on the pavement. Mr Softee was doing his best to knock the living daylights out of Mr Whippy. Apparently the young upstart Whippy had encroached on the Softee patch. They went at it blow for blow for quite a time as a sizeable crowd gathered. I thought it was brilliant. Ray laughed his socks off. It didn't end until Mr Whippy stopped one too many and withdrew with his van, leaving his opponent to serve up the cornets with an ever blackening eye.

By and large the 15 months spent at Ganges was a great time for a youngster who wanted to learn a job and enjoy sport. But one officer in particular proved to be the bane of all our lives - Squeegee. He gained his sobriquet by way of a pair of large rubbery lips that looked like the implement we used to dry out the bathroom.

Lieutenant Squeegee had the most worrying stammer. Worrying because you never knew what was going to appear from those huge lips. Communication from him began as a low growl emanating from his jowls and then began the gestation period of his pregnant stutter, an effort that left him looking as though he was on the verge of apoplexy. As the volcano finally spewed out its message, a look of relief swept over his drained features.

Punishment was Squeegee's thing. His favourite mode of chastisement was the cut across the bare bottom with a wet lanyard, the thin piece of rope worn around a sailor's neck and tied with a gallows knot to enhance the sting. You could get half a dozen cuts for the most minor of misdemeanours, like talking or being caught reading after lights-out or not having your footwear in a dead straight line under your bed when he did 'rounds'.

The most infamous incident with Squeegee came right at the end of my time at HMS Ganges. Our class broke the Signal School record for achievements at final exams. As well as our certificates and the giant trophy for our mess cabinet, we were awarded a huge cake in celebration of our achievement, baked by our instructor Tony Cokes' wife. We were handed it on the Friday evening of our last official day of instruction. The class was supposed to eat it on the Saturday afternoon following 'rounds' when we knocked off for the day. But the promise of chunky icing and all the thoughts of what lay beneath it proved far too much for always starving youngsters.

Paddy Bates, our chief honcho, had been put in charge of the cake. He was a bit wary of doing anything daring in case he lost his rate because it provided him with all sorts of privileges not available to the rest of the class – going straight to front of the enormous dining-room queue was one. However, we cajoled him into producing the mouth-watering cake after lights-out.

We all gathered in the airing room, always as warm as toast and perfect for lads clad in pyjamas, and Paddy cut the cake with a knife purloined from the dining-room in anticipation of the tasty treat. Slices of the delicious largesse were only just reaching mouths when the door of the mess was flung open. Our bête noire, swinging a lanyard, came bursting into the airing room. Mouthing spluttering orders like an-out-of-control machine-gun, Squeegee looked as though he was going to have a heart attack. We all had to throw our cake slices into the dustbin.

It was going to take a marathon lanyard session by Squeegee if he were to punish all 22 of us. Possibly fearing tennis elbow he ordered us to collect our oilskins and fall in outside the mess. We were then ordered to put on the oilskin back-to-front, very uncomfortable around the throat especially. Then came the order "double march". Running around the parade ground in the dark was bad enough but with an oilskin the wrong way round, it was purgatory. Round and round we went until several dropped to the ground because of sheer exhaustion. Our finale at Ganges was anything but a piece of cake.

Mum and my brother John made the trip down to Ganges again to watch my passing out ceremony. After we had our march past it was tea and sticky buns for Mum, John and me with all the officers and NCOs who had been responsible for my 15 months of training. After a mass picture of all the 31 Recruitment boys and the Ganges hierarchy, we had the afternoon and evening free. Mum took John and me for lunch (no chips) and then I was allowed to choose a film for us to see at one of the Ipswich cinemas. I opted for *The Rebel*, starring Tony Hancock. I was a great fan of 'Hancock's Half Hour' – the lugubrious comedian was up there for me with the Goons. I enjoyed the film immensely. It wasn't really Mum's cup of tea but she pretended to enjoy it just for me. My brother slept all the way through it.

Fond farewells were made to HMS Ganges in the summer of 1961 (you only remember the good times) and I said goodbye to Slinger, who had been chosen to stay on as a junior instructor at the annex.

By this time I had grown a couple of inches to 5ft 10ins and filled out by a stone to 9st 7lbs. There was more growing (to nearly 6ft 2ins) and gaining weight to come over the next few months as our class, along with the bunting-tossers, headed for HMS Mercury, a sort of finishing school for communicators.

Chapter 16

SEA FEVER

HMS Mercury was in the wilds of Hampshire, in the Meon Valley and comprised a signal school and barracks, with Nissan Hut classrooms. Here we were to learn more about telecommunications, how to tune radios, listen in to shipping broadcasts, use cryptography and capture electronic signals which, as if by magic, produced taped and hard copy messages.

I gained my first promotion, made class leader. This earned me a pair of white gaiters instead of the normal khaki ones, the responsibility of marching and doubling the class around at parade and going from class to class. I had to make sure our mess in the junior intake quarters was kept spotless. While we were not housed in one of the six blocks where the more senior ratings lived, there was a relaxed atmosphere in our hut now that we were on the brink of joining the fleet as fully-fledged communicators.

Rather excitingly, our divisional officer was a sub-lieutenant Briggs who was, of course, nicknamed 'Basher'. Well, Basher was an enduring celebrity. He was one of only three survivors from HMS Hood when she was sunk by the Bismarck. For many years he featured in documentaries and films, although I don't remember him ever talking about it to us lads. Over the years, I would be proud to reveal that Basher was once our divisional officer.

We had nowhere near the constant supervision we'd had at HMS Ganges. After work and parades and such like, I was supposed to be the authority in the mess. I was hardly a Captain Bligh. In fact I was probably guiltier of horseplay than most.

Denis Lloyd had been a bosom pal all through training at Ganges. We were both goalkeepers and found ourselves in constant opposition to play in teams on several occasions throughout our Naval careers. I have to admit that Denis probably had the edge over me. I was more spectacular but, and this won't come as any surprise, I was more prone to the sudden inexplicable boob that could cost the team dearly. I'd had that fault since schooldays, probably nerves, and it lived with me through all my goalkeeping career.

On this Sunday afternoon Denis and I were practising goalkeeping moves in the corridor of the washrooms of our mess with a tennis ball, making exaggerated leaps and each trying to outdo each other. The tennis ball ran free as we tried to wrestle it from each other and I made a lunge at it. I missed and carried straight on – through a window. I didn't really feel any pain but was alerted to the fact that I might be seriously hurt by Denis: "Norm, you're bleeding like a stuck pig." I looked down at my wrists, which had led me through the window, and blood was spurting out of them like geysers. I was rooted to the spot. "What do I do?" I quivered as blood spattered the washroom floor. I had sliced into the arteries of both wrists. "We're going to have to stop it somehow," Denis said, looking nervously over at his pristine bath towel nearby. I decided that I'd sacrifice my own towel for the sake of first aid and wrapped it around both wrists, with Denis holding it in place. We were both in just underpants so we made a comical sight shuffling up to the mess together like OAPs doing a barn dance. "Somebody run and tell the duty petty officer," I barked at my goggling messmates, switching from frightened wounded lad to class leader.

After somehow managing to put on deck slippers, Denis and I waddled along together to the Mercury sickbay. By the time the duty PO met up with us on the way, both towels were soaked. I'd lost a fair bit of blood by the time a ferocious looking SBA (sick berth attendant, a sort of paramedic) inspected me. I was whipped straight into the surgery and stitches were put in the wounds. Finally the bleeding stopped. I then had to sit quietly for an hour, having been given a huge mug of tea, presumably to help my body make up for the blood I'd lost.

Denis and I both got it in the neck the next day, when the report from the sick bay went in. I sported wrist bandages for a few days and the whispers went around Mercury – I'd tried to commit suicide by slashing my wrists over a Wren who had spurned me. For years I had to explain how the scars on my wrists came about.

We weren't men but as 16-year-olds, going on 17, we were starting to be treated as such. We received a ration of cigarettes called 'Blue Liners', lethal jobs that took your breath away. From smoking the occasional fag at Ganges, more as an experiment than anything else, I became a serious, although always guilty (Mum wouldn't approve) smoker. Then there was proper leave. At weekends we could catch a bus into Portsmouth, for instance. The rest of the class had to be back 'on board' by 2200 hours but, as class leader, I didn't have to get back until 2230.

Pay increased, so you could enjoy your time off in Pompey, where we soon learned that the NAAFI Club was the place to go. It was a great venue, the centrepiece of which was a huge dance floor where we bopped and rocked to a huge jukebox, sometimes to a band. Well I would have done if I could have got a girl to dance with me.

The first time my friends and I went to the club in a leafy lane in suburban Portsmouth, 20 or 30 girls were queuing up. "Sign me in, Jack," came the plea, as the girls tried to gain admittance to the club. The NAAFI was for service personnel only but one girl per serviceman, mostly Navy lads, could be signed in for the night. Imagining all sorts of pleasures to come, I did indeed allow a young filly to clasp my arm as I walked her into the club, ignoring warnings from older sailors on their way in who had spurned the sirens. I signed for her on the door and the girl made for the cloakroom to deposit her coat. That was that. The next time I saw her she was dancing with an older bloke to an Eddie Cochran number. "Can I have a dance, being as I signed you in?" I asked wistfully. "Sod off Jack," came the withering reply as the girl looked at me as if I was something she had trodden in while waiting in the lane.

Money was always tight but I hit on to a way of making an extra few bob by scouring HMS Mercury's grounds for empty 'Fling' bottles. The orange drink was a great favourite among the sailors and the Wrens, who were not exactly ecologically sound in those days, when a rubbish bin was a fairly scarce commodity anyway. I'd devote lunch breaks to wandering around Mercury looking for the empties, which, when returned, brought in two pence a bottle. I'd learned the trick from taking back beer bottles as a kid.

It very nearly led to me getting a good working over, however, in an incident right out of *The Godfather*. Unbeknown to me, I had muscled in on somebody's perceived monopoly of the Fling province.

One day, as I started my rounds, this be-whiskered tramp grabbed me in a vice-like grip by the arm. "What do you think you're up to sonny?" growled my assailant, who, to my great bemusement, was actually wearing Naval number eights (blue denim shirt and trousers). "Them Fling bottles are my business and nobody else's, so leave 'em alone, see, or you'll be in for it." Shaking myself free from his hold I looked him up and down and fancied I could take him. "Who's going to stop me?" I reposted belligerently. "You'll find out sonny," said the hobo, slinking off.

I was determined not to be frightened off, even if this vagrant did seem rather confident with his threats. It did at least put me off from Fling collecting that lunchtime. I decided to investigate.

The hobo was called Wally and he was something of a long-standing character at Mercury. Wally was actually a sailor, what is appealingly called in the Navy a 'three-badge fuck-all'. This is a rating who has been in the RN for donkey's years, gaining three long-service stripes, without achieving any rate above able-seaman. He'd been at Mercury for longer than anybody remembered. And he wasn't just the Fling King. Wally, with various cohorts, was into several scams. I was warned not to meddle with him and to give up my lucrative little sideline or I might be found with a broken nose (another one) and no front teeth, down in the woods by the wireless station. I huffed and puffed about not letting anybody frighten me. But I knew I'd had my Fling.

Back at camp we had some light relief from daily training when 'work ship' week came along, just before we were due to leave and join the fleet for six months' sea training. This entailed doing all sorts of duties around the establishment while the senior ratings were home on leave. With only a skeleton staff on duty, nobody really stood over us to ensure we were actually working.

Denis Lloyd and I were given a classroom to paint and we duly set to work. As the day wore on the task became highly boring. We slowed right down and then decided to paint a few faces on the walls. We knew it wouldn't matter because tomorrow we would be finishing the job and we could just paint over it all. Trouble was, we were assigned a different task the next day. When the petty officer in charge of us went along to the classroom to check our work he found the wall with faces on it. I think he was a bit paranoid because he imagined one of the faces was him.

That resulted in Denis and me being awarded a week's stoppage of leave. Never mind, we could save our pennies for our great adventure, flying to Malta to pick up our respective ships. I had been assigned HMS Battleaxe, an old 'Weapon' class destroyer which was laid down at the end of the Second World War. I was joining Battleaxe with Paddy Bates, our old leading junior from Ganges. Denis was to join HMS Ursa, an equally old frigate. Those two ships would prove mighty infamous later on.

Before our 'drafts' (postings) to Malta, however, there was embarkation leave to be had. I enjoyed a fortnight of sheer celebrity, telling all my old school-friends and pals about my coming adventure.

On my penultimate night's leave I enjoyed a convivial evening at the Horse and Groom pub of back-slapping and hand-shaking and innuendo on what I might get up to now I was a proper sailor. I inadvisably downed four halves of mild ale, more alcohol than I'd ever consumed before. I was also bought a large panatela cigar and I felt really grown up.

Grown up? It was a case of thrown up when I got home. Mum and Ray were apparently really concerned when they spotted me weaving my way up Plummer Lane. I was quite merry – until I was put to bed. Then I had my first episode of 'spinning bedroom'. I felt really sleepy but as I tried to drop off the room went into a spin. Giddiness then turned into nausea. I leapt out of bed and fled outside to the toilet. I spent the next two hours either talking into the big white porcelain telephone or sitting moaning by candlelight.

I had just about recovered when I set off on my exciting journey (accompanied by a large chocolate cake, of course) from Kegworth station with Mum, Ray and my brother waving me goodbye. I met up with Denis and Paddy in London and the three of us, along with several other sailors, were taken to Hendon 'trooping' centre before moving on to what was all part of the old London Airport, to embark for our trip to RAF Luqa in Malta.

I had never flown before but the civilian flight on British Eagle Airways was an unforgettable experience. Getting airborne never bothered me in the slightest but it did Paddy. He spent most of the journey talking into the big white air-sickness bag.

Having never been to foreign climes before, my breath was taken away when we arrived. Not because of the scenery, because it was about three o'clock in the morning. It was the heat and humidity which hit me.

I said goodbye to Denis. For a long time I'd only meet up with him on rare occasions from then on, when both our ships pulled in to Malta. Paddy and I were whisked off to a shore base, Royal Naval Air Station Halfar, for a few days, which acted as excellent acclimatisation. I can remember waiting for the Naval bus which took us down to the dockyard. As I sat on a wall I was startled by two scorpions – must have been a mating ritual – circling each other at my feet. I was so transfixed it never occurred to me that I could get a dangerous sting to celebrate my first week in Malta.

We were taken down to HMS Battleaxe, which was in the last throes of its refit in Valletta. My first ship looked pretty impressive, although I felt it was a little top-heavy with its massive '965' radar.

Paddy and I were subjected to all the humiliating rituals on our first day. We were handed clipboards with tasks to fulfil: 'Report to the pay office to collect Mediterranean Phobia "Medphobia" pay; report to the sick bay to pick up your salt tablets.' These two missions seemed quite reasonable to a naive young lad not yet 17. In fact I got quite excited about the 'Medphobia' pay, imagining an extra few bob in my pocket. Salt tablets I wasn't sure I really wanted.

On arrival at the respective offices I was greeted with knowing wide grins and comments like: "Not today lad; come back when you've been on board a few weeks," accompanied by giggles at my earnest requests. Looking further down the list on my clipboard, my suspicions that I was being had, grew. I was supposed to fetch 'navy cake' during the morning break; go to the chief engineer to pick up a 'golden rivet'. While the first task also appeared genuine, leaving me hoping it would be chocolate cake, I couldn't imagine what a golden rivet might be. Every enquiry brought gales of laughter from the people I approached. It was only a few weeks later when I became more worldly-wise that I found out this was all to do with the Navy's reputation. I'll have to let you work that one out for yourselves. Anyway, when I was told to get a bucket of blue steam from the Chief Stoker I told the guffawing apes that enough, was enough.

I looked in wonderment at all the dials and machinery in the wireless office but it would be a little while before I was let loose on any of it. My first task as a junior radio operator on board ship was to climb up above the forward gun turret and clean the HF DF 'loops'. These were four brass poles used for radio direction finding. That would be my job for a few weeks, no matter what the weather. I would clamber out on to the turret and rub the loops vehemently with brass polish until I could see my face in them. Then the first big wave would drench them in salt, spoiling all my handiwork almost instantaneously.

Because the Battleaxe was pretty ancient, there were no bunks for the ratings, only hammocks. I was taught how to 'sling' a hammock. "It's like riding a bike son; you'll never forget it once you've learned," I was told. I'd proved I wasn't that tricky when it came to riding bikes. I felt like slinging it all right. It all came undone easily but, with your pillow, sheets and blankets in, it was a beast to get into. Many was the time I swung straight out the other side. Men learned not to be underneath when I was embarking lest they got a foot in the face or a body on their shoulders. Even when ensconced I rarely slept well. When we got to sea, the hammock would sway around if we hit even the slightest of swells and threaten to eject me onto the mess floor. And because I had to situate my hammock right at the sharp end of the ship in the radio operators and stokers' mess next to the paint store in the bow, it was like being on a switchback every time we went up and crashed down in the waves. Until I finally did get a bit used to it, I was walking around with huge bags under my eyes.

Then there was the purgatory of 'lashing up and stowing' your hammock. When the mess loudspeaker's bugle played 'Charlie', the wake-up call, you only had a few minutes to roll up your hammock, tie it up with wrist-breaking and palm-tearing rope, and get it stowed in the cage that housed the bedding. If you lagged, not only were you in for a tongue-lashing from the messdeck leading hand but, much, much worse, the gannets that lived with you had scoffed nearly all the breakfast by the time you had lashed and stowed. I longed for a comfortable bed.

Life on the Battleaxe was a daily routine of preparing the wireless office to go to sea when the ship's refit was complete. It was really hard work and long hours, learning how to tune in the radios to receive shore to ship 'broadcasts', the Battleaxe's lifeline, and putting into operation what I had been taught about cryptography. However, relief came from the ship's intercom that belted out records being played on the American Forces Network station. This proved to be my initiation to country and western music. Even more than 50 years later I can whisk myself back to Malta 1961 whenever I hear Patsy Cline sing 'Crazy' or Johnny Cash growl 'Walk the Line'.

A much-anticipated break from a morning routine came around 10am. This was 'stand easy' time. We'd had stand easies at Ganges and Mercury but they were just short breaks between lessons. The grown-up stand easy was a different matter altogether. Having worked from breakfast time my hunger had built but it was appeased by various mouth-watering snacks that were sold on the jetty by mobile catering vans. Pasties, pies, sandwiches and cakes were on offer and I made sure I always had enough to make my mid-morning purchases. When you consider we had three large meals a day, stand easy treats and what we called 'nine o'clockers', more sandwiches, buns and the like, at, well, nine o'clock, it was hardly surprising my weight soared to 10 stone. I was still skinny, however. It was not the last time I'd be likened to a 'racing snake'.

My first experience of sea time was memorable for all the wrong reasons. I had looked forward to it immensely, a life on the ocean wave at last. A chance to get some time in on the gleaming radio sets in the wireless office and somewhere new to enjoy when we got shore leave – Naples. It didn't work out too well, though.

I had been ashore in Malta a few times but restricted my leaves to scrambled egg on toast at the Vernon Club, which was an opulent serviceman's haven set on a promontory above Valletta and close to the Barraca Lift that took you up and down from the Maltese capital and dockyard area. My meal was normally followed by a flick (movie) at one of the two cinemas. Even though the films were sometimes in a foreign tongue and you had to frantically try and catch the subtitles before they disappeared, I loved watching movies. I remember Steve Reeves, one of the early muscle men, being popular in Malta.

Corrodina Canteen, the opulent-looking fleet club just up from the dockyard, also had a cinema. I remember watching _Breakfast at Tiffany's_ there. It was a bit slushy but I was into romance at the time – possibly because I didn't have one.

Sometimes I'd watch one film in the afternoon and another in the early evening. Then it would be supper at the Vernon Club and back on board. I couldn't afford to drink much. I did have the occasional beer but up to then I didn't really have a taste for the Maltese brew, 'Hop Leaf'. I could manage a glass of the brown ale, curiously called 'Blue', but – I shudder to remember now – only if it was laced with Coca Cola.

It was because I diversified from my normal routine that I suffered a horrendous start to my first sea trip.

On this night, because we would be sailing the next day I wanted to appear grown up, a jolly Jack Tar. Instead of going to the pictures I followed some of the lads to Valletta's notorious 'Gut'. This was actually a collection of sordid bars, cafés, night clubs and brothels in a long lane, split by steps, called Strait Street. The Gut was about half a mile or so long and was an absolute den of iniquity. Sailors began at the top of the street in the Bing Crosby Bar and made their way from bar to bar down to what I think I remember was the Empire Bar. By the time the merry matelots had reached the last bar they'd had a skinful. Some could hardly crawl back up the street; some didn't even bother and crashed out in one of the dodgy boarding houses or pensions at the bottom of the Gut. Many had already succumbed to the harlots that teemed in the Gut to pay for 'all night in'.

It was a wide-eyed Dabell who wandered down the street, accosted by numerous brightly made up ladies of the night at every doorway and every bar. You were called by whatever ship's name was on your cap tally (the gold braided band on the rim of your sailor cap). "Come inside Battleaxe, all your ship's company in here," would be the siren call made with flashing eyes and very often flashing other parts. "Queen Victoria fucking good bloke," was often added, to put you at your ease. No amount of cajoling would part me from my meagre earnings, though. "Why you no want jiggy-jig Battleaxe? I very cheap." For goodness sake, I wasn't quite 17. If I was going to lose my virginity, it would be to a nice Kegworth girl. Anyway, I, as the old hands on the ship would often point out, still thought it was for stirring my tea with. And hell, I hadn't even properly kissed a girl yet.

As the rest of my older shipmates dispersed to sample the dives, I went into the cleanest restaurant I could find and polished off a huge spaghetti Bolognese, drank a cup of coffee at the Vernon Club and headed back to the ship. I was only allowed out until 2300 hours until I reached the dizzy heights of radio operator third class, in about three months' time.

After the usual hammock ritual I was sound asleep when at about midnight I felt myself being swung back and forth at quite a violent rate. A few of the stokers in the mess opposite, drunk as skunks after celebrating their final night in Malta for some time, had decided that tipping the junior out of his hammock was a great idea. I hung on like dear life but I suddenly started feeling really queasy. In a moment of pure justice I honked up all over one of my persecutors. That soon scattered my tormentors.

Unfortunately that was not the end of my woes. I felt really violently ill and spent the next few hours talking on the big white telephone in the forward heads (latrines). By morning I was in a right state with acute sickness and diarrhoea. I was warned not to trouble the sick bay as I may get myself into trouble. The Navy had little time for sailors who it was felt had brought their illness (including sunburn, I discovered later) on themselves. You could be put on jankers for what was termed 'self-imposed punishment'.

When we sailed for Naples I was in a terrible state. Then, as we encountered a force eight gale, seasickness kicked in. I wanted to die. Luckily the Petty Officer Telegraphist running the wireless office, a really nice chap called Harry Julian, who would later become a chief coastguard in Cornwall on his retirement, took pity on me. I was excused duties. It was no good trying to see out my illness and seasickness in my hammock, though. The swaying would only make me worse. I was given permission to lay out my bedding on the floor near the paint locker. There I lay for nearly 24 hours, apart from dashes to the heads, occasionally stepped over and checked once or twice to make sure I was still alive.

Eventually the sickness passed. I rose from my pit and managed to keep down a mug of 'pot mess'. This was a thick stew that the chefs kept on the go on a stove in the galley during bad weather. It was accompanied by 'hard tack', biscuits that were so unyielding they could shatter a row of teeth with consummate ease. The meal was brought to me by our concerned leading radio operator Frank Younghusband. He was concerned at getting me fit because we were short-handed in the wireless office. My fellow junior Paddy Bates had also succumbed to sickness, although his was purely mal de mer. It was the only time in my life I was ever sick at sea, though. Over the years I often came in for extra duties because I was one of the few men left standing. I developed a great fondness for pot mess and hard tack and the steaming cups of 'Kye', a thick, sugarless chocolate drink, which you could stand a spoon up in, also doled out during gales.

I was raring to go again when we pulled into Naples harbour. It was a fantastic spectacle, with Vesuvius above Pompeii actually spewing out smoke. Once I'd established this was quite normal, I was able to put my mind to shore leave when my duties in the wireless office and mess were over.

Even though we were in the land of pasta, spaghetti Bolognese was not going to be on the menu. I decided to take one of the trips called, for some reason unknown to me, 'grippos', arranged by the locals for our ship's company. It was fascinating looking around the ruins of Pompeii. Of course some of the lads had done the tour before and directed me to the spot where the couple who were making love were when they were overcome by the lava flow. I must admit I could hardly tear my eyes away from the scene. What a way to go. The moment was soon shattered, however, by some insensitive vendor trying to sell me a key ring in the shape of a flying phallus. I didn't actually spot that's what it was. I thought it was some kind of long-necked bird. I really was that naive.

My sexual education was to be furthered terrifyingly, however, the next day. I went off on my own to watch a flick. The latest one was on, too, called *Come September*, starring Gina Lollobrigida, Rock Hudson, Sandra Dee and Bobby Darin. It was dubbed in Italian but that didn't spoil my enjoyment. However, the film would become etched in my memory forever, for all the wrong reasons.

I was deep into the movie, watching Dee and Darin shooting about on scooters when suddenly I felt a hand on my leg and then a grab of my groin. I squealed in panic and started beating my assailant. There followed pure pandemonium in the picture house. The lights went on with me yelling blue murder and pointing at the miscreant, who was trying desperately to beat a retreat for the cinema exit but had been grabbed. Even my cries in English were understood. The perpetrator was apparently well known as a local groper and was frogmarched to the manager's office. The kindly manager offered soothing words: "Vary sorree about thees Jack. We will takea care of thees. Plizza enjoya the rest of the film and hava nicea icea creama on me."

I'd had enough of being in the dark with strange people, though, and I decamped hastily. When I got back on board and related my story, it was explained to me what kind of person

this was that had interfered with me – interspersed with great
hilarity and jokes about 'golden rivets' and 'navy cake', all to
my great embarrassment. I'd had no idea.

Chapter 17

THE LOST COMMAND

From Naples it was on to Sicily where I had my second experience of volcanoes, watching Mount Etna belching out smoke as we arrived. I wondered if one of these days I was going to get unlucky. I didn't fancy having my Naval career cut short by a lava flow. While we were in Messina, my messmates decided it was time I became a little active myself.

Word had got round that I was a virgin. They were going to make sure I 'lost my cherry'. Of course I'd thought about the big day often but it was far from my mind when accompanied ashore by two of the radio operators who had taken me under their wings. I thought they were being a bit generous when they paid for a couple of beers but the alcohol lulled me into a false sense of security. "Right Dinger," – my new nickname – "it's about time we looked for some Italian lovelies," said one of my escorts, a pleasant lad from Liverpool, nicknamed, of course, 'Scouse'. This seemed a good idea to me. I had visions of doing the twist with some sultry young Sophia Loren. We walked on into the back streets of Messina and I began to feel a little uneasy. "Don't worry Dinger, you're going to remember this night for the rest of your life," said Jim, Scouse's mate. I started to lag behind, with my fate beginning to dawn on me. Scouse pushed me towards this whitewashed house. The lads went in, leaving me trembling outside. This house had a peculiar door to it, split in half like a stable door. As I eyed it dubiously, the boys came out with smug expressions on their faces. "We've taken care of everything, Dinger." With that, over the stable door leant a very large woman with long black hair and a face painted garishly with bright blue eye make-up and lurid red lips. She had a huge smile on her face as, through gravestone sized teeth, she spoke to me in a tone which she considered tempting. I had no idea what she was saying but then I wasn't looking at her lips for long. With a flourish she whipped out a huge pair of breasts and, with arms outstretched, beckoned me into her house. It would have taken four Navy patrolmen to hold me. With a face virgin white, I burst free from Scouse and Jim and ran and ran for the dockyard until I thought my lungs would burst. I scampered up the gangway of the Battleaxe like a scalded cat. I was the laughing stock of the ship that week when Scouse and Jim related the story. I didn't care. I was saving myself for a nice Midlands lass.

By the time we left Sicily, the only thing I'd tried for the first time was a pizza (this was in the days before there was an Italian restaurant or delivery service in every village, as there are now). Having steered clear of spaghetti I was, thus, unmoved when a storm began to whip up in the Mediterranean on our way back to Malta. I just relished the thought of slurping pot mess and Kye and watching the huge goffers (waves) crashing over the ship's bow. Soon, though, everyone was nervous. The heads were awash with vomit as the seas got larger and the wind stronger. We hit 12 on the Beaufort Scale as I lurched my way to the wireless office.

I hadn't been on duty more than an hour when all hell broke loose. The bridge had spotted a merchantman, a timber carrier, in the distance that was obviously in great difficulty. Harry ordered us to go to emergency channels on the UHF (ultra high frequency) bands. Sure enough, we soon heard a frantic SOS: "Mayaday, Mayaday, Mayaday, this isa the capitain of the Federico Bartoli. Our cargo she hasa slipped and we shall sink." I'm one of the operators taking the emergency call and passing information on for Harry to report to the bridge, via our voice pipe. We have the only link with the stricken vessel and we send back to the captain of the Federico Bartoli that we are going to try come alongside.

A coston gunline (a line fired from a rifle which was attached to a rope that could then be hauled aboard) was fired over the heaving timber vessel and grateful hands grabbed it. I can't relate exactly how this was done because I was in the bowels of the ship in a safe, warm, if a little frantic, wireless office while all this was going on. By now our captain was down in the wireless office talking to his opposite number on the Federico Bartoli. "We must attach a tow line," our captain told the Italian ship's skipper. The Bartoli captain refused to do this, point-blank. I couldn't understand this until it was pointed out to me that this would render the timber ship 'salvage' if we towed it into port. HMS Battleaxe would be then due salvage money, presumably from the insurance company insuring the timber vessel. The Italian captain must have thought it was more than his job's worth to allow this and he held out for some time. In the end he had to give in when his cargo slipped even more. A tow line was attached and we started to head for safe waters. We hadn't gone that far, however, when the timber slipped even more in the churning swell and waves. The Federico Bartoli started to slide under and we had to release the tow. The vessel sank and the captain went down with it. The terrified calls of "Mayaday, Mayada, Mayaday," from that subsequently doomed skipper haunted me for years.

The Battleaxe resumed its course for the Aegean after this very disturbing incident. We headed for Piraeus, the main port for the Greek capital Athens, then moved on to Crete for further courtesy visits. My main Greek memories are of a trip to the spectacular Acropolis, a tortuous bus ride and ouzo, the fiery aniseed drink. The bus ride was another 'grippo', this one to Marathon and to what we were told was the site of the original Olympic Games. It took most of the day to get there and back to Marathon in a bone-shaker of a bus with no air-conditioning. I couldn't really afford to lose any more weight but I think I must have sweated quite a few pounds by the time we arrived. No problem, though. An oil company that was hosting the trip had laid on a magnificent banquet which entailed seven courses.

After the meal we were offered a glass of ouzo. Now I had been warned off this highly potent beverage by way of the ship's noticeboard. And according to the old sea salts, when you drank ouzo it could not only go to your head pretty quickly but if you had a glass of water in the morning you would be drunk all over again. However I chanced a small tot of ouzo and it enabled me to sleep on a rattling bus on the way back to the ship. I was very nervous when I drank my cup of tea at breakfast the next morning but I was relieved to find that I didn't keel over.

Incidentally, the noticeboard warning about ouzo was a similar one repeated at nearly every port I pulled into during my time at sea. Greece it was ouzo, then a little later in my career in Sweden, aquavit (a type of Swedish schnapps). When we pulled into Split in the then Yugoslavia it was slivovitz (a sort of plum brandy) and then in the Far East the ship's company was strongly advised to avoid Thai whisky. It was usually the first drink sailors looked for as soon as they got ashore.

After a few more weeks in Malta learning my trade, it was time to return to Blighty to finish off my training and wait for my first real full time 'draft' as a fully-fledged radio operator. I was still a junior but it wouldn't be too long before I attained the dizzy heights of radio operator third class (equivalent to ordinary seaman) at the age of 17 ½. You were then considered a man. Then I didn't have to be back on board until just before midnight when I took shore leave and my pay increased significantly.

When I returned home for leave it was to a new house. Our family no longer lived in the rented triangular building at the entry to Plummer Lane. Mum and Ray, using his lifetime savings, had bought a house at the top of the hill going out of Kegworth in Ashby Road. Soon it would be quite close to the M1 which was to be built a couple of miles away and it wouldn't be far from the East Midlands Airport, which wasn't then even fully mooted. But at that time it was a tranquil haven for Mum, John and me who had never known what it was like owning our own home. Good old Ray. No more outside toilets. We had a bathroom, a big garden, a garage and our own car. And I had my own bedroom. The view, looking down rolling hills and fields towards Derbyshire, was stunning. I knew what this all meant to Mum. I was ecstatic for her.

It was hard to tear myself away from home life when the time came to go back from leave.

I had only been at my new posting for a couple of days when news filtered through that HMS Battleaxe had been in a collision with Denis Lloyd's old ship, HMS Ursa. There were chilling reports of the collision up in Scotland. Ursa had smashed into Battleaxe with some force, caving in the side near the bow. My replacement was in his hammock, in my old spot, when the crash happened. The paint store had caved in and his legs were crushed in the twisted metal, crippling him for life and, of course, ending his Navy career when he was invalided out of the service. I shuddered when I heard the news. This time fate had been on my side. My old ship never recovered from the collision. Battleaxe was deemed beyond repair and scrapped.

I don't believe in ghosts or paranormal happenings really, but there was something eerie about that hammock position on the Battleaxe. While I was in Malta I was once awakened from a deep sleep with my mother's voice, screaming "Norman" in my ears. It was as if she were standing next to me, calling me in distress. It so alarmed me I couldn't get back to sleep and it moved me to tell Mum about it when I next wrote to her. I found out that on that very night Mum and Ray and Aunt Jessie had been travelling back to Kegworth with my Uncle George at the wheel, when their car overturned on a bend. As she was thrown out of her seat, Mum had screamed out my name, thinking she was going to be killed.

My next stint of training and duties, while I awaited news of my draft, came at HMS Drake, a shore establishment near

Devonport dockyard in Plymouth, which you'll remember was my preferred home port. I met up with some of my old Ganges shipmates, who had also returned from sea training. We filled in the time waiting to be sent to our next ships, working at the signal school at St Budeaux. I did my best to overcome my shyness with girls and even had a couple of dalliances with the fair sex, Wrens of course. But nothing significant came of it, except making me more out of pocket, frequently standing for their port and lemons and getting very little in return – not even a proper kiss.

Our next postings came up. A large section of my friends were going to be heading for two carriers, the Centaur and Hermes. That sounded really exciting. My name appeared at the bottom of the list: 'RO3 Dabell, to HMS Rampart'. I'd never heard of it. I had to consult *Jane's Fighting Ships*. It was a 'Landing Craft Tank', another ship that had been commissioned just after the Second World War. She had been in the thick of battle in the Suez Crisis of 1956. I was hugely disappointed until I realised that there would be only two radio operators on board, me and a more senior radio operator second class. A leading tactical operator, the 'head of department', made up the communication numbers.

When I arrived at the jetty in Poole Harbour, Dorset, on a Sunday late afternoon it was with a kitbag filled with all my worldly belongings. I was filled with trepidation. The Rampart looked a proper scruffy ugly duckling. As I struggled up the gangway the first person I saw I presumed was the ship's cook, standing outside the galley, smoking a roll-up and wearing a grease-stained T-shirt, chequered trousers and an equally grubby chef's hat. Nobody else seemed to be around. "Hello, I'm the new radio operator, name's Norman," I said nervously to this grizzled individual. "Bloody war baby, I suppose," came the snarled reply, "they're getting younger." He disappeared through a screen door that had acrid blue smoke pouring from it. "Don't worry about Norman," came a voice from behind me. "He's never very happy about anything." As well as the chef being called Norman I was to discover that at least two more of the crew had the same first name. The Rampart was a sort of floating Battle of Hastings.

One of the ship's quartermasters was delegated to show me my billet, down in a mess at the aft of the ship where all but the NCOs and officers lived. I had a lower bunk close to the ladder of the mess in a sort of metal cage and an inadequate locker where I was expected to keep all my kit and belongings. The mess was deserted and felt damp. I felt totally dejected.

After sampling chef Norman's supper, a stew swimming with grease, I got my head down. Not for that long, however. Throughout the evening and night my messmates, who had been on long weekend, came clanking down the metal steps to the mess and noisily found refuge in their bunks. It was just my luck. The occupant above me snored like a buzz-saw. And it was not just the racket he made. A badly aimed boot, designed to halt the flow of the vibrating cacophony above me, missed him and struck me on the elbow.

The next morning I found out that the blowing whale above me was a Scottish stoker who had been re-bunked on several occasions in a bid to locate him where his snoring had least effect on the rest of the mess.

It was a bleary-eyed Dabell that reported to the navigation officer on Monday morning. He was responsible for the communications department and introduced me to the leading tactical operator in charge of signals. The radio operator second class who would be working with me had apparently taken ill ashore at his married quarter. It wouldn't be the last time. As I could hardly be left alone with the radio equipment, most of which I didn't recognise from any of my previous tuition at Mercury, I was put to work cleaning the bridge. Further dejection set in.

When the senior radio operator finally returned from shore I was heartily sick of cleaning off rust and corrosion on the bridge and repainting it. At last I could get my teeth into some proper duties. As we were a small ship our communications was all Morse- and voice-based, no telecommunications. I would have to sit at the radio and type out every broadcast that involved the Rampart.

There was going to be plenty of time to learn the ropes in the tiny little compartment laughingly called an office, though. The Rampart went in for a refit. It meant I had other varied, menial, duties. But there was one I really took to. Our captain, Neil Durden-Smith, was a sports nut. He played for the Navy at cricket and hockey and was rarely around. But when he was, his other sporting penchant was golf. I was appointed his caddie several times. Little did I know that Neil and I would become a more infamous duo, suffering an escapade on the Rampart that we would still be talking about 40 years later when we had carved out careers as sports journalists. Neil's girlfriend at the time, who often visited him on board for cocktails, was Judith Chalmers, who would become a famous travel writer.

My luck and success rate with girls didn't get much better. A long-term, although pretty chaste, relationship with a veterinary assistant (female) in Clevedon, Somerset, foundered eventually because her mum thought she should be learning how to be a vet rather than getting petted by me.

This break-up I took particularly badly. It had taken a mammoth act of bravado to even go with my pal Doug Skeen on weekend leave to meet his girlfriend's friend on a foursome. Pauline and I got on like a house on fire and I'd enjoyed meeting up with her every weekend I could, even staying in a damp and cold boarding house with blankets that smelt like sweaty feet, near to Clevedon Pier. I even put up with her taste in music, being dragged to listen to 'trad jazz'. Acker Bilk, her favourite musician, who came from not that far away, was a regular turn in Clevedon. I found his music almost impossible to bop to.

My few months with Pauline nearly landed me in real hot water. I did smoke at the time and I had a duty-free allowance. However, we were only allowed to take one packet of cigarettes, I think they came in 25s, off the ship for the weekend. I decided one weekend leave to take a chance and try and smuggle four extra packs out for Pauline's dad. I devised a scam that would have earned the approval of Long John Silver. I placed each of four packs of Players between slices of bread, wrapped them up in brown paper and placed the contraband underneath my weekend clothes in my holdall.

I walked up to the dockyard gate at Portsmouth, looking as nonchalant as I possibly could. I'd never been stopped before by the dockyard police on the gate. That was why I'd decided to take the chance. Whether it was my white, sweating, face or my nervous tic, or my vibrating Adam's apple... I don't know what could have possibly have given me away. "Right lad, over here," commanded the stern dockyard policeman. "Let's have a look in your bag." My heart sank. I was mortified. It was only by sheer sphincter control that my resigned walk over to the search desk wasn't my only movement. The policeman rooted around in my holdall and then held up my brown paper parcel. "What's this then?" he queried. "It's my dinner to eat on the train," I replied, unable to suppress a nervous gulp. "Let's see what you've packed yourself up then," he said with a malicious wink. The game was up. "Well, what do we have here?" said the policeman triumphantly as he discovered my tobacco sandwiches. He marched me off to the customs officer on duty. "Well I've got to give you ten out of ten for ingenuity," the customs officer said. "You obviously knew you were taking out more than your allowance, though, or you wouldn't have gone to these lengths. Who are they for – or do you smoke a lot?" Like LJS I didn't have a leg to stand on. I apologised profusely, assuring the officer that I had never tried to do anything like this before and would never again. My grovelling paid off. I was given a caution instead of being locked up to face subsequent Naval discipline. My cigarettes were confiscated, including my legal packet, and with enormous relief I was allowed to go. As I exited the dockyard gate I heard the customs officer and policeman chuckling behind me. Good try but no cigarette.

Soon the Rampart was ready to go to sea. For me it was a torrid baptism of fire when we sailed for Norway and Sweden.

My senior radio operator pal was again sick on shore. I was in at the deep end. It was a good job I'd learned how to operate everything. We had to sail and there was no chance of a replacement for my senior colleague.

All went well at first. The leading tactical operator and I handled the harbour to ship voice operation satisfactorily. When we headed off for the North Sea I felt fully in control of communications. That was until I missed an afternoon weather forecast for our region. I had been in the office for several hours, taking down reams of messages and weather forecasts but ours wasn't one of them. Whether it was fatigue or not, somehow it had come through and I'd missed it. I got a fearful bollocking from the first lieutenant on the bridge. However, as all the forecast areas I had picked up were for fairly calm seas, I thought it might not matter too much. A gale blew up. It was only force seven or so but in a flat-bottomed landing craft it was like being on the big dipper. When the buzz got around the ship that it was my fault we weren't in calmer waters, my name was mud. Only my youth and inexperience saved me. The first lieutenant stopped short of putting me on a charge but decided it best to tune into the BBC for the shipping forecast for the rest of the trip, just in case.

Heavy weather at sea was to prove the least of our problems, though. It was snow, ice and fog, well low-lying cloud, that caused a national incident involving the Ramps.

We had a contingent of Royal Marines on board who were to carry out a training exercise, part of which was up a Norwegian mountain. We duly disembarked them in Stavanger to begin their journey. My job was to keep in touch with them by radio. All worked well at first. At appointed times the cadre's radio operator reported in to the ship and I passed on the report to the duty officer. Then suddenly, nothing. When two situation reports failed to come in, our skipper Neil alerted mountain rescue. They came up with nothing, too. The Bootnecks (the nickname for the Royal Marines) had disappeared into thin air. Hours went by and nothing was heard. It meant another lengthy shift for yours truly. Neil was really worried. The rescue services hadn't located the marines for several hours and had to give up when night fell. He was even more worried in the morning when on the BBC Home Service crackling away in his cabin he heard: "Rescue services have been scouring mountains in Norway for a squad of Royal Marines who have lost contact with their ship HMS Rampart..."

When the marines' communications number finally contacted me, Neil nearly collapsed with relief. The boys had bivouacked down in an area where there was no signal for their radio while heavy fog cleared, to avoid the risk of falling off the mountain in the snow and ice. It wasn't my fault of course but the very fact that a bunch of Bootnecks had gone missing when it was my duty to keep in touch with them, had the Rampart's crew again muttering about a "Jonah on board".

I don't think Neil lost his command because of this incident but it was rather telling that soon after he was drafted away from the Rampart. I met up with him and Judith again about 20 years later when I covered a celebrity cricket match for my newspaper. He recognised me straight away and formed a cross with his fingers – just in case. Then another 20 years later Neil blanched when we met up again. We were both playing in a golf pro-am event at a tournament I was covering in Portugal. As Judith confided at the pro-am dinner, it was lucky we weren't on the same team or Neil might have gone to pieces.

Anyway, Neil's successor wasn't any great shakes. Our new captain must have been a bit short-sighted, we all felt. Every time we tried to come alongside the jetty at Poole Harbour, the ship bashed into it. After six months the jetty was at least six feet shorter than when the new captain took over.

Visiting Norway proved a delight. While we were in the small fishing port of Haugesund I was introduced (couldn't have done it on my own) to a lovely blonde girl called Vigdis. She was slim and very athletic looking – for a good reason. She was a nationally ranked swimmer with an ambition to represent Norway in the Olympics. I spent every minute I could with Vigdis who spoke English better than some of my messmates on the Rampart. When we parted she gave me a peck on the cheek. I went to 30,000 feet. Vigdis and I wrote to each other for two years. I still have a lovely little traditional Norwegian copper kettle, pressed flowers and a four-leafed clover as mementoes of an innocent time for two 17-year-olds.

My other memory of Haugesund isn't quite so fond. This was a football match between the Rampart and Haugesund who played to a very high standard in the Norwegian leagues and were to go on and feature in the European Cup on a couple of occasions. We lost by the odd goal in 11. Bill Stubbs, our stores rating, scored the odd goal and they scored the other ten. It was a complete mismatch. For some reason the crowd gave me a standing ovation as I walked off. They were either acknowledging that the score might have been 20-1 or it was pity.

All too soon we sailed for Bergen, Trondheim and Tromsø, which were all closed while we were there.

It didn't take long before I finally managed to get a bit further than a kiss, however. My great moment came by 'virtue' of a flame-haired Scots lassie. I'd plucked up courage and asked her for a dance at Dunfermline Ballroom and she suggested I walk her home. She was much older than me and did all the running of course. The lassie seemed tickled pink that she had led me astray on a hillside near her home, gushing "Can ye believe it? I found myself a cherry boy," when she kissed me goodbye. I was pretty proud to be become a notch on her gun but, with wet elbows and grass stains on my trouser knees, I felt, at that stage, losing your virginity was a bit overrated.

Chapter 18

TWICE SHY, ONCE BITTEN

Soon after my momentous occasion I took weekend leave back home in Leicestershire. I determined I would put my new-found sexual prowess to work and prove my shyness was gone forever. The girl I took out on Saturday evening in Loughborough was the sister of a school friend who I'd been informed confidentially was "up for it". She left me in no doubt that I would be in for more than just a cuddle back at her parents' house. "I hope you have some protection with you," whispered the little Jezebel as we groped on the settee. Her parents had discreetly gone to bed.

I'd nervously, and with a face as red as the pole outside his shop, purchased a packet of three from a barber's in Loughborough who didn't know me. If I'd tried to buy them from Bill Orme, our Kegworth barber it would have been all round the village. And I certainly didn't have the courage to buy condoms from our local lady chemist.

The seductive tones of the young lady served as a spur but I was a bag of nerves. "Yes, I've come prepared but it's still quite early, what if your mum and dad hear us?" I hissed as we settled on the carpet in front of the fire. "They'll never hear us upstairs," said my temptress. "We just have to make sure we don't wake the dog up in the kitchen."

We had been at our business for a few seconds when I heard a damn dog start growling next door. When the growls turned into yaps I was put right off my stroke. Seemingly unabashed, my partner leapt up and opened the kitchen door. The dog, a Yorkshire Terrier, tore in, but it at least it stopped its yapping when given a bit of attention. We got down to business again but I sensed it was a lost cause. "I can't do it with the dog watching," I protested. "Well I can't put it back in the kitchen or it will wake up mum and dad. Just get on with it." I resumed operations but it wasn't just my heart that wasn't in it, my whole libido had withered. I made one last valiant attempt at satisfying my fellow protagonist. That was a bad move. The dog, with flawed perception at my attempts at love-making, launched itself at what it thought was an assailant, biting me on my bare bum.

The night's proceedings were over. I hastily adjusted my clothing in case her parents came down to investigate what the commotion was all about. My lady friend had now transferred her affections to the canine that had ruined our carnal tryst.

It all went very badly. Even the condom (empty of course) wouldn't burn properly because the fire had nearly gone out and took an age to dispose of. In my eagerness to enjoy sexual pleasure I hadn't even thought about how I was going to get home to Kegworth, six miles away. I could have used the girl's parent's phone and rung my stepfather Ray to see if he would pick me up but I didn't want to put on him at that time of night. There was nothing for it but to walk home and hope I could thumb a lift.

I had walked – well, with a sore buttock, aching, tender, loins and wobbly legs it was more of a limp – half the distance to home when I was picked up by a lorry driver. "You're out a bit late lad," said the grinning driver, winking and nudging me. "Did you get any?"

A little while later a girl with whom I had become infatuated at HMS Mercury, a lithe and slim auburn-headed Wren writer called Jenny (the one gossips reckoned I'd slashed my wrists over), who I had never plucked up courage to ask out, came back up on the radar. We had often exchanged smiles and winks when we came across each other in corridors or out and about at Mercury but it never came to any more than that. When I ran into her in Portsmouth I found out she had been equally keen on me and had been most disappointed I hadn't made a move. We arranged a night out, unfortunately the night before the Rampart was due to sail down to Instow in Devon.

I was ecstatic to be going on a date with a girl I'd idolised a year or so previously. It called for a trip to the Naval tailors, with whom I had an account, and I bought an olive green bomber jacket for my date. It cost me more than I could afford but everything you bought at Naval tailors was on tick, so I'd pay it off over six months. I met Jenny and first took her to the cinema. She allowed me to put my arm round her and, joy of joy, she responded positively to a kiss. Not wanting to appear gauche, I left it at that. After the cinema, flushed with affection, if not with very much money, I suggested a visit to a pub. There I found out she didn't drink. I was still very nervous of making a mess of my date but I needed Dutch courage and ordered a pint of bitter. "Goodness, that's about four cups of tea," my date pointed out, casting a dubious eye over my pint, which I downed sharpishly, because the landlord was calling time.

The last of my rapidly dwindling cash disappeared with a taxi ride back to the girl's dormitory at her establishment on Whale Island. We cuddled at the doorway of her mess and then I nearly collapsed with disbelief when she whispered: "There's nobody about, do you want to take the chance and come to my room?" What an offer from the love of my relatively short romantic life. I desperately wanted to take her up on it but I had to demur. It nearly broke my heart. I loathed myself for being such a chicken. But I just couldn't. If we got caught my feet wouldn't touch the ground. My ship was sailing the next morning. And I was dying for a pee – after drinking the equivalent of four cups of tea.

Although we wrote to each other when she was drafted to Malta soon after, I never saw the very first real love of my life ever again. I had to sell my lovely green bomber jacket – to the snoring stoker who slept above me. He offered me about a quarter of the price I'd paid for it but I was seriously skint and had to accept. It wasn't even for him, well it couldn't be. He couldn't even get it on he was so plump. I suspect he sold it on for a profit.

There was plenty of chance for romance over the next few months. That was when my face had recovered from another broken nose, this one attained from falling into our tank deck. I had been sent down to collect some radio stores but slipped on the ladder down and fell on my nose on the tank deck. This, added to my chipped tooth, didn't exactly fill me with confidence about my appearance.

A few weeks later the Rampart pulled into the little Scottish harbour of Campbeltown. As my two pals on board, a quartermaster seaman and a young engineer, were on duty I went ashore on my own. I must have left the ship in some hope because I opted for full sailor rig. It was a well-known fact that the ladies would swoon over Jack in his bell-bottoms. It worked. Grasping my courage in my hands and a shilling in my sweaty paw, I gained admission to a big hall with a 'dance' slogan above its door, where music was blasting forth. I soon found myself a duck out of water.

There were girls in there, dancing around their handbags as was the wont in those days. Just two youths watched on, glowering at me as I walked into the hall. The rest of their mates were all either still in the bar or visiting a chippy. I wished the dance floor would open up and swallow me. I certainly wished I had cohorts alongside me. The two blokes looked very threatening. The music stopped. I made for the door. "Where youze going sailor?" queried a voice. I looked around and there was a cute little number – about five foot I estimated – with tight blonde curls. "Aren't you going to stop and have a dance? We won't eat you." I turned to jelly but blurted: "I do enjoy bopping. Do you want to dance then?" She did no more than grab me by the arm and march me on to the dance floor as the band launched into a fairly brave attempt at

'Peggy Sue'. Buddy Holly it was not but that didn't matter. I was dancing.

My efforts seemed to be going down well. Both of us became a blur of whirling arms and legs as the band played on, continuing with more rock music. When they launched into my favourite number of the time, 'Red River Rock' (Johnny and the Hurricanes would have approved) I must have looked quite a sight jiving frenetically in my bell-bottoms. But I had made a hit. When the music finally did stop I stepped back and gave an exaggerated bow to my partner. The lassie was enchanted with such Sir Galahad behaviour. Not so our two laddies watching on. They both whistled loudly and offered catcalls which went along the lines of "fucking Sassenach Jessie". When my diminutive dance partner turned on them and scattered them with her handbag I should have been warned that I had met a minx.

I danced happily with the lassie until a glance at the hall clock told me I had only half an hour to get back on board before my night leave ran out. My dance partner was disappointed that I wouldn't have time to walk her home but suggested we should meet the next night and go to the flicks. I was then relieved to find no-one waiting for me outside.

I met the lass at the designated hour the next night and into the cinema we went. Pure dread has played havoc with what I consider is a good memory. I have no recollection whatsoever what the film was we went to see.

Inadvisably, as it turned out, I was again in uniform. "Who's yer sailor boy?" the girl in the ticket box asked my escort. "Never you mind, eyes off," was the snapped riposte. There were no cheaper seats downstairs left so I had to buy balcony tickets. It was dark because the evening's programme was in full swing. The place was packed, so we had to stumble to seats right at the front. We finally got comfortable and I chanced my arm, placing it around her shoulders.

When the lights came on for the interval, I disentangled myself, recklessly got to my feet and asked the girl if she would like an ice cream. I stood out like a sore thumb in my Navy rig. I was spotted. A crowd of lads down in the stalls turned ugly (well some of them didn't need to turn actually). First of all abuse was hurled at me. Then it was an empty peanut tin. When a half-eaten choc ice projectile splashed onto her skirt, my wee partner went wild. She leant over the balcony's edge and screeched some of the choicest language I had ever heard, enough to make a hardened sea-dog blush. The whole cinema seemed to be in an uproar. But it got worse. As she continued her tirade I saw something fly out of her mouth. The lads down below scattered, then a huge cheer went up. She had shed a top row of dentures. I had somehow suspected her gnashers looked a little too even to be true but I'd preferred not to think about it.

The worst of it was that my little ball of fire was totally unabashed as she stormed off in search of her false teeth. I'm ashamed to tell that discretion overcame me, replacing valour. Instead of following her I made a quick exit. I told the girl in the ticket box that she might need to get the manager out. A hard-hitting flyweight might well be laying a few people out down in the stalls.

After trips all round the UK the Rampart ended back in refit in Portsmouth. My radio office was temporarily redundant and I was made the ship's postman. This was a highly enjoyable job, cycling around the dockyard collecting messages and mail. I took a pride in being the fastest postie in Pompey, riding a bike on which I painted the slogan: 'Mailstrom'. Calamity was lying in wait for me, though – inevitably. I was heading back to the ship with a heavy load of mail when the bag swung off my shoulder. As I frantically tried to maintain control of my handlebars, my front wheel got caught between the lines of the dockyard railway. Over the handlebars I went but I was incredibly lucky. My bike sailed on, down into a yawning, deep dry dock, to be mashed beyond repair. I escaped with a dislocated shoulder.

Bikes and boats were never kind to me as a young man. When the Rampart was invited to be the flagship for the annual

Isle of Wight Cowes Regatta, I should have known better than get in a boat again.

For the trip to Cowes we took a couple of yachtsmen and a dinghy that was to be the Royal Navy's entry in that class in the races that week. A stumble in the tank deck, though, earned one of the two dinghy crew members a broken arm. A volunteer, with some experience, was sought. "Well, I did a bit of sailing at HMS Ganges," I offered when no-one else came forward, blotting out all memories of sandbanks and stranding. My cox'n was a pretty proficient sailor but having me as his crew, inexperienced with dinghy racing and all arms and legs trying to keep control of the sail, was never going to work. We finished last in the first of our two heats. Then we capsized in front of the Royal Cowes Yacht Club in the second.

From Cowes we headed back to Instow to pick up another cadre of Royal Marines, this time with several DUKWs, amphibious armoured vehicles, which we were to drop off at Cherbourg in a re-enactment of Second World War landings. This all seemed an exciting prospect. It never occurred to me that this offered scope for yet another mishap.

By now I had been promoted to Radio Operator Second Class and with it a certain degree of responsibility. I didn't expect that to include carrying out one of the most hazardous jobs of the re-enactment. I was sent to the forward deck with the command: "As soon as the ship grounds on the beach, Dabell, you are to hoist the Union Jack. There will be television cameras covering the landing, so that flag must go up as soon as we land." That seemed an innocuous duty. However, it proved anything but. Try pulling up a bloody flag in a howling wind head-on to you – with thunder flashes exploding all around you and the ship's gun blasting off behind you. Somehow I managed to raise the flag, although I'm not sure of the co-ordination with landing. Our captain, the one who had a habit of nibbling bits off Poole Jetty, came in rather too quickly, hit the beach with a thump, and dumped me on my backside. Fortunately I held onto the halyard, preventing the flag from fluttering off to Paris, a flogging offence. As I regained my composure and whipped up the flag, I looked down in the tank deck. The cadre of marines had gone down like toppled skittles.

I looked a pretty sorry sight when the marines and their vehicles disembarked. I was a bit wild-eyed and scorched in a couple of places. Norman the chef took pity on me and invited me into the galley to finish off a tray of pork chops, knowing I'd missed lunch through standing for an age on the ship's bow waiting to pull up the flag. And things appeared to get better when one of the petty officers invited me into his mess to drink a tot of rum to celebrate my promotion. Trouble was, I'd never sampled neat Navy rum before. It took my breath away and caused me to choke, leaving me hurtling for the heads to bring up Norman's pork chops.

Because of my elevation to RO2, my time on the old rust bucket Rampart came to an end. It had been an influential part of my life and was a milestone in my career.

I returned to HMS Mercury for more training and to await my next draft. This was a time for catching up with old comrades who had similarly fetched up at Mercury. One night we walked down to the Rising Sun at nearby Clanfield to play dominoes. The night remains etched on my memory. I had just put 'Maria Elena' by Los Indios Tabajeros on the jukebox when the landlord strode out of the bar and switched off the machine. "President Kennedy has been shot and he's not going to survive," announced the landlord. We were all stunned and didn't have the heart to stay.

After a few weeks at Mercury several draft notices came in, mine included. I was to join a much more modern ship this time, a 'Rothesay' class, type 121 anti-submarine frigate named HMS Falmouth, commissioned in only 1961, which would also carry the command of the 30th Escort Squadron.

When I joined her in 1963, just before Christmas, the Falmouth was in Devonport Dockyard, Plymouth, finishing off a wholesale refit before going on sea trials with the whole squadron at Portland. This meant plenty of shore time before the Falmouth sailed for the Dorset coast and what is called in the Navy a 'work up', preparing ships for war.

I quickly made friends with the lads on the communications messdeck but, as Christmas approached, I was delighted to find my old pal John 'Slinger' Wood was in town. He had been on the Lowestoft and was billeted at HMS Drake, the Devonport Naval barracks. Like me Slinger had volunteered for 'retard party' over the festive season. The name is nothing to do with the characters employed, although some would call it apt. It just means that certain sailors stay on board during leave periods as skeleton crew until the main leave party returns. Then the retards take their leave.

Slinger and I were just a little into gambling at that time, nothing too serious but we did fancy ourselves as pontoon (black jack), and brag aficionados. We decided to visit a Plymouth 'casino', not exactly Monte Carlo but somewhere you could play cards without the law interfering. As the night wore on, Slinger wasn't too successful but I found myself on a bit of a good streak. I was holding what I thought was a winning hand. The only player left in the game had run out of money and couldn't even 'see me'. The rule of the house was that if you didn't have the funds to carry on, you lost. I looked up to see Slinger beaming, relishing the thought of splitting a pot with me that was at least twice our pay.

Suddenly, all hell broke loose. Slinger had dived at my opponent and was twisting his arm behind his back – which held a wad of notes. Somebody had slipped the player funds under the table. I jumped up from my seat. I was then grabbed from behind. The table went over and there were bodies wrestling with each other all over the place. The management and two bouncers came rushing up. But they didn't collar my opponent and throw him out for foul play. No, it was Slinger and I who were grabbed. No amount of protesting cut any ice. Without getting chance to scoop up any of my money, we were both hurled out into the street. It was about two o'clock in the morning and it had just started snowing. We didn't have a penny between us even if we could have found a taxi at that hour and it was a long way to walk to Devonport in the snow. Ever the resourceful duo, though, we found the answer. We squeezed into a telephone box together – and spent the rest of the night dozing off standing upright.

After Christmas leave the Falmouth left Devonport and we went through an exhausting spell in Portland, in which we sailed from port at dawn every morning and returned shattered at night. The process of 'working up' the ship took over a month. For the communications staff this meant endless monitoring of shore-to-ship broadcasts, hundreds of messages to encrypt and decrypt, countless squadron manoeuvres, air-to-ship exercises, action stations every day, everything that got us ready to take on anything an enemy could throw at us.

Camaraderie was high on our communications messdeck, with everyone appreciating we had to pull together. It definitely was a case of sink or swim but some of the friendships forged then have endured. Even though we all stuck together and watched each others' backs, four or five of us were really firm pals. My very best mate was Jim Sked, a radio warfare 'sparker', one of the little band of radio operators on the Falmouth charged with listening in to enemy broadcasting. Then there was Johnny Vear and Keith 'Scouse' Grattan, like me formal radio operators, and Roger 'Flook' Young, a 'bunting-tosser'.

When our month-long stint of sea trials was finished we were ready for the ship to 're-commission'. Everyone was very proud of the gleaming HMS Falmouth. Our messdeck looked modern, airy and highly comfortable when the ship opened to visitors, which included several of the communications staff's families. I wonder if our guests were ever told that there were 30 ratings living in our quarters – with only four bunks available. This meant that 26 ratings had to sleep in either hammocks or camp beds in this modern fighting warship. Even Colditz had had a bunk apiece.

With the re-commissioning ceremony over, we sailed for Liverpool to start a short stint of 'Home Sea Service', a series of exercises and some courtesy visits around Britain.

Liverpool proved to be what we sailors called 'a good run ashore'. It was crucial to wear your uniform while out and about in Liverpool. The girls came flocking round us. Everyone seemed to hit it off with a young 'Scouser' lady – everyone but me of course.

After various stints at showing the flag, we returned to Devonport dockyard, Plymouth. We spent the next few weeks there, preparing for the 30th Escort Squadron's forthcoming stint of duty on the Mediterranean station.

I had a short stay at home before we left but it proved a dismal one for our family. I came down one morning to find Ray standing mournfully with a very rigid Binky cupped in his hand. "I found him upside down in his cage," Ray said ruefully. "Keep it quiet until I've made your mum a cup of tea and broken it to her gently." Although Ray offered to buy another budgie, which I thought was a great idea and already had a name for him – Gordon Banks – Mum wouldn't hear of it. There was no replacing Binky.

For the last part of my embarkation leave I was invited by fellow radio operator Johnny Vear to spend a long weekend at his home at Bisham, near Marlow, in Buckinghamshire. Marlow is notable for its 'Compleat Angler' pub, named after the book on fishing by Izaak Walton, situated by the river Thames. It is a perfect spot for angling – and boating.

On the Saturday we met up with Johnny's girlfriend and her friend and he announced that he'd fixed up a treat for us in the afternoon after lunch. Johnny was going take us on a cruise on the Thames. He'd arranged to hire a small motorboat – well you could hardly call it a cabin cruiser – for the afternoon. The four of us piled into it and Johnny took the helm, starting up the engine first time and looking every bit the master mariner as he ordered me to haul in the rope holding us to the jetty.

Off we went onto the waterway, with Johnny looking mighty confident in what he was doing. I had had no idea he could even steer a dinghy. My initial nervousness subsided and I concentrated on trying to melt the snooty ice maiden Johnny had paired me up with. No dice. She was decidedly frosty. I decided to enjoy the views and look for kingfishers on the riverbank. As we ploughed along, not exactly racing at any great knots, I noticed people waving at us from shore side. "What a friendly lot they are around here," I thought. I waved back. Johnny gave a sort of lazy, imperious salute from the helm.

This went on for a good few minutes. The waves to us seemed to get a little more animated. We waved back enthusiastically. Suddenly a voice boomed out from the shore: "Turn back, turn back, you are on a direct course for the weir." I spotted an official with a loudhailer in his hand. Realisation dawned on Cap'n Vear. Frantically he flapped for reverse. There was an awful grating noise. Then our engine cut out. No matter what Johnny did in his panic, he couldn't get the engine to restart. The girls squealed. I felt like doing so, too, envisaging our small and inadequate craft being dashed to pieces on Marlow Weir. At least my partner had warmed up a little.

Just as a large cruiser came alongside us, our recalcitrant engine tried to kick into life. Our rescuer was taking no chances and attached us to a hawser. We were then hauled humiliatingly back to the jetty from whence we came. Johnny was read the riot act by the chap from whom he'd hired the boat. Our two lady friends fled in shame.

It was not the final time that Johnny and I got into a real scrape. But a few days later it was with a lorry, not a boat.

With the prospect of a long spell away from home as the ship prepared for its service in the Med., we all made sure that we enjoyed our last nights in Plymouth, our home port. I think it was the second-last night before the Falmouth left Devonport. Johnny and I were on late duty and so we were only able to go ashore at about eight o'clock in the evening. We decided we would do no more than have a quick drink, maybe two, in the nearest pub to the dockyard, the 'Keppel's Head' and then visit 'Frank's', the pasty and hot dog wagon near the dockyard gates.

Johnny and I didn't have much money, so, being a 'flip to the front' (Naval slang for someone canny and astute), I suggested that it would go a little further if we drank the local 'scrumpy' (rough cider) which, although it was often unpalatable, was dirt cheap. Then we'd definitely have enough for a pasty apiece on the way back on board.

I had limited experience with scrumpy but I knew of its dangers, so I warned Johnny: "Let's just have a half and no more; it comes up and hits you under the chin if you're not careful." Vear, ready for anything after a trying afternoon and early evening on duty, pooh-poohed such an idea. "If I can't drink a pint, whatever it is, then I'll give in drinking altogether," he said sneeringly. Johnny downed the pint almost in one, swallowing the lumps of apple and finings with it. "See, what's the problem?" he queried. He commanded the barman: "Set them up again." I stayed with my half.

Johnny's second pint took a lot longer for him to negotiate and I knew the scrumpy was having an effect because his eyes took on a glassy look. I was relieved when the barman called "last orders". Johnny was beginning to have difficulty standing up. I knew that pasties or hot dogs were now out of the question as I steered a lurching Johnny out of the door of the pub. When we hit the fresh air, Johnny's legs collapsed from under him. After a couple of vain attempts at standing, he allowed me to drag him up from the deck. He had an ominous daft grin on his face. Nothing he said was intelligible.

It wasn't too far to the dockyard gate and I somehow managed to haul Johnny along, helping him past the dockyard sentries who looked on knowingly. They'd seen all this before on hundreds of occasions. I assured them I was capable of getting my pal back on board. I steered Johnny along, weaving and staggering, until he collapsed once again, dissolving into a fit of giggling. I couldn't take him back on board like this. We'd have to find some shelter until he'd sobered up a little.

Close to where Johnny had buckled, I spotted a dockyard crane wagon with an inviting-looking cab. When I tried the door, it opened. I heaved and dragged Johnny over and somehow managed to haul him into the cab. He may well have already passed out by the time I got him sitting upright. Emitting loud snores and wheezes, my friend slept,

I think we'd probably been in the cab about two hours when I was awoken by Johnny thrashing around in his sleep. He tilted towards me and bashed into the lorry's hand-brake. The lorry gently moved forward. I tried valiantly to grab the hand brake but Johnny was slumped over it. We gathered a modicum of speed and then – crash. Our journey came to an end at one of the dockyard's small storage buildings. I was certain somebody must have heard the din and I jumped out, pulling Johnny out of his runaway bedroom. He was finally beginning to ease out of his drunken stupor. With his legs now responding, I marched him away from what I imagined was a scene of destruction and got us both safely back on board.

The next morning Johnny had a huge hangover. The usual "never again" was promised. He didn't remember a thing about the previous night. It was a blessing he didn't. Later that day the dockyard police came to the ship. They interviewed everyone who was ashore the previous night about damage in the dockyard. When it was my turn to be questioned, I brazenly denied any knowledge of any incident. Johnny wasn't able to help them with their enquiries either.

Chapter 19

DANGEROUS DAYS

With our replenishment complete in Plymouth the Falmouth and its squadron headed for the Mediterranean station.

Our immediate boss in the wireless office was Chief Radio Supervisor Victor Smith. The chief had taken a dislike to me. He kept calling me 'Dabble'. I hated that pronunciation. I called him 'Schmidt the Shit' behind his back. Somebody snitched on me. "I don't like you Dabble and I'm going to make life hell for you," Schmidt warned me. And he did. When it came to making up the squads for 'landing party', 'boarding party' and 'emergency aerial repair party', Dabble was always on the list. Schmidt had a death wish. I was it.

Those extra duties that Vic Smith embroiled me in had little significance as the Falmouth sailed around the Med. Landing parties were always put ashore on friendly territory; boarding parties were carried out on small craft serving as stooges to our exercises. The weather at that time in the Mediterranean was benign. There was little problem when carrying out emergency repairs to our aerials on exercise. That, though, would all soon change.

Malta became our base and life was pretty good. We had plenty of time to play football and dance at Manoel Island, in Sliema, near where we were tied up. I also had chance to revisit Valletta. Inevitably we found ourselves down the 'Gut'. I was an experienced Strait Street sailor now though. "Come inside Falmouth, all your ship's company in here. Queen Victoria…" I wasn't playing ball this time either.

By now I was allowed overnight shore leave. It was great not having to belt back on board before midnight like some bell-bottomed Cinderella. You could flop into a room in a boarding-house on the harbour front at Valletta, nicknamed the 'Barbary Coast', for half-a-crown. The bedrooms were basic but always spotlessly clean. And you were given a wake-up call with a glass of coffee and condensed milk to make sure you got back on board on time. I occasionally did the overnight stay in the vain and unrequited hope that I'd get lucky with some young lady at a dance or a function.

Our two favourite modes of transport in Malta were the daighsoe, the island's version of a gondola, and karozzin carriage, fondly called a 'garry', We boarded the daighsoes to get backwards and forwards from the ship, when we were tied up in Valletta Harbour for instance. Part of the fun taking a daighsoe was negotiating a fare with the daighsoeman. There was always much swearing and cursing from boatman and passengers haggling. Sometimes the daighsoeman refused to go any further if he thought he was going to be swindled out of the fare he'd demanded up front. A stand-off in the middle of Grand Harbour was a regular occurrence. This was because the daighsoemen had got wise to the trick of pulling in to the jetty and seeing jolly Jack Tars leg it ashore without paying their fares.

How those little craft stayed afloat, especially with some of the drunken passengers they had aboard, is beyond me. But we actually had a great rapport with the daighsoemen. They would, for a good upfront price of course, occasionally arrange to pass in bottles of Marsovin, the cheap and very sweet white wine of Malta, fondly and aptly called 'screech', through ship's messdeck scuttles (portholes), to the more alcohol-dependent ship's personnel. Frankly I couldn't abide the stuff, unless it really was a last resort on a non-pay-week – and heavily topped up with lemonade. I'd seen metal buckets gleaming as if new after being cleaned with it.

The karozzin drivers were wise to matelots' tricks too. The horse-drawn vehicles could take five passengers, four inside the lovingly cared-for carriage and one up alongside the driver. A shotgun passenger was always mandatory. He was the driver's insurance. Inside passengers were likely to thin out during the journey as the destination approached.

The daighsoemen and karozzin drivers often used to enter into the spirit of the occasion and seemed to take delight in races back to the ships, driven by the promise of a large tip if our daighsoe or karozzin beat the opposition back. Once again, how those carriages stayed on the road is a mystery.

From Malta the Falmouth went on idyllic sojourns to such places as Marseilles, the Greek island of Argostoli, Bari, Venice and Naples (again for me) and the seaside port of Split in Yugoslavia.

Argostoli was a marvellous experience, right out of a holiday brochure. Of course it had been anything but a few years before our visit, suffering a catastrophic earthquake. Split still showed the signs of the Second World War and I remember one cafe we frequented being actually in the bombed-out ruins of a building the Nazis destroyed.

Venice was a particular delight. While we were there the spectacular Water Carnival took place, with highly colourful boat races in traditional costumes. A few days into our visit there was another aquarian spectacle – St Mark's Square under water, where only the day before we had wandered amongst the tourists on dry land. The Bridge of Sighs, a trip to Lido across the bay, a ride in a gondola: we did it all.

Malta was always our base and I had at last found a girlfriend there, a pretty Wren called Margaret from Boulmer who I called 'George' because of her Geordie accent. Jim Sked also had a friend at 'Whitehall Mansions', the WRNS quarters in Sliema Creek. Neither of us had got past snogging goodbye on the mansion steps, but we were looking forward to enjoying life as normal men instead of floating monks when we pulled into Malta after one of our trips in the Mediterranean. On about the second night back a gaggle of us were enjoying a night out in a little hostelry in Msida Creek, just up the road from the Wrens' quarters, where you could buy good food and drink not too expensively.

Our little party was in full swing when suddenly a Naval patrol burst into the bar. "All men from the 30th Escort squadron report back to your ships immediately," rang out the chilling command. "Don't ask questions just do it. Anyone not reporting back immediately will be in serious trouble." Then off went the patrol to the next bar. As well as being dismayed we were baffled what this order was all about. Reluctantly saying goodbye to our girlfriends, we dolefully made our way back to the Falmouth.

When we arrived back at the ship all hell had broken loose. There were huge steam clouds billowing all around the ship and men scrambling about all over the place. "What's going on?" I asked the quartermaster on the gangway. "Don't ask me son," he said curtly. "We're getting ready to sail as soon as we've upped steam. No idea where to though. Better get down to the mess and get into your number eights."

Within about half an hour of us getting back, the tannoy crackled into life: "Do you hear there? The ship will be ready to sail in one hour. You will receive further information shortly." We had no real idea what was going on. I just knew that at least half the ship's company had been dragged off shore well pissed on Hop Leaf and screech. I hoped we'd get out of Valletta harbour without a collision with anything.

Soon we knew our fate. The three lads on duty in the wireless office were in the know. "We're heading for the Far East," they informed us. "The Indonesians are attacking Malaysia." And that was it. The 'Indonesian Confrontation' had begun. The 30th Escort squadron was to be part of a protection force from the RN to try to protect Malaysia. We were heading for the Indian Ocean and Singapore. This was bad news for the lads who had their wives living in Malta and for the Maltese chefs and stewards, who had to bid their loved ones a hasty and unexpected farewell.

It was a gruelling trip to the Far East. Communications work was always a tough slog at sea, spent working the traditional Naval watch-keeping system. There were three duties to work in rotation over 24 hours by nine of us, three to a watch. Three would do the afternoon (1200-1600hrs) and middle watch (midnight-0400hrs); three would do first dog watch (1600-1800), first (2000-midnight) and morning (0400-0800), while the remaining three had the easiest watch of last dog (1800-2000) and the following forenoon (0800-midday). Chief Smith and the senior leading radio operator, 'Bungy' Edwards, shared the running of the wireless office during the day. LRO Edwards was also on call out in case an emergency came up during the night. The chief was only to get a 'shake' from his bunk in the direst of situations and under pain of joining RO2 Dabell on every dangerous assignment going.

Remarkably, the chief radio supervisor appointed me senior hand of a watch. This was quite a responsibility, a post held on most ships by a more senior or experienced rating than me. Was Smithy mellowing? No chance.

The squadron was at full speed, carrying out regular 'action stations', with periods of 'darken ship', when the ship was plunged into, well, darkness, to try to avoid it being spotted during countless manoeuvres. We had a short stop at Port Said, where I had my first experience of 'bum boats', canoes with traders aboard trying to sell you all kinds of goods: souvenirs (camel whips by the thousand and plastic pyramids), fruit and smelly delicacies that would be sure to have you spending at least a day in the heads.

Going through the Suez Canal was a slow but memorable experience and I did actually witness eggs being cooked on top of a gun turret in the blazing sun. The messdeck was like an oven due to the heat and humidity. Of course the air conditioning unit in the mess chose this time to pack in. Some of us took our camp beds up top and slept on the upper deck when we were off 'watch', our duty in the wireless office.

On arrival in Singapore after taking just over a fortnight to get there, to our dismay there was no shore leave. There had been rioting and clashes between Chinese and Indian fraternities. It was only going to be a brief stop, anyway, to refuel and take on stores. We had to settle for several games of crib and 'uckers', a sort of Naval ludo, and watch a couple of movies for a second and third time on the quarterdeck. Then, as soon as we had refuelled, taken on victuals and swapped the movies for some new ones, the squadron was back at sea, either patrolling the Malacca Straits between Indonesia and Malaysia or in the South China Sea between Borneo and Malaysia and Singapore. This was called Strategic 'Reserve' Service, as I remember. Don't know why we didn't make the first team.

We were on the lookout for a squadron of warships that the Indonesians had bought from the Russians. Silhouettes of Sverdlov cruisers and the like were displayed everywhere, so we knew what the enemy looked like. Our other duty was to sweep the seas for sampans who were either gun-running or carrying insurgents who were trying to land on Malaysian shores.

We spent our time watch-keeping and time off from duties mostly at action stations. It was an arduous few weeks. Every time I heard the call on the ship's intercom: "Boarding party to muster," a chill went through me. I'd collect my portable radio and head for the craft to be dropped down into the ocean.

I was incredibly lucky, however. Not one of the sampans we boarded had anything more on it than boxes of fruit or catches of fish. I spent weeks terrified over what we might come across. My fears were hardly assuaged when news of a terrible incident came in on the radio. A midshipman leading a boarding party before us off another ship had been killed when a booby-trapped sampan blew up. It was the luck of the draw.

Landing parties from the squadron were a bit like scouting parties in the old Western movies. My job was to link up with the ship when we landed personnel on the myriad islands in the straits between Indonesia and Malaysia. Again, I escaped unscathed without being involved in any really serious incident. Schmidt must have been beside himself with frustration.

Our reward for completing our stint patrolling was a trip to Hong Kong. With nothing much to spend our money on, apart from Coca Colas from the ice tub by the laundry, we'd saved up a tidy sum to change into Hong Kong dollars. We all enjoyed a wondrous break, scaling the peak via the funicular, shopping in the markets where you could buy everything from a snake to a sailor suit and of course, enjoying 'Wanchai Street', an incredible thoroughfare of night life.

After the visit to Hong Kong our unscheduled stay in the Far East was over and the squadron was ordered back to Malta. Soon we were into the Indian Ocean, where sleeping on the upper-deck then became just a little fraught. Flying-fish don't sleep. I awoke with a jump one night when a flapping, wet object smacked me neatly between the eyes.

This time we crossed the equator. It gave rise to an uproarious event on the upper-deck as 'King Neptune' christened all those who had never 'crossed the line' before. I was one of them. Neptune, complete with crown, trident and fish head, slapped you around the face with a brush and sloshed you with foam before you were tipped unceremoniously into a makeshift pool off a custom-made 'crossing the line' stool. As you spluttered to the surface you were handed a can of beer. Your 'crossing the line' certificate was then presented to you as proof so you didn't have to undergo the indignity ever again.

Soon after a brief stop at the island of Gan in the Maldives to refuel I attained my 20th year, a notable landmark in the life of a sailor. I was now old enough to draw my 'tot' of rum. At first I was wary of the grog, a mixture of strong rum and water, which came at 'Up Spirits', about half an hour before lunch, and was dealt out by a 'trusty' wielding a grog cup. I had to learn how to drink the stuff and at first I only drank half. That was enough to make my head spin. I soon learned not to just give the other half away, however. The tot, or half of it, even just 'gulpers' or 'sippers', provided great bartering power. You could get somebody to do your harbour duty for you for a tot of grog for instance. If somebody was a bit of a 'rum rat', you could get them to stand in for you for a mere half a tot. If you wanted a favour done, the traditional way of asking was to show your index and little finger, with your other two fingers clamped by your thumb. This meant the favour was worth half a tot. I often used the ploy.

About halfway between Gan and Aden the ship came to a halt in the Indian Ocean and all the hands off duty were given permission to go for a swim. Imagine the delight at diving off the side of the ship into endless fathoms of deep blue water. It was a bit scary diving or jumping off the side but my flag-wagger friend Flook Young had to go one better and plunged in off the flagdeck, quite a feat, about the equivalent up of two Olympic diving-boards.

While we splashed about and enjoyed the cool water a patrol boat with a rating armed with a rifle kept an eye out for sharks as he circled around we ocean swimmers. Suddenly I felt something wriggling around my legs. I was terrified. "Something's got me," I screamed out as I tore off in an explosion of arms, legs and foam for the climbing net on the ship's side, hardly touching the water and resembling an aquatic Speedy Gonzales. As I frantically scaled the net with whimpering relief, the patrolling rifleman, who had followed me in, held out a boathook on which dangled a length of toilet roll. "Here's your shark Dabs," he guffawed.

When we arrived in Aden there was plenty to look forward to. Life seemed idyllic for us off-duty radio operators as we delighted in the joys of the beach at the shore establishment HMS Sheba. The only thing we had to worry about was whether we might get stung by the sun or a stingray, or lose a foot to a voracious barracuda. We weren't warned about sharks as they rarely came near the beach. It was definitely the lull before the storm, though.

Later in the day, bosom pals Dabell, Sked and Grattan, in the company of a young newcomer to our mess, 'Ginge' Langseth, decided to go on a shopping expedition to the

Casbah. A similar quartet of electricians from the next mess to ours decided to do the same. Fate decreed that we would opt to wear 'civvy' clothes; the electricians had decided on their white number one 'duck' suits. Both groups took taxis to the Casbah and both arrived about the same time. The sparkers headed into one bazaar and the electricians made for an adjacent shop.

I'll never forget what happened then. As the last man wandering into our bazaar I, for some reason, looked behind me. Mesmerised, I saw an arm snake out of a clapped out old Mercedes and hurl an object out of the car. It was a grenade. It went rolling into the electricians' bazaar rather than ours. Next, there was an almighty bang and blue smoke billowed everywhere. We four radio operators were rooted to the spot for a moment before hitting the deck. Then there was pandemonium. An army patrol came from nowhere and grabbed us, forcefully chucking us out into the street and telling us to get scarce. Our bazaar owner scrambled to close his shop. As we tottered into the street, it was all happening – an armoured car screeched up, men spewed out; then an ambulance and a police car, both with flashing lights and sirens, also screamed to a halt. We weren't allowed to check up on next door which, from a nervous glance, I could see was wrecked. We were just yanked by our collars and ordered to get to HMS Sheba "as quick as Christ will let you."

We ran for the taxi rank, convinced our electrician mates were all dead. There were service personnel everywhere, all being thrown into taxis by armed Navy patrol men. Ginge and I were bundled into a cab and a voice inside bellowed: "Go, go, go – HMS Sheba." The cab driver burned rubber. He was not hanging around. On gaining HMS Sheba, Ginge and I tumbled out of the taxi and ran up the steps of the shore base. Jim was just ahead, going through the main door. Inside it was a seething mass. "Where's Scouse?" I blurted fearfully. "There was no sign of our lanky Liverpudlian mate. We frantically ran around checking on every group of men in the rooms. No Scouse. "We were pushed into a taxi which already had two blokes in it," I said quaveringly. "The taxi shot straight off. We thought Scouse was with you Jim." "No we got separated in all the chaos," said the worried Scot. "I thought he was with you." We were mortified now. Where was our mate?

Suddenly the main door opened. In slid a wide-eyed, blanco-faced, shuddering heap. It was Scouse. "Where the bloody hell were you all?" the shaking Liverpudlian blurted. "I got grabbed by a patrol van and brought here or I might still be wandering around wondering where everybody was. It was bloody awful. I've come close to crapping myself." We did our best to excuse ourselves but each one of us felt mighty guilty at Scouse's misadventure. Soon, though, the bar in HMS Sheba was in full swing. A couple of brandies calmed the nerves a little. We could not, though, get this awful vision of our electrician friends being blown to pieces out of our minds.

However, in the end, somehow, by a miracle and an act of great bravery, they all survived. They had been picked out for the grenade because they were easily identified as Navy boys in their white uniforms. That was possibly a fact that saved us sparkers next door. Would I have had the presence of mind to do what the last man in the next door bazaar did? When the grenade came rolling into the front of the bazaar he ran forward and threw himself at his three colleagues, pulling them to the floor with him. He was the only one to get injured – mainly his back and buttocks – but he survived and eventually came back to work on the Falmouth.

Of course that was it. Aden was now off-limits, even HMS Sheba. Insurgents and Yemeni tribesmen had upped the stakes. We were all told to be on our utmost guard. This included being ordered to move sharply about the upper deck of our ship and take cover behind its superstructure at every opportunity. The rebels had decided it was a great idea to take a pop at anyone standing still down in the dockyard. They had taken up positions in the hills above where our ship was lying alongside the jetty.

Well Smithy had it in for me again. At the outset this time it didn't seem such an onerous task. I was to dispose of the confidential waste from the offices, all the restricted, secret and coded messages that had come into the ship which had been shredded. "Right Dabell, you are going to have a little trip to the dockyard incinerator. You'll have two Bootnecks with you and they'll be armed – so no need to worry."

Worried? When the gravity of the job hit home, I was petrified. I hauled myself reluctantly to the ship's upper deck with two huge sacks of shredded confidential waste which bowed my back, sweating 'neaters' (a Navy euphemism for perspiring profusely). I met up with the two Bootnecks and made my way over the gangway of HMS Falmouth. They wore steel helmets. I was in denim shirt and shorts with a plastic cap on my head. We made it to the incinerator without any incident. On the way back though I was sure I heard a couple of pings as we dodged along using the monster gash bins which lined the jetty, as cover. I threw myself to the floor. The lads guarding me chuckled, assuring me it was just rubbish blowing about. Smithy looked quite disappointed when we got back to the ship and saw that I was unscathed – apart from two grazed knees.

From Aden we made our passage through the Suez Canal again, on to Port Said and then the 30th Escort Squadron called in to Beirut in the Lebanon to show the flag. At that time there was still a sizable ex-pat contingent in Beirut. The ambassador and his team were major players in cocktails in the Falmouth ward-room. The ratings were happy to play in a football match – Beirut City versus the 30th Escort Squadron. I was chosen as goalkeeper for the squadron.

We played on the City pitch, a venue in the hills high above Beirut. It was hard going on the old knees because there wasn't a great deal of grass. But it wasn't dissimilar to the Manoel Island ground and the squadron was more than holding its own at half-time, with the teams going in at 0-0.

I was always a bit nervous playing in goal but my upset tum leant itself more to the spicy dish I'd eaten the previous night than any nerves. I spent half-time in the toilet. However, when I tried to get out of the lavatory the door refused to budge. I just couldn't shift it, even with a hefty shoulder charge. I shouted and shouted but nobody responded. It had gone ominously quiet in the changing-rooms. I was then reduced to panic. Still no response. I looked up the wall – a small window. I grabbed the toilet brush and smashed it open, yelling at the top of my voice. Suddenly the toilet door was wrenched open. "What the bloody hell are you playing at Dabs?" said our team captain angrily. "We're a goal down now."

Nobody in our team had noticed I had not retaken up my position between the sticks when the referee blew the whistle to start the second half. The Beirut side did. With delight at spotting there was no opposition custodian between the sticks, their centre-forward, straight from the home team's kick-off, lobbed the ball accurately into an empty net. The referee refused all protests from the visitors. His opinion was that if the stupid Brits didn't know where their goalkeeper was, then it was their fault. We lost the match 1-0.

Christmas was approaching as we forged on to Malta. While we were at sea we had a special 'treat'. The British Forces Broadcasting Service had set up a link relaying messages from home to servicemen abroad, accompanied by choices of music. We all listened raptly in the mess in the hope that one of us got lucky and had a message. I was amazed to hear my name read out. Mum's message to me was typical of her but while it had my messmates in fits it had me squirming with embarrassment. "I hope you are looking after yourself and not getting too sunburnt. You know how you burn. Remember our holiday in Rhyl when we had to cover you in calamine lotion?" My messmates hooted with delight, suggesting I should see the sick bay wallah and get myself some calamine lotion. I could tell Mum was losing it. As she was dedicating her record to me she really broke up. I could hear my stepdad Ray comforting her in the background. I felt really miserable that I wasn't back home with them. On came Mum's choice, an old favourite of mine, 'In the Hall of the Mountain King' from Grieg's 'Peer Gynt' Suite. Cue more catcalls from my messmates, who were actually quite relieved that they didn't have to hear any more Cilla Black music. I used to turn up the mess radio when the lovely little Liverpool red-head was on. I still had to suffer, though, as a trio of my pals stomped around the messdeck tables going: "Duh duh duh de dih dih dih dih", simulating the opening bars of the Grieg piece.

Chapter 20

DIRTY DANCING

I had to settle for Christmas in Malta, which wasn't such a bad thing. It wasn't the same as being home, though, and a few days after the festive period I had to stifle a little sob when I received a photo in the mail of Mum, Ray and John and several of our relations drinking my health in our front room.

Christmas Day was spent on board. We all had a lie-in and there was the usual tradition of the captain swapping places (very briefly) with the ship's youngest crew member, namely exchanging headgear, to do rounds of the messdeck. The skipper was not the most effusive of men but he did his duty in the galley, stirring the sauce for the Christmas pudding with a glassy stare and fixed smile of which Vincent Price would have been proud. He later wished us all a merry Christmas when we gathered on the quarterdeck. The call 'up spirits' came after the skipper's rounds. We all offered 'sippers' of our tots to the younger members of the mess. Then the beer ration came out before we all got stuck into a festive lunch.

This is the Christmas Day programme and menus:

0800: breakfast: Fruit juice, cold gammon, fried egg, bread rolls, marmalade and coffee. 1000: service of lessons and carols on the quarterdeck. 1100: messdeck rounds. 1130: up spirits. 1200: Christmas dinner (lunch): Tomato soup, roast turkey with bread sauce, ham, chipolatas, roast and creamed potatoes, cauliflower and Brussels sprouts. Christmas pudding and rum sauce. 1630: Tea: Christmas cake, mixed nuts, fresh fruit. 1900: Supper: Turkey soup, cold roast pork, cold roast beef, salads. Cheese and biscuits.

They say an army marches on its stomach. The Navy did no marching this day – we would have been incapable.

After Christmas we moved on to Naples. Flook and I wandered around Pompeii where some artful thief managed to slip Flook's watch off his wrist without him even realising it. I wasn't wearing a watch. Mine had been shattered during a one-day exercise with other service personnel in Maltese countryside a couple of weeks before. I'd jumped over a low wall to avoid being spotted by our 'enemy' and fell down a hillock of 20ft or so, on the other side. I avoided serious injury but the watch, an Omega bought by Mum and Ray, got shattered as I protected the radio I was carrying.

Soon we were able to sail for the UK and the bulk of the ship's company could enjoy long-awaited leave. I tried desperately hard to find a girlfriend. On my first Saturday at home four of us did the rounds by way of my pal Jimmy Sibson's Morris Minor shooting break, finishing the night off at the Sherwood Rooms dance hall. First we enjoyed a cheese and onion 'cob' and a sherry at Yates's Wine Lodge while we watched the little combo that used to play there, a violinist, pianist and formidable lady playing the harp. Very rarely, though, did we get to try out the Sherwood Rooms' sprung dance floor when we got there. I think it might have been our cheese and onion breath that put the ladies off.

On the last Saturday of leave I went to the Kegworth Carnival Ball at the new village hall. For once I did plenty of dancing and got on really well with the younger sister of one of my old classmates at Kegworth School. I bashfully arranged to take Jill to the cinema the next evening. We were to meet on the Kegworth bus to Loughborough. The next day my dreaded shyness overcame me. I knew that a couple of my pals were also going to be on that bus to Loughborough. I couldn't stand the thought of the ribbing I'd get from them. Besides, Jill had probably thought better of meeting me and wouldn't be on the bus anyway. Then I'd get even worse treatment from my mates. She was on the bus. I had no idea, though. It was a miserable wretch that left for Plymouth the next day, Monday, to return to my ship. I had so wanted to see the girl but I'd funked it.

It must have been terrible for her. My pals had to console her. I was supposed to be paying her bus fare as part of our night out, too. When I next saw the lads at home they called me all the names under the sun for being so heartless. I never saw Jill again. About 40 years later I happened to be checking 'Friends Reunited'. Under my name I got a message saying: "I'm the girl you stood up in 1965. I've been living five miles from you for the past 10 years. Don't worry, though. I forgive you – and I've moved."

On return to Plymouth I was greeted by Smithy on my first day back. "Had a good leave Dabble?" I couldn't believe his bonhomie. I replied: "Yes chief, I went to…" I was cut off in midstream. "Well forget it, you're back. Make sure the aerials are in good shape."

The ship's company had a good deal of work to do. HMS Falmouth was smartened up in readiness for a trip to where it was built: Barrow-in-Furness.

News of our visit had obviously been very well publicised because a huge crowd stood on the jetty as we arrived at the north-west of England docks, waving flags and cheering us in. A dance had been laid on but I decided to take up the offer of a free entry to watch Barrow play football. I thought it was safer.

Another dance, though, was to provide me with further disappointment.

Our next port of call was Invergordon, then a thriving Naval base in the Highlands of Scotland. As part of a programme of events, designed to show off the ships to the locals, a ball was arranged at the Strathpeffer Pavilion a few miles away from where we were tied up. An advertisement was run in the local paper which read something like: "Girls, girls, girls, the Navy's in port. Come along and meet the boys at Strathpeffer Pavilion for a Grand Ball". A charabanc packed with eager sailors from the Falmouth left the jetty at Invergordon with expectations high. When we arrived at the ballroom our hopes of meeting a fair young lassie rose even higher. The room was full of gorgeous girls. They spent the night dancing with each other. I can't remember one of us even getting onto the floor.

From Invergordon the Falmouth crossed over the North Sea to Bergen, which was still closed. Our next stop was Hamburg. It was definitely open. Especially at night. The usual warning had been put on the ship's noticeboard: "The Reeperbahn area should be avoided..." It proved to be a magnet for the crew who went ashore en masse around 2200 hours as the bars, night-clubs, strip joints and worse, opened up. It was a real education in German decadence. No wonder the Beatles set up shop there.

A whole fortnight's pay got blown by many of the ship's company and at least three men went AWOL. For Jim and me there was a rather healthier attraction. We were selected for the 30th Escort Squadron football team to play Hamburg Police and, joy of joys, the game took place at the famous SV Hamburg Stadium.

We lost a hard-fought match 3-2 and then we were entertained by the policemen to a lavish banquet. When we sat down at our places each of us had a 'boot', a one litre 'stein' drinking glass, which waiters filled with frothing lager before the meal and speeches. The policemen watched in glee as we Brits tackled our boots. What we didn't realise was that an air-lock gathered in the heel of the boot as the lager was downed to cause a splash-back. Our thirsty team finished up covered in German beer, much to the delight of our hosts. We soon got the idea though and the boot was then on the other foot as the away team nearly drank the club dry.

Soon it was clear that the 30th Escort Squadron would be returning to the Far East. The confrontation by Indonesia had heightened and we were needed to relieve the squadron out there doing patrols between Malaysia and Singapore and looking out for the foe, an Indonesia backed by the USSR.

First we took Easter leave. At the start of it I was entrusted with Mum and Ray's new house, while Mum, Ray and my brother sampled the delights of Whitby. I was not the best of guardians. It all went badly.

My good friend Mick Snape and I decided we should have a party. He didn't want to hold it at his house because his parents were at home and felt that wouldn't be much fun. With great reluctance I agreed to be the host. I invited my cousin Gill and a few pals from Gotham and Kegworth.

We were having a great time, jiving to records on my Dansette, when to my horror I saw a burn hole in Mum and Ray's new corduroy sofa. I immediately switched to panic mode. It didn't ease when Gill, the culprit, just flipped over the tarnished cushion and said: "There. Nobody's going to know now." Some chance. Sherlock Holmes had nothing on my mum.

Sure enough, within half an hour of the family returning home from Whitby two days after, there was a shriek from the front room. Mum, with her unerring sixth sense, had found the burn in the settee. I got it in the neck. Ray tried to smooth things over for me. Then he found out that five of his bottles of home-made grapefruit wine were missing.

Before leaving Plymouth we said goodbye to some of the communications staff, who were replaced by new crew members. Then the squadron prepared to set off again for the Far East station, via Gibraltar, Malta, the Suez Canal, Aden and Gan.

We had several days in Malta to take on stores and tighten a few nuts and bolts. A few of us did some shopping then went for a swim before rounding off the day with a meal. We didn't feel like a long walk back to the dockyard, so to get back to the ship we called a karozzin. Four of us piled into the back, leaving a rather weary 'That is' Jones to clamber into the shotgun seat beside the driver. Jones, who'd joined the ship a few weeks before, got his sobriquet because his initials were I.E.

Our carriage shot off at a rate of knots but soon had to slow down at a bend. As the driver concentrated on negotiating the road, one of our number quietly slid out of the carriage. Then the next time we eased up, another of our quartet jumped ship. Over the next ten minutes or so, the last two inboard passengers departed.

By the time the garry arrived at the dockyard, only 'That is' was left of its crew. Poor old I.E. had dropped off to sleep. As the carriage drew to a halt, 'That is' awoke with a jolt and then realised it was awfully quiet inside the cab. Slowly it dawned on him in his fuzzy brain that he was on his own. The garry driver demanded his fare. 'That is' had to tip up the money, no amount of protestation cutting any ice with a whip-wielding driver.

On our way to Singapore there was an incredibly tragic piece of misfortune. The squadron was being refuelled at sea by one of the Royal Fleet Auxiliaries and it was the turn of HMS Aisne to receive the pipe that carried fuel across from one ship to the other. This was a highly tricky operation. To get the fuel pipe over, first a line with a metal rod on the end of it was fired from a rifle onto the receiving ship's deck. This line was then attached to the fuel pipe which would be hauled in on the receiving ship and fed into a fuel inlet valve. Whenever the rifle was to be fired to send out the 'coston gun line', a whistle would be blown to warn the ship's company on the receiving ship to take cover. Well, apparently everyone did take cover accordingly but one unfortunate lad, who had ducked behind a gun turret, was hit by the metal rod. His temple was pierced as the rod ricocheted down from the barrel. The lad only survived a few minutes. I didn't witness the incident but I read the report on the broadcast. Everyone was dumbstruck at such an incredibly unlucky tragedy.

From around July the squadron spent a good deal of time at sea, scouring horizons, looking for Sverdlov cruisers which never materialised. There were a couple of little breaks from the punishing routine, however. This was after we had switched our patrolling duties to the other side of Malaysia to keep a lookout for trouble at sea emanating from the Borneo area. This meant a stint in the South China Sea.

When there was a short hiatus in routine, the call would go out on the tannoy "Hands to make and mend". Up to about the end of the Second World War this announcement signalled a break from duties and the crew did exactly what it said – made and mended their clothes during an unscheduled afternoon off. For us modern sailors, whose clothes all came from 'slops', the clothing and kit stores on board, this unexpected time off meant a chance to go ashore, get some welcome kip, play cards, write letters, or watch a film on the quarterdeck. I for one had got out of the habit of darning socks.

Because we were at anchor, out in the South China Seas, any thought of shore leave was out of the question. We were seemingly miles away from proper human habitation. Not to be deterred and fed up with crib championships, some of us off-duty communicators were allowed to take a boat from the ship on a 'banyan', a Navy picnic, to Pulau Tioman. At the time it was a small island with only a very few proper buildings. We enjoyed an idyllic few hours swimming, sunbathing and eating a barbecue on a deserted beach.

Our second banyan was to an even remoter island in the Perhentian chain. The atoll we picked out seemed pretty deserted. About a dozen of us who landed in our banyan boat prepared to set up a barbecue and tackle the two packs of beer we'd brought. We were interrupted by an impressive-looking chap in local dress who spoke English of a sort. "You blokees wanna playa the footiball?" enquired our visitor. "My village take you on. We play every time sailor come to island."

We were more than pleased to take him up on his offer, feeling it would make a change from taking in rays. All of us were brown as berries anyway. "You bring beer with you," suggested this self-styled village official. We followed him into the jungle that fringed the beach. After a trek of about 20 minutes we came to a village, comprising the usual huts on stilts. The villagers seemed highly pleased to see us and we were directed further into the jungle where we came across a clearing. In this clearing were two bamboo goals and a pitch perfectly marked out for football. Within a few minutes our opposition arrived. They were wearing shirts and shorts and football boots, the old leviathan ones with big hard toe-ends and nuggs. Apparently the kit had been scrounged over the years from various Navy ships that pulled in near the island. The shirts were a bit ragged but each one had 'Blackpool' spelt perfectly, scrawled on the front, with numbers similarly drawn on the back. One of the village players proudly told us he was "Mr Stanley Matthews", pointing eagerly to his number seven on the back of his shirt. We, of course, were just in swimming trunks with bare feet, but we fancied our experience would show.

It was no contest. As the goalkeeper I was the only one not to suffer a mashed foot in the heavily one-sided encounter. Instead, I finished the contest sporting a black eye after coming into contact with one of those fearsome boots. Mr Stanley Matthews was the star of the show. I think he scored five goals. It was a massacre. After our serious thumping, the chap who'd approached us for the game, announced grandly: "We now have prize-giving for winners." The prize was our beer.

We never did come across even one of the Sverdlov cruisers with which we had been threatened but the powers-that-be did their best to get us embroiled in some skirmish or other as we spent hours and hours scouring the seas around Malaysia. When our squadron was relieved by another flotilla, it was back to Singapore.

I'd given up trying to find a girlfriend in Singapore or on our trips a bit further away to Johor Baharu, the border with Malaysia. I'm ashamed to say I did what many a red-blooded young tar did at the time – on the advice of the older members of the ship's company. I visited a brothel. This one was called 'The Tokyo Nights'. It was a bar and dance hall, with bedrooms at the back, a really plush little palace. For several visits I chickened out of going any further than a couple of beers, a dance and a free grope. Inevitably, though, I succumbed. One of my dance partners invited me to her bedroom. She told me her price and her name. "I am Suzie Wong," said my rather attractive hostess demurely and proudly, although not as proudly as Mr Stanley Matthews. She'd come a long way from Hong Kong I thought.

I wouldn't say it was the perfect liaison but it was exciting enough for a 20-year-old to want to come again, so to speak. The next pay day I made another trip to the Tokyo Nights. Like William Holden, I got to know Suzie Wong pretty well.

Our break from patrol was soon over and it was back to sea again for a few more weeks of hard graft. It was at this time my nickname changed from 'Dabs' to 'Snags'. My colleagues had noticed on too many times for comfort that when I tuned in a radio it invariably lost signal or the paper in the teleprinter machine jammed.

I got my nickname baptism the day a flying-fish suddenly came flying down the pipe connecting the wireless office to the bridge, flapping about on the office desk and rendering unreadable a message that had taken my watch an absolute age to receive in Morse code and decrypt. I don't know how I was supposed to be responsible for our finned friends' activities up top. Anyway, I suspected it wasn't just an unlucky flight that had sent the fish unerringly down the pipe. I felt my chum Flook, always on the lookout for a jolly jape, had something to do with it. Of course, he denied it.

Chapter 21

THE OWL HAS LANDED

The next time we pulled in to Singapore my feet hardly touched the ground. My pal Punchy Bowman, a handy pugilist and fellow 'sparker', and I were 'volunteered' for duties at the Naval wireless station Kranji, a former Japanese prisoner of war camp not far away from the Johor border with Malaysia. It was another of Vic Smith's schemes to persecute yours truly. Punchy had upset our boss by calling him a "pot-bellied, drunken old bastard" when Schmidt came into the wireless office one day worse for wear after tot time in the chief's mess and completely disrupted the watch.

Punchy and I settled into our duties at Kranji and made the best of what was a boring stint at first. We'd be working in the wireless station on shifts and also had to patrol the fenced perimeter of the station. It was a rota of four hours on and four hours off for two days, then we'd have a day and night off. This enabled us to get to the little village about a mile from Kranji where you could get a 'nasi goreng' (chicken fried rice) and a beer and chew the fat with the locals, albeit mostly in a sort of pidgin English which both parties struggled to understand. The walk down to the bar was via a well-worn path through the jungle. The outward journey was full of trepidation, wearing the gaiters we'd used for patrol and a wielding a hefty stick. This was protection from snakes, of which there were at least five absolutely deadly species in the

Kranji region. Coming back we lighted our way with Naval issue torches but a couple of bottles of Tiger always seemed to lower the inhibitions as far as worrying about snakes was concerned. I often used to wake up the next day and shudder at the thought of what might have taken a shine to a Dabell calf. Somehow, though, neither Punchy nor I ever got bitten by anything more than a mosquito.

We slept under 'mozzie' nets at night. Well, I did. Punchy said he would sooner get bitten than suffer the stifling heat inside the net enveloping his bunk. One night I was awoken by a terrific screeching above me and to my great alarm I watched my mosquito net being torn from its moorings. It was a terrifying few moments before I realised an owl had somehow flown into our hut and got itself entangled in my net. Even when Punchy and I managed to free it the panicking owl flung itself around the hut, causing mayhem until we finally ushered it out of the window. "Why is it always you it happens to?" queried Bowman, aggrieved to be awoken by what initially had seemed to be some eastern banshee. "Why did you bother putting up the bloody net in the first place? They're a waste of time."

I thought it was particularly mean of Punchy to feel he had to get some kind of revenge for this interrupted night. The next morning I was sitting in one of the stalls in the bathroom block when, to my horror, a thin black snake, of the type we used to call a 'bootlace' and particularly venomous despite its size, dropped into my lap, seemingly from the roof slats above me. Brushing the bootlace off in panic, I shot out of the toilet like a scalded cat, my trousers and underpants around my ankles. I was absolutely petrified. Then I saw the treacherous Bowman, doubled up with laughter, standing a little way from the stall. "It's a dead 'un," gloated the evil Bowman. "Thought that would get your attention, though. You should have seen your eyes, standing out like chapel hat-pegs. And your face. You're as white as your mozzie net."

I vowed vengeance. I knew that Punchy, despite his cavalier attitude over mosquitoes, hated most insects, particularly spiders and the like. A couple of days later he was snoozing peacefully on the bench outside the mess. "Punchy, Punchy, wake up but don't move too quickly," I crooned in his ear. As he came to, he whispered nervously, "Waazup?" Then he saw it. On the window ledge in front of him, inches from his face, sat the most enormous praying mantis ever known to man. It was at least eight inches in length. Naturally in an aggressive stance after being released from the shoe box I'd snared it in, it slapped its legs together like one of Punchy's former boxing opponents. It stared threateningly and hypnotically at the mesmerised Punchy. "Get rid of it for God's sake," wailed my paralysed pal. "They're completely harmless you softy," I chuckled, reaching over and grabbing for the massive insect before Punchy gathered his wits and smashed it to bits.

Not long after these incidents we were both under threat – our whole camp and wireless station was. Punchy and I were ambling around the perimeter as usual, feeling fed up at carrying out these patrols when most of the rest of our gang were enjoying a trip up to Mackenzie Camp, a services holiday resort near Penang. Suddenly there were explosions, gunfire and yells from just down the road. While Punchy and I debated what we should do and wondered what was going off, a petty officer from the guardhouse came running up to us. "Ready yourselves you two, the Indos have landed at the border and they're making their way up here," he roared. "Take up a position by the fence." This order was worrying enough but positively disquieting when we looked forlornly at our only 'weapons' – a pair of helving tool handles, a sort of weighted stave that fitted onto a ditch-building spade. True, they would produce a nasty, potentially fatal, wound if the metal end came into contact with a head. But we were hardly equipped to hold off a squad of fully-armed guerrillas. The petty officer did at least have a firearm, a regulation NCO's pistol. He, however, turned tail and made back for the guard house. "I have to go back and get permission to draw ammo," he shouted over his shoulder, leaving Punchy and me to take on Indonesia. Fortunately, the insurgents only got within half a mile of

Kranji before they were scattered by the real defence force protecting the base who had rifles and machine guns, rather than helving tool handles.

On our arrival back on the Falmouth there was no time to visit the Tokyo Nights before the squadron left for more patrol work. However, with the threat of any serious invasion by Indonesia on Malaysia receding, plans were afoot for the 30th Escort Squadron to wind down its patrolling duties.

This enabled the Falmouth to take in a few visits, a return to Hong Kong, on to the Philippines and then Thailand.

Chapter 21

The Vietnam War was in full swing at that time so we all hoped Britain would not be dragged into that show, too. We might not have been involved in Vietnam but we met up with a lot of US sailors who were when we pulled into Subic Bay, a Naval base in the Philippines where several US Navy ships were anchored.

My mate Johnny Vear and I made particularly good friends with one US sailor, who like us was a communications rating. Tom Mueller was a petty officer but in the US Navy he was really a senior radio operator rather than an NCO and he had no trouble mixing with the Falmouth erks. Tom took quite a liking to tot time at the weekend and would come aboard at the witching hour to sample some grog in our mess. All the US Navy ships were 'dry', so it was a novelty for Tom to be able drink on board our ship. He would stay for lunch and then we'd hit the town of Olongapo. I remember one great club in particular we used to visit. It was supposed to be a services club but it was overrun by dozens of extremely attractive raven-haired Filipinas, who helped the US matelots especially, temporarily forget about war. Dear old Tom couldn't get enough of the Filipinas and seemed to have a different girlfriend each night. He really let his hair down, particularly after he'd enjoyed my tot.

We had to be a bit careful, though, because leave was only up until 2230 hours and then there was strict curfew in place.

Well, one night Tom really did go too far. He was absolutely shipwrecked by the time we needed to be heading for our respective ships. No amount of cajoling, persuading and finally pleading, would stop him staggering off into Olongapo town with a voluptuous young thing draped around him. Johnny Vear and I gave in and reluctantly headed back on board.

That was the last I saw of Tom. I'd feared for his well-being, so I went on board his ship the night before we sailed for Thailand. I questioned one of the communication ratings as to what might have befallen Tom. "Oh, he's in deep shit," I was told by his shipmate. "Tom was spotted by a Navy patrol and the local police in the town. Apparently he ran off and the local guy let off a round at him. He got shot in the foot. He's now under guard in the sick bay, so you won't be able to see him. He's in for it big time."

Several weeks later I received a letter from Tom. He told me he would have got away from the patrol but they shot his shoe off as he tried to climb a wall to escape them. Unfortunately his injury wasn't serious enough to excuse him duties and patrols in Vietnam and he was back at work, having suffered a fortnight's stoppage of pay and liberty, while losing his good conduct stripes.

Tom wrote to me several times from Vietnam but suddenly his letters stopped. I wondered what had become of him. Then months later I received a letter from his parents. Tom had been killed in Vietnam but they thanked me for looking after their son and for a brief time taking his mind off the horrors of the war. They had traced me through the letters he had sent to them, talking about the fun he'd had with us all in Olongapo and how the "crazy limeys" drank rum on their ships every day.

From the Philippines we headed for Hong Kong. Johnny Vear and I decided we'd take the five days of 'station' leave we had left and booked in to the China Fleet Club, a huge hotel and leisure club for Naval personnel. If you couldn't enjoy Hong Kong then you were either a real misery or you were dead.

Even the teeming rain all week failed to dampen our spirits. Our 'Wanchai Burberries' kept us dry. (These were umbrellas made out of cane and paper. The expression comes from when sailors were caught in the rain without their Burberry raincoat and bought one of these bamboo and cardboard umbrellas from local Chinese traders.) They were quite flimsy and didn't last for long but saved you having to wear a raincoat in the humid temperatures and they were dirt cheap.

One of the nights we spent at the Singapura Hotel, where Acker Bilk was appearing. I'd last seen him three years or so before when he was appearing in Clevedon. Listening to 'Stranger on the Shore' again made me feel a little sad. I wondered how Pauline was getting on now.

Next stop after Hong Kong for the Falmouth was Thailand and the port for Bangkok. I'd only just got used to calling it Thailand, preferring the much more romantic sounding 'Siam'. As quite a film buff, my head was full of memories of *The King and I*, a marvellous musical (one of the few musicals I actually liked) which starred Yul Brynner and Deborah Kerr. I was all set to visit palaces and temples similar to the ones I remembered from the film. I expected to see my fair share of Siamese cats and bald-headed royals.

There were myriad bars and dance halls in the port but I was determined to have my cultural visit. Everyone was really friendly at the bus station, telling me where to locate various sights. I got chatting to one girl in a café as I waited to catch a bus into the city. She seemed really taken with my white tropical sailor suit. I decided she must have seen *South Pacific*. She was quite forward and took my mind off sight-seeing. She suggested we might go dancing that night if I let her accompany me. Completely smitten and overcoming my innate shyness with the opposite sex, I acquiesced. I suggested I could skip the bus ride. We could perhaps go for a meal and then a dance, instead. I could visit temples and palaces another day.

We had a splendid time. I was really taken with her. She wanted to know all about me and listened to my life story avidly. Things got quite cosy. Then she suggested I might go home with her.

I thought I'd twigged what was going on. "I no have money to go home with you," I said. She exploded: "You no need money to go my home, what you think I am, call girl?" whacking me across my shoulders with her handbag. "I just like you and wanna be friend and for you come meet my family," she added. Obviously I'd misread the situation. I didn't have to be back on board until 0800 hours, so, after she'd calmed down, I agreed.

I was highly nervous as we trekked out of the dockyard area, wondering if I was walking into a trap and I was going to get mugged. They wouldn't get much. I only had only a few bahts on me. I didn't want to lose my new watch, though. I'd bought another on tick from the NAAFI.

Despite my nervous glances around me my escort urged me on until we arrived in a compound of about a dozen huts. I was ushered into one of them, where we were met by an enormous lady, with an equally enormous smile, more of the Cheshire variety than Siamese. "This my mother," I was informed. I could only guess that a visit like mine had taken place before. But what the heck. I was in this for the experience. Her mother nodded in what I took to be approval after she was informed who I was and I was allowed in their home. After mother and daughter had come out of a huddle I was directed to a corner of their hut where, from the signals I was getting from mum, it was expected daughter and I would spend the rest of the night.

I was given a chair on which to hang my uniform and I flopped down on a reasonably comfortable bamboo bed. Then my inhibitions returned. I wanted to enjoy my good fortune but with a big fat momma in the house and two of my young lady's sisters in close proximity – one of them was actually sleeping under the bed – it was hard (or not, as the case may be) to concentrate on the job. But it was Bangkok. I was determined the night shouldn't be a flop.

I was awoken quite forcefully at what I felt was not that long after dawn, by my partner hauling me up from the bed. A study of my watch through bleary eyes, told me it was 5am. To her great amusement I tried to cover myself up. "You come for bath," said my Siamese kitten, handing me a sort of flimsy kimono to protect my modesty from her family.

The family 'bath-house' was a sort of tall standpipe in the middle of the compound. I was nudged under the tap and my young host then whipped off my robe. "I wash you," she said, wielding a small brush. I was not as delighted at the prospect as she seemed to be. I did my best to cover up but my hands were continually brushed out of the way of my parts. I chanced a glance around me. Sure enough, the whole compound seemed to be watching from every doorway. My scrub down completed, I was wrapped up again in the kimono and I scrambled for my suit. Navy 'duck' suits are difficult enough to get on anyway, but it took some effort to get my clothes on over a damp body.

I didn't feel sartorially elegant but my young lady was impressed. "You have meal with us before you go back to ship?" I wanted nothing more than to get out of there. Anyway, my stomach was lurching from the smell of food coming out of the end of her hut. "No, I have to be back on ship soon," I said anxiously. "And I do not know where I am." That brought great disappointment from the family when she explained this to them. "OK, but I show you way back to docks," she said, much to my relief. I really did have no idea where I was.

My hostess looked a million dollars in her cheongsam type of dress. I was quite proud to be kissed goodbye on the jetty before striding up the gangway in my creased suit with my cap on at a rakish angle. In fact I felt a little bit like Yul Brynner when he finally got a dance with Deborah Kerr.

I think I was something of a trophy, though, for my young Siamese friend. Although she said she would meet me on the jetty two days later when I next had leave, she wasn't there. I guessed she'd found another white suit and another young body to scrub. When I realised I'd been stood up, I caught the bus into town and headed for the Golden Temple. I never did see a Siamese cat.

When another changeover of staff on the Falmouth came about I was delighted to discover my old pal Slinger Wood was going to be joining the ship. Slinger embarked at Singapore during a small refit and before we finished our time in the Far East.

During the refit the Falmouth played in one of the Navy football cup competitions. After coming through the qualifying matches, sometimes in the broiling heat and humidity of Singapore afternoons in the monsoon season, the Falmouth team made it all the way to the semi-finals. We took part in a real humdinger of a match at HMS Terror stadium, against HMS Barossa if my memory serves me well.

About 20 of their supporters gathered behind my goal and gave me hell throughout the match. "Shaky goalie, shaky goalie," was the favourite cry whenever the ball came into our penalty area. For once though I wasn't convulsed by the nerves that usually visited me on these big occasions and I played a blinder. I twice saved at the feet of the opposing centre-forward, sliding across the unyielding bone-hard 'turf', ripping all the skin off my knees. It was not until after the 0-0 draw that I realised my knees were in quite a state.

The day after the match the Falmouth put to sea and by then my knees were extremely painful and already showing signs of infection. I had to report to the Falmouth's sick bay for treatment. This treatment was pure torture, administered by a particularly sadistic sick berth attendant we all called 'the doc', even though he was nothing more than what would be termed, in this day and age, a paramedic. The doc first scrubbed my wounds clean of torn skin, congealed blood and seeping pus, then sprayed my knees with a hideous concoction called 'plastic skin'. I don't know whether this medication is even legal. I can remember its effects with stark clarity. As the plastic skin bit into my wounds I let out a less than muffled screech. When the doc eased me down from his ceiling light I then tried to stand. It was as if my knees had been cemented. I staggered out of the sick bay like the tin man in *The Wizard of Oz*. You can imagine how I looked trying to make my way around the ship as it rolled with the swell. I drew much derision particularly as I staggered, stiff-legged, down the passageway past the queue at the NAAFI hatch. The doc's cure, I must confess, did the job however. Within a week I was raring to go and ready for the cup replay when we pulled alongside the jetty for another short stay in the dockyard. The replay never happened. Neither ship was available at the same time. The other two teams in the semi-finals qualified for the final instead. My agonies had been for nothing. I still have the scars to this day.

With the new intake of crew now fully briefed the Falmouth said goodbye to the Far East Station and set sail for Blighty around October time 1965. Our passage through the Indian Ocean was a particularly poignant one for me. I celebrated my 21st birthday during the crossing.

The lads made as much fuss of me as was possible but it wasn't a great celebration because we hit a gale on the morning of November 9. Many of the mess were in their usual throes of mal de mer, especially poor old Jim Sked, who never did master seasickness throughout his Naval career. The gale got worse. Several of my messmates urged me to share their tots but I demurred because I was on duty for the afternoon and middle watches.

A small 21st birthday cake had been baked for me but I think I was the only one that ate it. The night of my birthday was spent trying to keep the broadcast signal in tune and sympathising with my new young operator, 'Bozzy Buesnell', who spent most of the watch talking more into a bucket than a radio set.

We had all the usual stops on the way home: Gan for refuelling, Aden, where we were confined to the ship, Suez

Canal, into the Mediterranean and then quite a lengthy stopover in Gibraltar.

Chapter 22

BANK ROBBERY

Because of the circumstances Slinger and I had still had no chance to go ashore together on a night out. Our stop-off in Gibraltar changed all that. Our short stay on the 'Rock' proved to be a typical Woods-Dabell affair.

Having invested heavily in 'rabbits' (souvenirs) for Christmas presents for our loved ones, in the Gibraltar shops in the afternoon, Slinger and I were not exactly skint but not exactly loaded when we went ashore late on the Friday evening. Our intention was to enhance our finances – with a visit to the casino.

To save as much money as we could we spurned taking a taxi. But it was a heck of a slog to our destination. The casino was all the way up the road that ran out about three-quarters of the way up the Rock and it took about an hour to get there, hauling ourselves, eventually breathless with effort, along the winding route from the dockyard.

It was getting on for midnight when we arrived at the casino steps. There we were greeted by a doorman dressed more like a colonel in full mess-dress than the flunkey he was supposed to be, all gold braid and epaulettes. I say greeted. It was more of an interception before we could go through into the casino foyer. He looked at Slinger and me as if we were escaped convicts. Admittedly we did look a tad dishevelled after our long hike up to the casino but we were both wearing sort of 'smart casual' – jacket and grey flannels in my case and a suit in Slinger's. "Excuse me, you can't go into the casino without a tie," he simpered, giving a passable impression of Uriah Heep, wringing his white-gloved hands in sheer pleasure that he had at last been able to act out his perceived role of keeper of the gate.

Both of us had actually gone ashore wearing ties but during the strenuous climb, perspiring heavily, we had taken them off. We triumphantly whipped them out of our pockets and added them to our ensembles. The doorman was racked with frustration as he grudgingly allowed us in to the foyer. "You need to be wearing a tie when you come in here in future," he bleated after us.

We didn't get very far inside the casino as first we found we had to register ourselves at the concierge's desk. Fortunately this gentleman was not so pompous or pedantic, accepting our Naval identity cards in lieu of passports. Filled with hope we made for the tables.

Within half an hour we were broke.

Slinger lost all his money almost immediately at Blackjack. Mine drained away on the roulette wheel. Crestfallen, we headed for the door. As we looked down on the twinkling lights in the dockyard, we were filled with dread. It was around two o'clock in the morning. This time we had no money for a taxi. "I can't face walking all the way back down that road Dabs," Slinger said, his shoulders sagging. I agreed. "Let's sit in the foyer for a while," I suggested. "That armchair over there looks awfully comfortable."

As Slinger made for the gents I sank into the plush upholstery. I fell asleep almost immediately. I was jolted awake by an arm furiously pumping at my shoulder. "You can't sleep here Jack," barked our fake colonel doorman, full of bravado now he knew he was on safe ground. "Let's have you out of here." I groaned: "Hang on a minute, I'm just waiting for my pal to use the toilet." "Your pal's over there," the doorman bayed, pointing an accusing finger over at the foyer's huge settee. Where Slinger was stretched out. "Your mate is refusing to budge, but you had both better get out of here before I call the management," warbled on the colonel. "Call the bloody management," growled a supine and irritated Slinger, who had long ago decided that "a while" represented a bed for the night. "We've spent good money in here." "That doesn't entitle you to spend the night on our sofa," responded the colonel. "I'm going for security."

Recognising we were in a no-win situation, much like a couple of years or so ago in Plymouth, Slinger and I prised ourselves out of the casino furniture and wearily made for the exit. I vowed I wouldn't be going ashore again until we got back to UK.

But the call of Gibraltar was too strong. Having borrowed a couple of quid apiece, ever the gluttons for punishment and with energy renewed, Slinger and I decided we would have a quiet 'run ashore' that Saturday evening. No frills, just a couple of pints, maybe the cinema, then back on board.

With only innocent thoughts in our minds we sauntered out of the dockyard gates. The Gibraltar NAAFI Club was our first port of call. We knew we could buy a couple of pints and get ham, egg and chips there fairly cheaply. As we walked in the NAAFI main door we read a notice that there was to be a live combo that night. The NAAFI nearly always laid on something at the weekends, a cabaret or dance or something. Even at NAAFI prices, though, we'd be lucky to make our money spin out long enough to spend all evening there.

On the way to the bar Slinger grabbed my arm. "Look over there Dabs, food." Wood was positively salivating. No wonder. In the corner of the NAAFI dance hall was a large table. Although it had a loose cover over it, obviously to deter flies, you could see it was laden with luscious fare: sandwiches, sausage rolls, pies, chicken legs, you name it.

The mouth-watering spread was unattended. "Wouldn't mind some of that," hissed my diminutive and ever-hungry comrade. "Wonder if we can sneak something before anyone comes in?" "Erm, perhaps we'd better not," I replied nervously. My anticipating, grumbling, stomach, though, gave us the go-ahead. "But there's only one way to find out."

Glancing anxiously around us and listening hard, we crept up to the banquet and lifted the cover. Juggling with the protective sheet, I had a vol-au-vent halfway home. Then a body came swishing through the curtains near the ballroom stage. "Who the blazes are you?" the body, a fairly mature body with an official look about it, barked. "Ahem, aah, er, ulp, aargh," I spluttered, showering him with regurgitated pastry. Slinger had already absorbed a pickled egg. His throat was clear. His mind was even clearer. "Oh, hello old chap; we're the band," said Slinger confidently, switching from broad Derbyshire to his posh voice. "He's the drummer and I'm the guitarist." My admiration for Slinger's sheer balls knew no ends. I warmed to the con. "Yes, we've come a bit early. The organist's on the way. Don't mind if we fill the tanks up first do you?" "Well OK, but tidy up after you. And don't scoff too much. We're expecting a big crowd tonight," said this harassed-looking body.

Slinger decided to go for broke. "You couldn't get us a couple of pints of bitter to wash it down with, could you?" said the brazen Wood. As we tucked in with gusto, up came a couple of pints. "You'll be wanting to practise then," said the body earnestly. "Yes, but there's plenty of time," said Slinger, a ham sandwich in one hand and pint in the other. The body was obviously the manager, a busy man. He disappeared to manage.

A few minutes later he reappeared. "Christ, are you two still eating?" I could tell he was getting suspicious. Slinger gave him a withering look. The manager was not abashed. "Where's your gear, anyway?" he challenged. "I don't like your tone," said Slinger, putting on a highly aggrieved air. "Well I've got my doubts about you two," responded the manager. "Right, that's it; we're off," said Slinger, his voice loaded with hurt. I nodded in agreement and we strode off. As we marched out of the club the manager, now regretting he had doubted our credentials, wailed: "You can't go; what am I going to do for a band?" A replete Wood and Dabell marched on, noses in the air. Unlike Lot's wife, we didn't look back. Our gait turned into a trot, then a dash.

The next day we sailed for home and the Falmouth's base at Devonport, Plymouth. There, we went through the process of turning over our duties to new crew who would augment the men who had joined the ship earlier in Singapore. Then it would be time at last for leave in the UK.

It was quite amusing when the Falmouth tied up in Devonport. All the crew who were domiciled in Plymouth, the 'RAs' (it stood for Ration Allowance and meant that you received expenses for living ashore with your family) were all lined up on the gangway in their best bibs and tuckers. They hardly gave the ship chance to touch the dockyard wall before they were pouring ashore. It was an unkind thought but to me they resembled rather large, well-dressed, rats deserting the ship.

My old mate Punchy was one of them and he leapt ashore with a spring in his step, heading for his married quarter, where his wife had lived while we were away. Punchy was a bit of a rogue and had fallen foul of the Navy a couple of times in the past, so he was pushing his luck by taking more than the legal amount of cigarettes ashore with him in his brown 'RA' case. He got through the dockyard gate without being challenged, though. He was so smitten with seeing his wife again after being away so long, he forgot all about his small haul of contraband and accidentally brought the cigarettes back on board the next morning. When he tried the same trick the next night, he got caught. Because he was a previous offender, poor old Punchy got banged up and his wife had to wait a few more weeks before she saw him again.

Christmas, some much-awaited leave with my family and farewell to the Falmouth were approaching fast. I was trying to save money but Slinger persuaded me we should have one good 'run ashore' before we parted company. He was staying with the Falmouth while I was moving on to pastures new after Christmas leave.

It wasn't much of a farewell at first. The Plymouth NAAFI Christmas dance was a write-off – we couldn't find anyone to dance with. As we wandered back on board our route took us past the National Provincial Bank. "Here Slinger, the lads haven't got a Christmas tree, how about this one?" I suggested, pointing towards the decorated fir outside the bank's front entrance. Slinger never did need any encouragement when a dare was on. He walked up to the tree and heaved it out of its pot. We headed for the dockyard with it, proud of our booty. As we walked down the main Plymouth parade, though, we spotted two policemen on their rounds, checking shop doors. I hurriedly secreted the tree inside my coat. Trouble was, my coat was about five feet in length and the tree was at least eight feet long. The Fuzz were not fooled. Our collars were felt and we were marched off to Plymouth police station. There was little sympathy or Christmas spirit on offer as we were hustled into a cell. There we stewed for a few hours. At least we had somewhere to sleep, even if the beds were very basic and the mattresses looked as though they might earn you a nasty disease.

After a fitful night, during which Slinger cheerfully pointed out that our cell door hadn't been locked, we were charged – with larceny. Our fingerprints were taken. "Bloody hell that's a bit steep isn't it?" I conjectured to the desk sergeant charging us. "We aren't exactly the Jesse James Gang." We were told we were bailed until two days later, when we would appear before magistrates at Plymouth Court.

We both made it back on board without overrunning our leave but our big problem was how to prevent the Navy finding out about our misdemeanour. If it were found out that two of its men had been charged by civilian police then there would be double the punishment. Slinger and I were both in quite a state, worrying especially about how we were going to make our court appearance in late-morning the next day. We hatched a cunning plan. That night we went ashore in uniform, carrying out our civilian clothes in our holdalls. We secreted the bags in a dockside toilet block. We then just had to hope that nobody discovered them.

Next morning we ambled innocently over the gangway in our 'number eights', our working clothes, having made some excuse or other to the quartermaster for needing to be dockside. To some relief our civvies were where we left them. We quickly changed clothes, made our way out of the dockyard and caught a bus to Plymouth Magistrates Court.

On arrival, Slinger and I were given the running order for the miscreants waiting to go in front of the bench. While we waited a heavily made up female with a lived-in face asked us what we were up for. "We robbed a bank," offered Slinger proudly. "My God, how much did you get away with? You'll cop for a long stretch for that," warned the woman, somehow lifting eyebrows that looked as though they had been plastered on with black cement. Slinger actually knew her and told me she was 'Big Sylvie', a legend, apparently. She was one of the platoon of women who plied their trade in the notorious Union Street area of Plymouth. "I know what I can expect," Big Sylv said. "This is the tenth time I've been caught. They'll give me a month inside. It'll be a nice break." With that we heard the call for "Wood and Dabble" to go into court. I hated my name being pronounced that way. "Excuse me but my name is pr..." My mild protest was cut short by Slinger. "Don't antagonise Plod; you'll only make things worse." I thought that was a bit rich from a prisoner who had gleefully warned the desk sergeant that our cell wasn't locked.

As we shuffled into the dock we looked across nervously at the grim-faced bench. Their chairman was an incredibly stern-looking woman who would have made an ugly man. After we had taken our places in the dock there were giggles from the gallery, in which sat a row of law students. I suppose it was a bit funny: Five foot Slinger and six foot one and a half Dabell, trying to look as if butter wouldn't melt in their mouths. "Stand up when you are in court," snarled the gorgon magistrate. "I am standing up," retorted Slinger. This brought even more titters in the gallery. "Wood and Dabble are before you for stealing a Christmas tree from the doorway of the National Provincial Bank ma'm," said the prosecuting officer. As he read out the charge, he held aloft our swag triumphantly. Earth from the roots and several decorations fell down on to the two court reporters. When one of the reporters jumped up scrabbling at his collar, the law students could no longer suppress their mirth and fell about in fits. The immortal phrase "Silence in court!" rang out. The magistrates chairman was not amused. "If there is any more commotion then you will all be ejected," she barked, resembling an angry mastiff.

"One of you, Dabell, explain why you are in court today," said the chairman when she had regained her composure. "We both want to plead guilty. We took the tree because we didn't have one in the mess for Christmas," I said, with a genuine tremor in my voice. "We're really sorry but it was because we'd drunk a bit too much Christmas spirit and it seemed a good idea at the time." I added, with a bit of a whine: "We've neither been in trouble with the police before." The sour-faced chairman snapped: "Stealing is never a 'good idea'. We take theft very seriously. Christmas does not give you an excuse for doing what you did." She bent over to confer with her colleagues.

After an agonising age while the magistrates buzzed and whispered, the chairman announced in a mournful voice: "You do not deserve leniency." Cue wobbling legs for Wood and Dabell. "But, in the light of this being your first offence we have decided that this can be dealt with by way of an absolute discharge. You will, though, both pay 7/6d costs." Slinger and I nearly collapsed with relief. We were nearly broke though and the costs would clean us out completely. "Can we have a fortnight to pay?" we asked. The students broke out in further gales of laughter. They were told to leave the court. We were told we had to pay the costs immediately.

While we were paying in our costs and filling in the appropriate forms to confirm the court's finding, Big Sylvie was escorted into the room. She was a bit downcast and looked very aggrieved. Before she was marched off, she told us she had first been awarded one month in prison. "A month?" she had sneered. "I told them I could do that standing on me 'ead. You know what that hag of a chairman said? 'Right,' she said. 'Well you can now do two months – and you can do that standing on your feet'."

Having managed to work the clothes switch in reverse without a hitch and sneak back on board without being missed, Slinger and I thought we were now in the clear. That was until the Plymouth evening paper came out, telling our sorry story – and naming names.

Whether it was because everybody was too busy preparing for leave to read the papers or not, we didn't get our collars felt a second time. But there was no escape for me. My Auntie Blanche, who lived in Plymouth, sent the newspaper cutting to Mum. I thought I'd really be for it when I got home on leave but Mum and Ray thought it was hilarious. I made them promise not to let my Uncle John see it. He was a policeman, much feared by me. He may not have seen the funny side.

Mum and Ray wanted me to have the 21st birthday party I had missed by being at sea and they put on a big do for me at Kingston Village Hall, just a couple of miles away from Kegworth and urged me to invite two of my pals to stay at our home and take part in the festivities. I plumped for Jim and Scouse. I would probably have invited Slinger and Flook but I was scared what they might get up to.

It was going to be mighty strange not returning to the Falmouth. It had been my home for over two years and provided me with vivid memories for the rest of my life. It was probably the most formative period of my life. And for the most part the memories are fond. But then you only really remember the good times, don't you?

Chapter 23

DOGGED BY SHYNESS

After a wonderful Christmas in the bosom of my family at last, I received notice of my next draft. On January 13 I was to join Whitehall Wireless. I was overjoyed. I would be living in the 'Smoke', London, and working at the communications centre near the Admiralty.

Before going to Whitehall I was ordered to report to a huge Naval living quarters called 'Furse House' in Queensgate Terrace, Kensington, not far from the Albert Hall, a block of apartments grandly called HMS President. This was where I was to be accommodated. It not only housed a large contingent of Navy lads – it was also the home of the Wrens who helped run the quarters and the girls who worked at Whitehall. Joy of Joys. My cup ranneth over.

After being assigned a plum billet, a single room, which was directly above the Wrens' quarters windows and, subsequently ominously, right next to the dividing door to the girls' rooms, I moved in. This was sheer heaven – a room on my own, dining room, lounge, television room and a basement snooker table. All this and London right outside the door.

The next morning, following a splendid breakfast, I set off on the underground for Whitehall Wireless. Just doing that without having somebody breathing down my neck gave me great delight.

Remarkably I made it to Whitehall without trouble, plotting my way from Gloucester Road to Westminster tube station with ease. I reported to the communications centre and was designated a 'watch'. Duties were carried out by four watches over 48 hours.

I didn't even get started. A pain I had been experiencing in my rear end quickly became agonising. The next day I couldn't even drag myself down to the Furse House sick bay, instead lurching to the door of my room and waiting for someone to go past in the corridor to get them to ask for a doctor to come up. I had suffered discomfort for several years but, with the problem being in such an undignified area, had kept quiet about it. After the sort of inspection I had dreaded, it was decided I should have to go to hospital as soon as I was comfortable. A few days of complete bed rest was ordered. I was in abject misery. Out there was London. In Furse House were Wrens and snooker. I was stuck in my room without even a book to read.

Rescue was soon on hand, however. News of my incarceration must have got about. I just hoped and prayed that my Wren friends did not realise what the cause of my disability was. The girls sent me up a couple of Micky Spillane books, a basket of fruit, a card wishing me a speedy recovery – and ecstasy, a transistor radio. Radio Caroline was back in full swing after its little debacle running aground.

A couple of days later, when I was able to limp and go to the toilet without leaving fingernail imprints on the door, I was driven over to the Royal Navy hospital in Brompton. Further indignity followed before a kink in my sphincter was diagnosed. It was decided that medication should keep it in check, however, causing waves of relief to overcome me.

Soon I was watch-keeping at Whitehall. I loved the work in the busy communications centre where messages came in from the fleet to be either acted upon or sent on their way around the world. Even the 'all-night-on' was bearable, knowing then you would have two whole days off to explore London. The capital was throbbing. It was the 'Swinging

Sixties'. I was keen to swing. The newspapers were full of mini-skirts, decadent rock stars, Carnaby Street was in. I wanted to sample all of it.

I quickly made friends with the gang of Navy lads in Kensington who took me under their wings. They told me how I could get free tickets for the theatre and shows that the Navy received daily. I was given a thorough education on where to enjoy London cheaply too.

Three of my new friends were considered the 'in-crowd' of the Kensington Navy lads. They were an extremely jovial Petty Officer Telegraphist called Jan Pauley and two senior RO2s, a witty fellow with a whole lexicon of jokes called Davie Dodd and a sardonic lad who was a Goon Show and Tony Hancock fan like me, called Jim Nolan. They rented a three-bedroomed flat in Kensington, 15 Ashburn Place. I was soon a regular visitor and frequent overnight 'guest' of the trio, who seemed to throw a party nearly every night.

The parties went on until the early hours. First there would be a few drinks, then the occasional canoodling for the fortunate lads who had a Wren for company. The Wrens all had to be in for midnight although occasionally the more daring ones managed to sneak out of their quarters. We would listen to great music while the girls were there – The Beatles especially. However, sometimes, after the Cinderellas had left it was time for 'Churchill and choo-choos'. Jan Pauley had several records of steam trains and Churchill's famous speeches. We'd sit around enraptured by the great man's pearls of wisdom and sounds like the Royal Scot belting its way up north.

Jim Nolan was a real lothario. He always had at least two girlfriends on the go, juggling so adeptly that none of his squeezes knew about their opposition. He seemed to have means that came from more than his Navy pay, too, so he could afford to run his little harem.

When I first started working at Whitehall I was still, despite occasional experiences like my little escapades in the

Far East, rather shy with girls. On my watch there was a gorgeous little Wren with marmalade hair and freckles called Sheila who I fancied like mad. The watch grapevine let me know she fancied me. She was less than five feet tall, however, and even shyer than me. The nearest we got to any kind of relationship at first was sharing a cup of tea on the night watch or chatting and passing goodies up and down from our windows at Furse House. Sheila and her room-mate were in the flat directly below mine. We did eventually pluck up courage to go out. But we suffered so much ribbing when my mates spotted us together – me the beanpole trying to hold hands with wee Sheila – that we quickly lost heart.

It wasn't long before I realised that time off in London was going to be expensive. So I did what many a serviceman stationed in the 'Smoke' did – I got a second job.

Just around the corner from Furse House in Petersham Lane was the Harrington Arms, a bustling pub that was always full to the brim with a real cross-section of people living in Kensington, many of them lads like me commuting to work in Whitehall. The barman was a Scot called Tommy who had recently retired from the Navy but had decided to stay down south. Tommy got me a part-time job when I was off-duty, as barman at the Harrington Arms.

I'd never been a barman before but I'd watched a few. I soon got the hang of things and I found the job enabled me to make loads more friends. I worked alongside a rather voluptuous girl called Gloria – well woman really, because she was at least 10 years older than me. Gloria, who was the live-in barmaid, kept all the boys in the bar very happy with her low-cut blouses and flirting. She made quite an impression on me. I couldn't draw my eyes away from her bosom. Whenever she spotted me ogling she would flutter her eyelashes and give me a very seductive smile. I did a lot of blushing and farting whenever I got caught giving her the once-over. My shyness wasn't really getting any better.

One night Gloria and I worked late, cleaning the glasses and tables, me doing my best to cover up my bashfulness with meaningless chit-chat while I occasionally sneaked a look at her main attributes. As we were finishing the cleaning up Gloria said: "I've got to take my dog for a walk now, he'll be dying to go. Do you want to come with me?" I froze with indecision. There seemed to be touch of innuendo about Gloria's voice. But was I reading signals wrongly? I was terrified of making a fool of myself. So I demurred and sought the sanctity of Furse House.

The next night I was on duty at the Harrington Arms again and I mentioned to Tommy what had happened with Gloria. "Bloody hell man, you must be daft in the head," said Tommy incredulously. "You were in there. I've been waiting for that kind of offer for months. How slow could you be?"

From Tommy's remarks I deduced that being "in there" meant that if I'd gone for a walk with her the dog wouldn't be the only one getting his leg over. I cursed my stupid affliction. I was filled with regret. I'd looked a gift bosom in the mouth.

I made a life-changing decision. I had got to be a bit more like Jim Nolan.

Another night, after finishing sweeping out the bar I was beside myself with excitement when Gloria said: "Would you be a love and fetch Fido (not his real name – I've changed it to protect the innocent) while I finish off the glasses?" I was full of anticipation as she handed me the key to her flat. I rushed down to her flat and ushered the bewildered Fido up the stairs. "Thank you darling," said Gloria, walking off with her dog. "See you next time you're on." I was totally deflated – and I mean all of me was deflated. You only got one chance with Gloria.

Onwards and upwards though. My barman job at the Harrington Arms brought me out of myself more and with the help of the girls in Furse House I did begin to lose my inhibitions. I revelled in the freedom that working in London gave me. And I spent more nights at Ashburn Place than I did in Furse House, sometimes crashing out on the lounge floor and on several occasions, sleeping in the bath.

This lifestyle was costly, so I took on more part-time jobs. The owner of the Harrington Arms offered me barman duties at his other pub, the Redcliffe Arms, a real opulent hostelry on Fulham Road near Chelsea Football Club. As a football nut I was 'over the moon' because most of the Chelsea team would come into the bar while I was working.

I found out, too, that you could get casual employment by going to the Union Jack services' club at Waterloo. We would wait in a queue in the foyer of the club until jobs were called out or a notice was put up explaining what work was on offer. You needed to get there early to land the plum jobs.

My first position was as a general kitchen and scullery hand at the Savoy Hotel but I didn't last long there after inadvisably reporting spotting mice when cleaning out a store cupboard. "We do not have mice, this is the Savoy," the kitchen manager said loftily, looking at me as if I were the rodent. When I was paid that night I was informed my services were no longer required.

My next casual job was waiting at tables at the Express Dairies restaurant, somewhere near Petticoat Lane. I didn't last long there either. On about my third shift I was captivated by a lovely blonde customer while carrying a tray of sandwiches and banana milkshakes to her table. I confess here and now, my mind was not totally on the job. As I bent down to place the order on the table the milkshakes took off and splattered all over the blonde's sheepskin jacket. The woman with her at the table (her mother, I soon found out) went, well, bananas. "You clumsy idiot," she shrieked, as the pair of them danced around the table, trying to avoid more milkshake slopping onto their shoes. The rest of the customers downed knives and forks and cups of tea and stared over at the hapless, miserable beast who had committed the felony. "That coat cost me a fortune," continued the ogress. I then made matters worse by trying to mop off the milkshake from the blonde's jacket. She leapt away from me in disgust. "Take your hands off my daughter," screamed the virago. "Fetch the manager."

There was no need to fetch him. He appeared like a wraith on my shoulder and grabbed my cloth off me. "Get out of the way and leave this to me," he snapped. "Now madam, I can see the problem. Let me have the jacket and we'll have it dry-cleaned for you. If it isn't satisfactory we'll have to buy a new one. Of course your meals are free of charge." With that he ordered me into his office. "Don't think you're going to get a penny of your pay until I get the dry-cleaning bill and dock it from your money," he growled. "If we have to buy a new jacket you'll be working for Express Dairies for nothing until it's paid off." At the end of my shift I slunk off payless, never to return – just in case the coat didn't clean up satisfactorily.

The milkshake spill, though, didn't cause a stain on my employment record because all the jobs were casual labour. I was soon happily making up Welsh Rarebits at a coffee bar in Maiden Lane. I even spent some of my precious summer leave working there because I became a little star-struck. That was when Joe Brown became a regular customer. I'd seen him on television a few years before when he appeared with his 'Bruvvers' on 'Six-Five-Special'. Joe was appearing in *Charlie Girl* at the nearby Adelphi Theatre. Most of the cast came into the coffee bar, including a huge, blond man-mountain with whom I became quite friendly and who later appeared as one of the heavies in the James Bond films. I never saw Anna Neagle in the restaurant, though. I suppose she opted for caviar in her dressing-room rather than Welsh Rarebit.

I had to work hard in my spare time to pay for my party lifestyle. I hauled crates of Schweppes drinks from a delivery lorry around Southwark for a time. Then I had quite a long stint doing odd jobs at the ladies' department store Dickins and Jones. Here I couldn't help talking to girls, girls, girls and I realised how easy it was to do the chatting up. My shyness with the opposite sex was over. My new bravado, though, nearly got me into a whole heap of trouble.

My room, as I pointed out earlier, was right next to the dividing door between the men's and women's dormitories.

One of the girls with whom I'd become very friendly got hold of the dividing door key so I could visit her room after lights out.

I had just eased through the dividing door when I heard someone coming along the passage. I bolted back through the door with a shout of "Hey!" from down the corridor ringing in my ears. I dived into my room and got under the covers virtually fully clothed. I expected the proverbial to hit the fan. However, all went quiet; nobody came into the men's quarters and nobody from our side came up to investigate from downstairs. I fancied I heard the door being locked from the other side. I felt deflated – I mean all of me was deflated. I waited for about half an hour and then quietly undressed and went off to sleep. It had been a frustrating exercise but at least I hadn't been rumbled.

The next morning at breakfast I was bending down to the grill to load up on spaghetti and sausage when a hand gripped my shoulder. A female voice quietly ordered me out of the dining-room. When we got outside she said: "You should have changed your socks, I recognise the ones you were wearing from earlier this morning when you scuttled through the dividing door." It turned out to be just a shot in the dark by this petite, rather attractive, PO Wren, but I decided to come clean. "OK, guilty," I admitted, adding: "but you don't need to take this any further do you?"

She let me off with a warning and I promised myself that there would be no more midnight jaunts in the Wrens' quarters. If I'd been hauled before my divisional officer at Whitehall it would have meant at least a fortnight's stoppage of leave and pay. I couldn't afford either.

It was now well into July and the World Cup was upon us, hosted by England. London was abuzz. My hero Gordon Banks, goalkeeper for my beloved Leicester City, was in the England team. I watched the drama of England versus West Germany unfold on a little black and white television which had been set up in the Furse House snooker room.

After that never-to-be-forgotten finale – "Some people are on the pitch; they think it's all over"; thump (Geoff Hurst smashing in England's fourth). "It is now." – I hurtled straight out of the door. The England team were staying at the Royal Garden Hotel, only a few blocks away from Furse House.

When I got to the street where the hotel was, it was chaos. Thousands of people thronged around the building, most of them well in their cups. The England team came out on the balcony. I've never heard such a noise. The cheers were deafening. I just stood there bellowing: "Gordon, Gordon, look down." Of course Gordon couldn't hear me. I stayed there for an hour. It was a wonderful, memorable experience. I was so proud of Gordon.

I finally got to shake Gordon's hand 34 years later when we played golf together in a pro-am. I got to hear his take on all the much-vaunted incidents from the final. He'd talked about them a thousand times before but Gordon went through the match as if it were yesterday. For me it was reward for all those times spent hero-worshipping behind his goal at Filbert Street – and for shouting myself hoarse under the Royal Garden Hotel balcony.

August came and went – and, so to speak, so did my little PO Wren, the one who had spotted me exiting in haste through the dividing door a month before. We had become quite friendly. On the night before she was drafted to Malta she paid me a visit in my room – through the dividing door.

As one door closes another opens. Within a couple of weeks I was on my way, too. It was goodbye to all the lovely ladies who had turned me from shrinking violet to budding rose. It was good riddance to the awful cucumber rolls and weak tea on the night watch at Whitehall. It was farewell to the good life in London. It wasn't going to be too bad, though. I had landed another plum draft. I was on my way to HMS Rooke and Gibraltar communications centre. Little did I know that it was going to be a life-changing two years.

Chapter 24

ROCK REVELS

Within hours of arriving at HMS Rooke I was playing football. After a five-hour flight I was whisked through the formalities of joining the establishment, a small barracks for sailors and Wrens down near Gibraltar dockyard. I was assigned a small room in an accommodation block which had a mere curtain at the doorway for privacy. This, I learned, was my 'casa'.

As I dumped my gear on the bed and decided where on earth I was going to put all my clothing, a familiar face peered through the curtain. "Norm old lad; fantastic to see you. Get your boots out, you're in goal for the comms team in half an hour." It was my old pal Denis Lloyd, the lad from Birmingham I'd joined up with at HMS Ganges; my old painting and decorating chum from HMS Mercury. It was wonderful to see him again.

Denis had been at HMS Rooke for over a year and was an experienced hand at life on the Rock. "We'll have a couple of drinks tonight and I'll fill you in on what to expect here," he chattered away as I searched for a second football boot to go with the one I'd already located. "But I told them you played in goal and you'd jump at the chance of a game. I would normally be in goal but I've got a groin strain."

As I followed Denis from our accommodation block we were joined by several Wrens who were on their way to the football match to support the comms lads. Denis introduced me to them all and linked arms with a couple of them as we walked out of the Rooke main gate. I fancied I knew how he'd got his groin strain.

The football was hard going – literally. The match was played on rock (there's a surprise) with only a thin covering of red shale. By the time the whistle went for the end of the match my knees were red-raw. I would be steering clear of plastic skin, however.

After the match I showered and found Denis waiting for me down in the little Rooke canteen. "Come on Norm, we're off to the London Bar," said Denis. "I'm going to introduce you to Albert."

We handed in our 'station cards', the little official document left at the guard-house to notify you were 'ashore', and headed across the road and up English Steps that led to downtown Gibraltar.

I discovered that the London Bar, owned by a wonderfully jolly Gibraltarian called Albert, was always the starting point for runs ashore by the inhabitants of Rooke and especially the communications personnel working in the bowels of the Rock. As we walked in the door a jukebox was blaring out. A gaggle of lads and lassies were singing along to '(It's been) A Hard Day's Night', swaying away on their bar stools. I found out this was a regular anthem for the comms personnel who were enjoying their first day off duty, to be sung between regular slugs of Bacardi and Coke.

The London Bar was quite an experience. The ceiling, a bit like a naughty Sistine Chapel, had huge copies of lewd seaside postcards adorning it. I'll always remember one of the pictures. It was the one where an elephant has stuck its trunk inside a tent to a bed where a couple were sleeping. The woman, in curlers, is sitting bolt upright shouting "Ye Gods Jack!"

Around the walls were pictures of hundreds of past visitors to the London Bar, mainly Naval of course, many of them from the Second World War. Among the various celebrities featured on the walls was, curiously, the Ivy Benson Band.

Apparently Ivy and her gals had been entertained royally by landlord Albert (he was in the pictures surrounded by the band, hugging Ivy) when they played in Gibraltar. The numerous shelves were filled with every kind of alcohol you could think of, including rare single malt Scotch whiskies. Hundreds of Haig 'Dimple' bottles lined the shelves.

I soon became a regular customer of the London Bar and I could write a separate book on all the goings-on that took place there. One day one of the larger, braver, macaques, one of Gibraltar's famous Barbary Apes, which used to wander down into the town from their quarters at the top of the Rock, stuck his head in the door of the bar and grabbed a steak sandwich out of a Wren's hands. The ape wasn't scared off too far and returned for more largesse. When he appeared this time at the doorway he was greeted by a punch on the nose from the Wren's boyfriend. This aggrieved primate didn't take kindly to this and ran amok in the bar, scattering tables and chairs and causing a right old mess until he was cornered and thrown out. Albert thought about hiring a bouncer, not for rowdy ratings but marauding monkeys.

It was not all beer and skittles, however. Work in the communications centre (comcen) was hectic, doing split shifts over three days – including the dreaded all-night-on. We would walk the half mile or so down a tunnel to the busy hub under millions of tons of rock, to do our work receiving and routeing messages from all around the world. Working all night was pretty arduous but we occasionally had chance for an hour or so break. Often we would persuade the security men to open up the old war room below the comcen where Churchill and the allies planned much of the North Africa campaign in the Second World War. The plotting table and radio booths were all still in place.

The two days off in Gib, though, were extremely enjoyable. You'd finish work at 8am, sleep for four or five hours, and then have the delights of the Rock beaches to enjoy. Catalan Bay, on the Mediterranean side of Gibraltar, was a particular favourite. You did have to make sure you were in the right place, though. A 'levanter' cloud used to appear in late afternoon over the top of the Rock that blotted out the sun.

I'd been in Gibraltar for about a month when an overnight trip was planned to Tangiers for a bunch of lads and lassies not on duty. We made the trip over the Straits of Gibraltar to Morocco in a Naval MFV (originally a motor fishing vessel but gutted to serve as a sort of large floating taxi), piloted by the officer in charge of the comcen, Lieutenant 'Tug' Wilson. Tug was nearing the end of his Naval service and didn't bother too much what we got up to.

On arrival in late afternoon we visited the Tangiers Souk, where stuffed leather camels and fez headgear were haggled for. We then headed back to the boat to lay out a beach picnic, having augmented the food with cheap, only just drinkable, Moroccan red wine.

All the while I had eyes only for a very pretty redhead called Dianne Whitelock. Di, a Wren radio operator, was on my watch in the comcen. She was, though, considered rather off-limits. She spoke, the boys reckoned, "a bit posh". I'd chatted to her a couple of times but, much as I'd wanted to, didn't have the courage to ask her for a date. And even though we'd now been thrown together in a slightly more intimate atmosphere we didn't get any further than perfunctory chit-chat on the trip over on the MFV or in the souk. I could sense there was a little chemistry between us. But was it wishful thinking?

As the evening on the beach and the cheap Moroccan wine wore on, things became a little carefree. The cry "time for skinny dipping" went up. The only light was moonlight, so I was far more devil-may-care than I would have been normally and shed my inhibitions with my swimming costume.

As I ran down to the sea a voice shouted out behind "Wait for me." It was Di, chasing after me in her knicks and bra. It must have taken a huge amount of pluck, and not a small amount of African plonk, for her to go that far. She joined me in the waves.

We did a bit of silly splashing about and then I put my arms around her. When she didn't squeal and slap my face I took heart and gave her a kiss.

Well it's not my intention to write like Barbara Cartland. Cut a long story short, Di told me, "I think you're great." I revealed I'd fallen for her as soon as I'd seen her. A romance was born.

I fully expected it was only going to be a shipboard romance, knowing Di's reputation for coolness towards the male section of HMS Rooke. But when she clasped my hand on the walk from the jetty to the barracks the next morning I was filled with optimism. When she asked me to help her make the tea on our first watch together in the comcen and allowed me to steal a kiss just before the petty officer of the watch came barging in, I knew this was for real.

As we moved towards the end of November 1966 there was a real buzz in the comcen. Telecommunications traffic was non-stop. Coded messages were flying around all over the place. We learned that talks were going to be held in Gibraltar between British Prime Minister Harold Wilson and the PM of Rhodesia, Ian Smith, who had led his country into a Unilateral Declaration of Independence (UDI). They were to meet on December 1 on HMS Tiger in Gibraltar to try to reach a settlement over Rhodesia's future. Work in the comcen was at an exhausting level. It really was a Hard Day's Night.

About this time money and valuables started going missing from the casas in Rooke. We had our suspicions who the culprit was but he was very sly and accomplished at thieving. One day I decided to lay a trap. I marked a five pound note and left it in my case while I went down to the television room. When I returned, sure enough, it had gone. I knew the thief was still in the building so I nipped out and fetched a patrolman. I told him if he searched this person he would find my five pound note on him and the rest of the lads in the building gave me their backing. He was a crafty so-and-so, though. My five pound note, with a tiny goatee marked on the Queen's chin, proving his guilt, was found tucked inside the miscreant's underpants. He was escorted to cells and 'weighed off' two days later, copping a three-month stint in Naval prison.

Di and I were getting on like a house on fire. Which brings me neatly to about four months on in our relationship.

We'd spent all our off-duty time together and became a firm 'item'.

It's hard to imagine going out with a girl for four months nowadays without getting any further than passionate groping. But that's how it was in a more innocent time. The battlements above English Steps saw plenty of service and so did the sofas of our married friends when doing babysitting duties. But it was all so undignified. Babies would always wake up and cry the house down just as we were getting to an important stage.

So when my pals Fred Torrison and Derek 'Knocker' White, who both also had serious girlfriends, suggested we should splash out on renting a flat up town with them, I jumped (perhaps wrong word) at the idea.

We rented a top floor two-bedroomed flat in a lane near all our favourite haunts, close to a bakery and winery. It was no Ashburn Place, Kensington, but it was cheap when the rent was split three ways. I was on a different watch to the other two; we each had plenty of privacy. At last Di and I could have a mature relationship.

All was going well. Fred, Knocker and I rarely met up at the flat because as I was leaving for Rooke to retake up residence and start my watches they were beginning their two days off. It was a case of finding the key under a flowerpot to get in.

One day, though, our routine fell by the wayside. I had flopped into bed after finishing an all-night-on and slipped into oblivion. When I came to go out for some croissants from the bakery, I found the door was locked. There was no sign of a key in the flat. It was a substantial door, even if the flat was a bit run-down. It would not be forced.

After shouting myself hoarse to no avail, bruising my shoulder severely and bending several items of cutlery on the lock, I gave in. I ruminated on my means of escape and decided I would climb out of the bedroom window, then drop down onto the balcony below it. I clambered out of the window. It was far higher up than I'd imagined. All the times I'd spent mending aerials on the Falmouth, though, stood me in good stead. As I tried to lower myself down to the balcony, however, some of the stonework I'd balanced my feet on gave way. I swung over onto firmer ground, but I was then stuck halfway between the window and the balcony. I was safe but in no-man's-land. I couldn't go up and I couldn't go down.

A small crowd had by now gathered below me. I assured them I was all right but could somebody fetch a ladder? I don't know whether my request got lost in translation but, after about half-an-hour doing an impression of a badly co-ordinated Spider Man, my ladder turned up all right – on a Gibraltar fire engine.

I suppose the brigade lads were grateful for something to do. Just as they were hauling up the ladder, though, Di arrived and, to my mortification watched my rescue. Apparently someone had seen the key in our flat door outside and, getting no response from within, had locked up and taken it to the landlord.

Di and I decided to spend our days off further afield. We often took the ferry from Gibraltar then the bus from Algeciras up the coast to Estepona and Fuengirola, sharing the journey with the locals – and sometimes their hens, rabbits and geese. On arrival we'd book into a pension for a couple of days and sample the delights of Costa del Sol beaches and restaurants for a change.

On one bus journey I remember stopping off at Marbella. This former small fishing port was just beginning to be the 'in' spot on the Costa del Sol after celebrities like Sean Connery built homes there. There was a little café at the bus stop, so Di and I disembarked for refreshment. On the way back to the bus I noticed that the concourse around the shelter had just been completed. There is something about wet cement, a bit like fresh paint, you just have to test it. I couldn't resist furtively dabbing down my shoe into the cement.

They all came to the area eventually, film stars, rock stars, racing stars. None of them had their footprint on Marbella's 'Walk of Fame', though.

Estepona, just a little fishing harbour then, was the favourite destination for Di and me. We had an idyllic time in Spain, visiting as many famous towns as we could. We marvelled at Granada's Alhambra Palace, looked around the sword museum in Toledo, saw the rock galleries of Ronda and enjoyed every beach and tapas bar we could find.

Mijas is one of my fondest memories. The trip up to the hill village, with its famous monastery, was a real experience. I'm sure there was no bus service. I remember walking several miles on foot, with our luggage carried by a donkey. It was on our visit to Mijas that I took the bull by the horns and asked Di if she would marry me.

Di said yes – provisionally. As she was an only child, the decision was not only hers, she explained. Her mum and dad would have to give their approval. How very old-fashioned. I was pretty sure my mum and Ray would be delighted that there would be a female in our family. Di phoned her mum Doris and dad Ted. Neither of our parents really knew we'd being seeing each other that long. I'm not sure we had even told them we were serious.

We had to inform the Naval authorities of course. This didn't present a problem for me but I know Di came in for a grilling from her officer in charge. Was she really doing the right thing? Did she realise that would almost certainly be the end of a promising career? Although I'm sure she had been earmarked as officer material, Di decided she would leave the Navy.

Not long before going back to U.K. for the big day I was playing in goal in an HMS Rooke cup final for the seamen and comms football team against the electricians. Just before half-time, with the score 0-0, I dived into a melee of players to grab the ball. A burly (and perhaps myopic) electrician centre forward called 'Jock' West drove his boot into the scrimmage of players at where he thought the ball was. His boot connected with my jaw.

It's hardly surprising that the incident is hazy now. It was then. Apparently I clung on to the ball even though my glazed eyes showed that I was not actually with everybody. The second half was a bit of blur. Despite obvious concussion I apparently put in a sterling performance for someone who should have taken a count of ten but we lost 2-0. As I wobbled off the pitch, the sick bay attendant who had been called to check me out at half-time insisted I went to the Naval hospital.

X-rays showed my jaw had a hairline fracture and was dislocated either side below the ears. The doctor told me I should have been a boxer not a goalkeeper with the ability I obviously had for taking a blow on the chin.

Poor old Jock came up to the hospital to see if I was all right, clutching a bag of grapes. As I had my jaw wired up I suggested (wrote) that he might return when they'd fermented into Rioja. Then this 16-stone pocket battleship Scotsman burst into tears, upset with what he'd done to the Dabell jaw. He wasn't the only one alarmed. When Di was told I'd been taken to hospital after being kicked in the face she wailed: "Oh, no. Please tell me he's not lost any teeth. We're getting married in six weeks."

I recovered fairly quickly from my jaw injury but unfortunately my eyes didn't. I was told by a Navy optician that the blow had altered my vision just slightly and I needed glasses. The news came like a kick in the teeth. Navy specs were definitely not flattering. I decided to soldier on without them. There was no way I was going to get married wearing spectacles.

Chapter 25

LIFE HITS A HIGH THEN A TRAGIC LOW

Di and I flew home and met both sets of parents. Mum and Ray were ecstatic about Di. Doris seemed happy with me but I wasn't sure about Ted. He came across as a dour fellow who wasn't too sure about me. That was understandable as he and Doris had spent all the money they'd earned on providing Di with a first-class education. Here was this erk about to end her Naval career.

Our wedding took place in Boreham Wood, with my old Kensington pal Jim Nolan as my best man. Di knew Jim as well, so his choice met with her approval. I don't think she would have been quite as happy with Jim if she had known what he whispered to me a few minutes before our wedding ceremony. "Are you sure you want to go through with this?" said confirmed bachelor Jim. "I can get you whisked away on a plane in no time." I was already desperately nervous and, like any potential groom I suppose, had had plenty of sleepless nights worrying about whether marriage was a good thing for either of us. Knowing Di was giving up everything for me didn't help my frame of mind leading up to the wedding. "For God's sake Jim, just make sure you've got the ring," the pale-faced Dabell hissed in reply. After all, it was May 13. Fortunately it was a Saturday, not a Friday.

Well, everything went off like a dream. We had a huge reception at Di's parents' house and then set off for a honeymoon in London. Knowing I would have limited leave before having to return to Gibraltar, Di and I had enjoyed a 'pre-wedding honeymoon' a few weeks beforehand in London Bar owner Albert's holiday apartment in Albufeira on Portugal's Algarve.

I'd booked us into the Cromwell Hotel in Kensington, an area I knew like the back of my hand. Our stay, though, didn't involve any visits to the Harrington Arms. Just in case Gloria still worked there. I could just imagine her thinking: "At last, I think he's found out it's not for stirring his tea with."

Our short honeymoon in London got off to an embarrassing start. A gaggle of supporters of one of the rugby league teams that had played in the RL Challenge Cup Final that day at Wembley was staying at the hotel. Forgive me for not remembering which one of the two finalists. There was a lot kicking off at that time.

As we checked in several of the fans came down the hotel stairs to the bar and gave Di and me knowing looks. A lot of nudge-nudging and wink-winking went on. I tried to look unabashed – until we were asked for our passports. As I opened our case a cloud of confetti showered the foyer. A cheer went up and it was back-slaps all round. I guess their team must have won. I'm sure they had a good night. So did we.

Di and I settled into a flat in Gibraltar and began married life together. It was idyllic for Di – clean up the apartment and then go for a sunbathe and swim before having a meal ready for me when I'd finished my comcen shift. We were happy little lovebirds.

I was still sport crazy. As well as playing though, I had a chance to show off my sporting knowledge one night. Another sports nut, one Tommy Bethell, and I were invited to form a two-man guest side to appear in a panel on Gibraltar Television in what was a sort of medieval 'Question of Sport'.

When we arrived at the television studio we were ushered into the station's lounge. Here, laid out on a table, were various bottles of spirits and mixers. "There's a little while to go before the programme is scheduled to start so have a little snifter to calm your nerves," said the chap who had welcomed us.

Well, I was keen to go over a few great sporting moments of recent times with Tommy, a rather grizzled Mancunian who had spent a number of years serving on the Royal Yacht Britannia. Tommy liked a drink. He was renowned for quaffing a couple of bottles of his favourite tipple, 'Cedaboa' white wine, most nights. He wasn't too interested in doing any swotting up. Tommy made straight for the gin and tonic.

I think Tommy had already had a bottle of Cedaboa before even setting off for the studio. His demeanour became more and more relaxed as the level in the gin bottle slipped to well below the Plimsoll line. By the time they came to fetch us to go to the studio Tommy was full of beans, slapping me on the back and telling me, in a worryingly slurred voice, "We're going to piss this Norm, no worries."

As Tommy got up from his chair I heard a sort of quiet 'twang'. Tommy's trousers started to fall as he rose. His belt had broken. "Don't fuss, I'll be all right," Thos assured our worried looking escort as my partner grabbed his waistband, hitched up his trousers and made for the studio.

As we took our places for the show, gravity again took over. Tommy's striped boxer shorts hove into view to the consternation of the nervous looking quizmaster. It was fortunate that we had a minute before going on air. After a few seconds of frantic scrabbling around Tommy was settled in his chair. Too settled. He started off reasonably well when it was his turn to answer. The quizmaster accepted 'Mobby Boore' as the name of England's football captain and 'Jack Nicholson' as the famous American golfer.

When there was no response from Tommy throughout the 'fingers on buzzer' round, though, I feared the worst. I glanced across at him and saw his eyes drooping. The hot studio lighting was taking its toll. Frantic digs in the shoulder failed to ignite Tommy. Then when I heard a gentle snore to my left I realised I was on my own.

The show was a great hit with all our Navy friends, if not with the television people. Everyone said it was the funniest thing they'd seen on Gibraltar Television. I suppose it did make a change from blurry grey images of Ena Sharples in the very first episodes of 'Coronation Street', or the unfathomable plots of 'The Prisoner'. There wasn't much excitement on the Rock's only, very parochial, channel. Needless to say, Bethell and Dabell were not asked to reappear.

The Navy found Di and me official accommodation up in the town and we were delighted with our new digs, a quite big apartment in an old colonial block. The Cannon Lane on which the block looked down featured a long wall stretching nearly the length of the lane. In more rumbustious times I had been one of many who tried to run as far along it as possible, trying to defy gravity by staying on as long as you could before toppling, or crashing in most cases, off. It provided great competition for the lads (and sometimes lasses) on their way back to Rooke from the London Bar. It was called 'Cracking the Wall' and it helped if you had big feet. Nobby Hall, from Sheffield, fitted that criterion to the full. Nobby would launch himself onto the wall from a few paces and flap along an incredible distance in his size 12 shoes. It was almost as if he had suction pads on his feet. He held the record distance by several yards. Even when Di and I went out for a civilised evening I occasionally felt I had to crack the wall. But I couldn't match Nobby.

As I came to the end of my first year in Gibraltar there was great excitement everywhere. With Spain once again laying claim to the Rock, a referendum took place.

I remember polling day quite vividly. It came on a day off work for me. I'd finished a hectic all-night-on, made even busier than usual with all the message traffic pouring in and out of the comcen before the referendum. Despite still feeling knackered after waking up about midday, I strolled along to the newsagent where I would collect my day-old *Daily*

Telegraph and occasionally a football or cricket magazine. As I came to the piazza which looked down on the harbour above English Steps, a scene of chaos greeted me. There were hundreds of Gibraltarians with banners, looking very threatening. A small band of Bobbies, a mixture of British and Gibraltarian policemen, were trying to bring order. The crowd, which got uglier and uglier as I looked on, turned into a mob and the gathering a riot. Shop windows were smashed and doors kicked. Then an officer in charge of the police, fearing for the well-being of his men, threw a tear gas grenade at the mob. They dispersed quickly, many of them in my direction. I decided to beat a hasty retreat. The *Telegraph* crossword would have to wait until a quieter time.

That evening the result of the referendum was announced and the remarkable scenes from the riot were shown on television. I pointed out to Di this lanky Herbert legging it down English Steps ahead of a small tidal wave of angry Gibraltarians.

The result of the referendum was the expected overwhelming majority in favour of staying British. It appeared that word had got round that two of only 40 who voted against were shopkeepers and they were the ones who got their shop fronts kicked in. The police inspector who threw the tear gas came in for much flak. In fact I was told he had been whisked out of Gibraltar on the first available plane.

Spain's reaction to the referendum was to close the border. The only way we could get to the Spanish mainland was by ferry to Algeciras. We made several trips over and one I remember starkly. We were queuing for hours to embark the ferry coming back to Gibraltar and after boarding Di and I looked down on the poor unfortunates who were still waiting in a huge line to get on board. One family had bought sandwiches and soft drinks and were carrying them as they came to the gangway. A Gaurdia Civil policeman started shouting at the husband and gesticulating at their food. He was telling them they couldn't take it on board. The husband looked at the policeman in disgust and threw the meal on the ground. He was then set upon by the policeman in front of his screaming wife and children and beaten to the ground. We were powerless to do anything but watch in horror. I ran to a deckhand on the ferry and demanded to know what the crew might do about it. The answer was nothing. The incident had taken place on Spanish soil. The last I saw of the hapless family was the husband being dragged away by the Gaurdia Civil. I've often wondered what happened. It didn't make the news on Gibraltar Television.

The whole Rock was buzzing soon after. The James Bond picture *You Only Live Twice* had some of its scenes shot in Gibraltar. One of our girls took star billing in the closing sequence of the film. Petty Officer Wren Jan Thomas was chosen to be the stand-in for Sean Connery's lady friend when the pair are hoisted up from the sea by a surfacing submarine. Jan looked every bit the star when we were all invited to the first showing of the film worldwide – in the little Navy cinema near the dockyard.

As the year wore on I spent nearly all my time off studying. I was down to take my examinations for promotion to leading radio operator. About half way through my studies, however, the second-worst day of my life came along.

Our officer in charge, Lieutenant Ken Scofield, who had taken over from Tug Wilson, sent word for me to come to his office. The lads with whom I had been working looked across in sympathy as I broke off from my tape-relay work. They had seen the message that would shatter my life.

Scofield gently told me to take a seat and sent a Wren to make me a cup of tea. I don't know how I knew but I whispered, "It's Ray isn't it?" Scofield nodded. I dissolved into floods of tears. It was the first time I'd cried since my father died all those years ago. I knew how much this would crush my mother, who loved my stepfather with all her heart. Ray had been so good for her. He had been a great father to my brother and me. Compassionate leave was quickly organised. Within two days Di and I were in Kegworth comforting Mum.

Ray had died of a heart attack while at his work at Rolls Royce in Derby. It was a harrowing time. Mum took it all very badly. I was grateful she had the shoulder of my uncle John, her younger brother, to lean on because just a day after the funeral Di and I were on our way back to Gibraltar.

It was difficult to concentrate on my studies when I returned and I was full of apprehension when taking my exams. However, I did reasonably well and, after retaking one of the ten sections of the exam, I was rated up to leading radio operator.

Eventually Di and I were finally allotted a married quarter in the block near HMS Rooke called Edinburgh House. I was relieved to move because there was a synagogue next to our old flat. It was quite remarkable. As soon as I laid my head on the pillow after an all-night-on walls would reverberate with all kinds of noises as the rabbi would launch into his routine. On top of that, once one of my socks dropped off our washing line down into the synagogue courtyard and it was confiscated.

Christmas came and went. I wished I could be home with Mum. She had an awful time without her own Rock.

Life in Gibraltar began to become claustrophobic as 1968 wore on. The border was closed and so was the ferry from Gibraltar to Algeciras. If you wanted to get to the Costa del Sol you had to take a ferry to Tangiers and then a ferry from Tangiers to Algeciras. We gave it up as a bad job. The Spanish made our lives as difficult as they could. They built a smelly gas refinery near La Linea so that the fumes would blow over Gibraltar. They parked a corvette, nicknamed 'El Pou' (the Flea), close to the end of the runway of Gibraltar Airport to try to obstruct planes taking off and landing on the Rock.

I was quite glad when my two-year stint at the communications centre drew to a close in September 1968, not long after my brother decided to follow me into the Navy. I was looking forward to meeting up with him some time. It would be rather novel to see him in his sailor suit.

As life would have it, though, we never did meet up. He was always away somewhere when I got home and when he took leave I was away. In fact the only time I saw my brother while he was still in the 'Andrew' was when I'd left the Navy. I went down to a 'Navy Days' in Portsmouth and arrived at his ship just in time to see him jump out of a helicopter in a search and rescue demonstration. We didn't get chance to meet up then either.

Di's parents' house in Boreham Wood became our home for the next couple of years. After a long period of leave I joined HMS Mercury, the Navy signal school, for my next draft. At Mercury I became part of the 'operations exercise pool', which meant that I could be sent anywhere at very short notice.

Before I got sent away, however, vanity finally got the better of me. I had a crown fitted over my chipped tooth. I was very happy with the result and couldn't stop smiling – now showing all my gnashers.

Vanity also played a part elsewhere on my face. As the months had worn on I had reluctantly realised I was going to have to wear my spectacles to turn blurred outlines into sharp reliefs. I hated the spectacles though. I thought they made me look like an owl.

After frequently being called 'Gig-lamps' or 'Four-eyes' and finding it impossible to play in goal wearing specs, I opted for contact lenses.

At first they were a great irritation but though they often caused a great deal of aggravation and demanded a high standard of patience, not my greatest trait, I soon mastered them. They nearly did for my mother-in-law, however.

Chapter 26

PUTTING THE BOOT IN

On one of my leave days, before setting off from my in-laws' home to catch the train to London to meet up with old pals, I inserted my contact lenses, putting the plug in the sink while I washed them, to avoid losing them down the drain. I can't remember what distracted me – the family dog Trudy barking for her Milky Way which I'd forgotten to give her after her morning walk, I seem to recall. I shot downstairs double-quick because it was going to be a mad dash to catch my train from Boreham Wood station.

I had a thoroughly pleasant lunch with some old Navy friends and then did some shopping. When I arrived home in early evening and opened the gate to the house, there up the path was the family standing on the doorstep, Trudy wagging her tail in expectancy of another Milky Way, was the only one happy to see me. Di, Doris and Ted were illuminated by a flickering lantern-light in the hallway. Otherwise the house was in darkness. "What on earth's going on?" I enquired. "You big clot, do you realise what you did?" barked Di, her mum and dad looking on with resigned expressions on their faces. "Mum came home, switched the hall light on and there was an almighty bang and blue flashes. It's a miracle she wasn't electrocuted. There was water pouring from the bathroom and into the lights. You and your darned contact lenses."

Doris had indeed had a brush with death. In my haste to get downstairs and out the door in the morning I had left a tap running – into a sink with a plug in place. Eventually the bowl overflowed of course. The bathroom became flooded and the water seeped through the floor, subsequently tracking down into the hall lights.

It was a fearful mess. We were without electricity for 24 hours and the house took a week to dry out. Fortunately Ted and Doris were well insured. Ted was just starting to warm to me, too.

I was at it again, though, in the spring to set myself back to chapter one in his good books. It was me that could have been electrocuted this time. I volunteered to cut the hedges around the front garden. Ted kept a beady eye on my clipping efforts from his bedroom. He watched in consternation as I neatly sliced through the cable of his electric hedge cutter. He was relieved (for Di's sake more than anything, I suspected) to see me standing looking forlorn at his cutter instead of lying on the ground. Rubber soles had saved me. His relief lasted until he realised I'd cut the cable only a foot or so from the cutter. At least I knew what to buy him for his birthday.

It didn't take a contact-lens for Ted and Doris to realise the evil-eye was on them – by dint of their son-in-law.

Calamity would not go away. My rear end problem resurfaced. After the usual embarrassing inspections it was decided I should go to the Royal Naval Hospital Haslar for an operation to stretch out the kink in my sphincter. If it had been undignified being diagnosed then the procedure after it was far worse.

I was placed in what Haslar in its delicate way called the 'dirty surgery' ward. My bed was next to a poor marine with a broken back and debris in his rear end. He had suffered terrible injury during an exercise. I felt a real fraud alongside this lad, especially as he had the sunniest of personalities.

On the morning of my operation, starving because I had not been allowed food for 12 hours, I was taken to a room next to the theatre and seated next to a doleful laddie who wanted to know what I was in for. I explained. Then he told me what he was in for (piles). Then he started to tell me what I was in for. "You'll need to be fast on your feet," he warned mystifyingly.

Before he had time to expand on his observation we were called forward and escorted by an SBA to a room next to the theatre. Here we were given some evil-smelling mixture which we were told was a strong enema to ensure our insides were cleaned out before the operation. "As soon as you've drunk your mixture, make straight for the lavatory," the stern faced SBA cautioned. I downed my glassful at the same time as my mournful mate. As soon as he'd finished his brew he leapt to his feet and shot off for the toilet just outside in the corridor. His words of warning came into my head at the same time as a frantic churning came into my bowels. I followed on, my hands desperately but unavailingly trying to wrap my hospital gown to my nether region. As I careered out of the door I saw with relief there were two traps, both with their doors open. I just had time to spot my pal sitting in one with a relieved look on his face as I hurtled into the other and squatted in the appropriate place in the nick of time. "Good job you both made it," said the brusque SBA, "or you'd be cleaning the passage yourselves."

I'd been warned by several pals that Haslar was not for the faint-hearted and now I knew what they meant. Once the SBA was satisfied that we had no more to give, so to speak, we were sent back to the waiting room. That's about all I remember until waking up in the ward.

When I was fit again the Navy decided I should be making up for lost time and exercises and loan-drafts came thick and fast.

Myself and another LRO called Micky Hook, a happy-go-lucky Brummie, were put in charge of a group of Mercury lads chosen to take part in a joint service exercise with the army in Wiltshire. While the cadre of communicators were to go down to Bulford by bus, Micky and I were allowed to travel down in his car. I was looking forward to the journey.

Micky's motor was not exactly a 'gran turismo' job. He was very proud of his first car but it was a bit of a banger if truth be told. It would be a far more comfortable trip than sitting in the front seats of an RN bus, though. So I thought.

The trip was about 50 miles and we set off in late afternoon with the sun just beginning to set. Micky had decided to take the scenic route to Wiltshire and some of the roads we found ourselves on were virtually single track. As darkness gradually shrouded us he turned on the headlights. They weren't exactly dazzlers. Every bend was an adventure.

Suddenly there was a bang as the car ricocheted from a pothole. The headlights went out. Mad Micky determinedly drove on. "Don't worry Norm, this has happened before," he revealed cheerfully to his passenger, by now sitting bolt upright, staring into the gloom, rigid with fear. "They'll soon come back on again. The moon's giving me enough light anyway." That was all right then.

After twice overshooting corners and with the lights showing no sign of coming back on, even the indomitable Hook had to grudgingly give in. He screeched to a halt, leapt out of the car and gave his headlights a good kick. The lights came back on. A triumphant Micky set off again confidently. We had gone about five miles when the lights went out again. Micky drove on with his head arched over the steering wheel, assisted by a pallid passenger with his nose pressed hard against the windscreen. Every time we hit a bump the lights either went out or came back on.

We must have gone off the road at least five times but somehow we made it to the army camp. As a non-driver I was a quivering wreck by the time we pulled up at the main gate. Micky was quite serene. It's never as bad when you're the one at the wheel.

The operational area was at an airfield and the Navy boys were responsible for the communications, with me in charge of the temporary comcen. The lads worked shifts while I was on duty during the day. It wasn't much fun. The Navy boys were bored and resentful of having to sleep in makeshift bivouacs near the comcen, with no leave during the exercise and no rum ration for the single sailors.

On the third day of our week-long stint I woke up with the 'blue meanies', filled with gloom. It was a Saturday, well only just. After tossing and turning for about four hours on my very uncomfortable camp-bed I gave up on Morpheus and got up. I looked outside our tent and dawn hadn't even come up properly. If I'd been on long weekend at the in-laws I'd still be tucked up in a comfortable bed with my wife. I would have woken up to enjoy one of Di's tasty breakfasts, taken Trudy for a walk and then caught a train into London to watch West Ham, Chelsea or Arsenal, a treat made 100 per cent better if any of them would be playing Leicester. Here I was stuck on some God-forsaken airfield. All I had to look forward to was an army chef's dog's breakfast and then begin work on whatever part of the exercise was to take place that day.

I pulled on my clothes and wandered out of the tent. I decided a walk was the best cure for the stiffness I felt in my back and legs, caused by my very uncomfortable 'pit'. It might give me an appetite. I struck out in the gloom and early morning mist onto the airfield and walked along its perimeter. Bloody hell I was fed up. I spotted a boot-polish tin lying on the deck near the perimeter fence. All my grievance at wasting a Saturday went into the kick I gave the tin.

Within a split-second of the object of my ire thudding into the fence a flare went up. Then all hell broke loose. Soldiers appeared from nowhere, guard dogs were going crazy and orders were being bellowed from every quarter. I was pretty sure the boot polish tin had something to do with it, so I slunk away as the airfield became a milling throng.

The makeshift comcen was all abuzz when I reported in for work. Everyone had been convinced we were under attack from an opposition force which had set off one of the booby traps on the perimeter. "Must have been a stray cat or dog," I suggested with an innocent air. At last things had livened up. It wasn't as good as Upton Park but at least I'd put the boot in on boredom.

When it was time to go back to HMS Mercury I was relieved it was during the day. Micky still nearly drove us off the road, this time because of being helpless with laughter when he found out who had caused the chaos on the airfield. He was sworn to secrecy.

It was extremely lucky for me that I was never found out because I had been recommended for a radio supervisor course for promotion to petty officer, which was due to begin at Mercury directly after my time in the operational pool was over.

The course was a hard slog, particularly the radio theory side. I was already pretty adept at Morse, voice and telecommunications, knew how to tune transmitters and receivers in (even if one glance from me seemed to knock them off wavelength) and how to organise communications for convoys and such like. Learning about the inside of radios, how the various layers in the atmosphere were used and how signals came in on certain frequencies was a whole new world. I spent hours over weekends with Di testing me on stuff that must have proved even more perplexing to her, before I was confident enough that lectures were sinking in.

Everything came together eventually and I passed the PO's course with flying colours. I then had a couple of months before I was found a ship that would benefit from my new expertise.

With moderately senior status my duties at HMS Mercury were very relaxed. I landed a plum job, that of manager of the Mercury Club. This was where dances, cabaret nights and discotheques took place for the ratings and Wrens working at the establishment. I really enjoyed organising some fun nights at the club, bringing various acts and pop artists in by way of contracts drawn up by the 'Melita Quintana Agency' in Portsmouth. I distinctly remember hiring a show headed by one Patrick Fyffe who brought the house down with his drag act as Perrie St Claire. He went on to greater things, becoming 'Dame Hilda' in 'Hinge and Bracket'.

Just as I was imagining myself becoming another Bernard Delfont, though, my draft to HMS Reclaim came in. I joined the Naval deep-diving vessel, which featured in the *Guinness Book of Records* for its feats, in September 1970. I took charge of a small communications department on a ship that carried out all the deep diving salvage, surveying, rescue and underwater repair and research work for the Navy.

I hardly had time for a full turnover of duties before we set sail for the deep-water Loch Ewe in the north western Highlands of Scotland, where our divers would be operating for a couple of weeks or so.

My first few days were a bit of a trial because the Reclaim's radio equipment was straight out of the Ark. The main transmitter, for instance, was one I hadn't used since HMS Battleaxe. I'd learned all about the Navy's latest integrated communications systems when doing my PO's course. Some good that was going to do me now. I had to delve into the far reaches of my memory to get communications in good order.

Working with the divers in the deep sea Loch Ewe, where during the war the Arctic Convoys used to assemble before their hazardous journeys to Russia, was really exciting. They were really tough and brave lads, whose leader, John Grattan, would later become heavily involved with finding the ill-fated Titanic.

There was much radio communications work to do in my office when the divers went on their underwater escapades. Their chief concern always was making sure correct diving and resurfacing procedures were carried out. The 'bends' was life-threatening decompression sickness caused by gas bubbles in the body forming during a dive, which affect the lads at any time. As a precaution, a diver would have to spend hours in the decompression chamber attached to the ship before he was cleared to breathe in fresh air. My admiration for the diving team knew no bounds and I was happy to be counted one of the team on our 'runs ashore', even if my head never once went under water.

It was a fascinating little stint in Scotland, made even more memorable by witnessing the Northern Lights for the first time. I'd been enthralled with the *aurora borealis* when I was a lad.

Job done in Loch Ewe, the Reclaim headed back to Portsmouth for a lengthy refit. We were all housed in HMS Victory's barracks.

With winter upon us, it was not a comfortable place. All the crew, apart from officers and the most senior NCOs, were lumped together in one huge, high-ceilinged, draughty, icy dormitory that was kept from completely freezing over by a massive cast iron coal-burning stove in the middle of it. The two most senior men housed in this large igloo were me and the chap in charge of stores, Derbyshireman Bob Henderson. We commandeered the billets nearest the stove. This came at a cost. We were expected to make sure the fire stayed in during the night. It didn't matter what your rank was if you wanted to avoid frostbite. At least our seniority excused us heaving the numerous buckets of coal up to the dormitory. But I wondered why I had bothered to do my PO's course if I were to be treated like a tar from the original HMS Victory.

I played a lot of football during the refit. However that eventually did me no favours and resulted in an injury that was to haunt me for many years.

I'd been spotted playing well for the Reclaim's team in our matches against other ships of similar size in the Portsmouth command and was subsequently chosen for HMS Victory, playing in the Portsmouth Command League. I think it was about my fifth appearance for Victory when we met the fly boys or 'hairy fairies' (Naval air servicemen) of HMS Daedalus. It was a tough encounter. Just before half-time I had to rush off my goal line to intercept a ball which had been punted into our penalty area. I dived down to collect at the same time as the opposition centre-forward jumped at it feet first. His lunge carried his studs at great force into my left thigh. It was a very nasty tackle. I was hurt quite badly but I didn't want to show the pain as I was helped up by the referee. When I tried to pivot, though, to take the free-kick awarded me, my leg collapsed under me. I had to go off.

I was strapped up at half-time and valiantly tried to play on in the second half, but one-legged goalkeepers are never very reliable custodians. Much as I loathed it I had to retire. The thigh, with five glowing red stud marks embedded in it, went from early numbness to agonising, throbbing pain by the time I was helped off the bus and into the Reclaim mess in Victory. I lay down on my bed to wait for the pain to go away. It wouldn't. Supper came and went and I just lay there, occasionally moaning as I tried to adjust my position. One of the lads went to the Victory sick bay for a codeine. It had little effect. Then the sick berth attendant who was in our dormitory came over, took one look at my by now heavily swollen and greying thigh and sent for help. I was stretchered off to the Victory sick bay where a doctor diagnosed acute haematoma. My leg was installed in a huge sling and hoisted up on a pulley.

After a couple of days I was able to limp out of the sick bay but I couldn't bend or flex my leg. I'd missed my long weekend in Boreham Wood and now my football season was over. I spent the next three months on physiotherapy. The injury was to have repercussions in later life. Di was happy I had my teeth intact but urged me to give up goalkeeping for good.

Chapter 27

RETIREMENT OF A SEA DEVIL

I hardly saw the Reclaim during this time, except to be given a run-through on where some new radio equipment (we were moving out of the carrier-pigeon age at last in the wireless office) was being installed. Still hobbling about, I began a GCE course in mathematics, having failed this particular exam twice in the past. I was being encouraged to try to elevate myself eventually to officer status and mathematics was a mandatory GCE in the process. I finally passed but that was only because I had a wise old 'schoolie' at Victory. He taught his class how to pass the exam rather than excel at it.

Other than sport, the days spent at Victory dragged by. One of the officers, chillingly also called Norman, was worried that the crew were idling their lives away. So he organised an 'expedition' for a 'select' group of us to go to the New Forest. His idea was not greeted with joy – especially by me. I remembered the calamitous 'expeds' we'd had at HMS Ganges.

Bob Henderson and I were put in charge of the jaunt. We were given two large tents and sleeping bags and backpacks containing rations for two days: tins of corned beef, beans, pre-boiled potatoes and the like. We would have to find water to fill our (circa World War II) water bottles. A lorry then came to pick us up and we set off for the New Forest, which we gauged was about 30 or 40 miles away.

The driver was under orders from Norman (our eager persecutor, certainly not me) to take a bewildering route in the forest, so we would lose orientation. After endless twists and turns, with all signs of human habitation gone, the lorry stopped and we were ordered to disembark. Bob and I were given Ordnance Survey maps. This filled me full of dread. It had been 10 years since I'd learned how to read a map. Protests from Bob and me, neither of us exactly Shackleton material, fell on deaf ears. Norm (again, not me) then told us we had to be at a certain location, marked on our maps, the next day at 1600 hours where we would be taken back to the barracks.

It all sounded a bit too commando for our liking. We tumbled out of the lorry grumbling and complaining. "I've marked on the maps where we are now. You'll need to do some walking first before you settle down for the night, to give yourselves plenty of time to get to the pick-up tomorrow," advised our half-crazed officer. "It's going to be a challenge; you'll get a lot out of it. Much better than sitting around playing cards."

The lorry drove off. We seemed to be in the middle of nowhere. Bob and I studied the maps. We deduced from the markings that we were about 10 miles from Lyndhurst. A sense of adventure kicked in. "Let's get walking and find a pub," Dave Titchen, a Brummie storehand suggested. This seemed an admirable idea, perhaps not in the spirit of Baden-Powell but pragmatic.

There was a great thirst upon all of us by the time we approached the outskirts of the picturesque New Forest town after about two hours route marching. Well, more ambling sluggishly with frequent arguments ensuing over whose turn it was to lug a tent. The tents were very lucky to go the distance.

With dusk not far away, it was decision time. "Let's have a pint," the ever thoughtful Titchen suggested. Henderson and I gave his suggestion the thumbs-up. We little band of outward-bounders trooped into the first pub we came across.

The landlord was delighted to have so many customers that early in the evening, enquiring where we were from. He was an ex-Navy chief stoker who reckoned he'd pulled every dodge in the book. We'd struck gold.

Titchen was delegated to run a 'Yorkshire', a pool of our funds, to buy the beers. Despite our adventure coming in a blank week, Dave collected a tidy sum. All leadership qualities which should have been shown by Henderson and me, dissolved in Friary Meux bitter. We did have to decide where we were going to camp down for the night, however. For my part, I was close to enquiring of the landlord if he might have a room. I decided that was not in the spirit of camaraderie, though. "Right, let's check the maps, Bob, and decide where we're going to spend the night," I said to my co-leader. "We'll have to make a move soon or it'll be too dark to put up the tents." This was greeted with hisses and boos from our cohort. An eavesdropping landlord came up with a brilliant suggestion. "There's a big field just below the pub, why don't you pitch your tents there?" Proposal carried unanimously.

And so it came to pass. Ten fairly chirpy and intrepid adventurers set up camp in a pub garden. Tents erected, a fire was built and a happy little band sat around it, making up camp fire songs. We all had a turn going solo. My song was inspired by the Cypriot sherry we'd bought from the pub to fill up our water bottles. "We are the team, but we're not what we seem. Full of good spirit and Emva Cream…" Bob Dylan eat your heart out.

The pub's steak and kidney pies had made our night rations redundant. When we woke up in the morning everyone was starving but the thought of corned beef and beans did not appeal. The landlord saved our bacon. We struck camp, cleaned up the field and went back in the pub for a hearty breakfast apiece. When we were met by our enthusiastic officer in the lorry that afternoon we admitted that, yes, we had indeed got a lot out of it.

It was a great relief to get back on board the Reclaim when the refit was over. I was delighted with my new equipment in the wireless office and happy to have a little privacy in my bunk bed as opposed to sharing a huge, often acridly smoky, dormitory. We set sail (metaphorically, but in fact the Reclaim had been the last ship in the Navy to use that mode of power) for the Scottish lochs again.

Work in the wireless office was tiring but not half as strenuous as it was for the divers. They were at it night and day – dive, work and then spend hours in the 'can', the decompression chamber.

We did have some fun nights ashore on the Scottish west coast, though. Dave Titchen was quite an accomplished guitar player and we would often spend an hour or two entertaining bar customers in the hotels around places like Aultbea near Loch Ewe, Tarbert and Lochgilpead with our repertoire of Beatles numbers.

I remember one night when there was a 'lock in' at one of the hotels. We were enjoying a few illicit drinks when suddenly everyone started disappearing out the back door. A police car had been spotted down at the harbour. As Dave and I sneaked out of the building two more police cars turned up.

The next day our divers were called out by the police. It appeared that a Scots lad had gone missing, feared drowned. His body was found and a lengthy investigation followed. Everyone on the ship was interviewed. One of our chefs, who'd fallen out with the victim, was a murder suspect for quite a time and held in the local police station cell. Attention eventually, though, switched to a civilian who was later charged with manslaughter. The two men had apparently been in a fight outside the pub and one of them had finished up in the loch. Our chef quite enjoyed the notoriety. Whenever you had a gripe about the food on board after that you were warned: "Shut it or I'll kill yer."

Our second long stint at Loch Ewe caused quite a stink. Weary of our chef's stodgy fare and tired of his threats, two or three of us ate ashore when we could. The hotel in Aultbea (Ault Bay) was a favourite eating house, especially for its succulent Sunday roasts. After lunch we would then have to go to the jetty on the small harbour in the bay and wait for the afternoon 'picket' boat from the Reclaim to pick us up.

On one of the Sundays I went straight ashore for lunch after spending the whole night working in the wireless office. I was shattered but the call of Highland beef and Yorkshire pudding staved off the need for sleep. After a glorious feed I made my way to the jetty, almost out on my feet. With the sun beating down I slipped into a deep sleep on a pile of pallets. I was awoken by a stench which assaulted my nostrils – bad fish. As I had lain in the arms of Morpheus my caring colleagues had thought it a great idea to cover me up with fishing nets. No-one would come near me on the boat, I stunk so vehemently. The stench stayed with me for days, no matter how I bathed and washed my hair. And I had to throw my lovely Double-Two best shirt away in the end when even three doses of Persil failed to prevent it smelling like a cat's dinner.

From Scotland we moved to Wales. The divers' task this time was to walk across St David's Bay, underwater of course. At some stage or other I remember a dance being laid on at Haverfordwest for the Reclaim. A piece was put in the local paper inviting the local girls to come along and meet the sailors. I had been down this road before in Invergordon. I warned the lads who were scrubbing up for the occasion that it would all end in tears. I was a happily married man but I couldn't resist going along to watch the girls dance around their handbags. Welsh girls were a lot friendlier than the lassies in Strathpeffer, however. It proved a triumph for the Haverfordwest mayor, whose idea the dance was. The divers were hugely popular. One of our boys later got married to a Welsh girl he met that night.

A few weeks later there was great excitement on board the Reclaim. We were to be used as a film set for shooting some episodes of 'Dr Who'. The ship was turned out immaculately when Jon Pertwee and his Tardis arrived to film shots for 'The Sea Devils'. The divers donned creepy rubber sea devil suits as stunt-men and we all appeared as extras at some time or other.

One of my young radio operators had a proper part, too, running up to the bridge with a message for the Doctor.

Dr Who's assistant Jo Grant was played by a very attractive actress called Katy Manning. Most of the crew spent the fortnight drooling over her. I remember her trying to look dainty tripping over the doorway of the ward room. I suspected gin and tonic rather than lack of sea legs.

About 25 years later I had chance to speak to Jon Pertwee about his time aboard the Reclaim. I say had chance. Mr Pertwee was staying in the same lovely country house hotel in Rutland where I had taken my wife-to-be Sharon to propose to her and present her with an engagement ring. While she said yes I got no response from Mr Pertwee when I walked into the dining room that night and said hello to him. He didn't hear me because he was too engrossed in his newspaper. I decided I wouldn't disturb him but I might chance talking to him the next morning at breakfast about the Sea Devils. It didn't happen. Dr Who had left the building by the time Sharon and I went in for breakfast. And it was my last chance. Tragically Mr Pertwee died the next day.

The Reclaim headed back to Portsmouth around autumn 1971 time for another, smaller refit. Thankfully we all stayed on board. I couldn't face more nights in cheerless HMS Victory.

One night my good pal Idris, the head steward, and I decided to go ashore quite late on and take in the last house of a film. Having enjoyed the movie we had no sooner left the cinema when we were confronted by a huge fellow swaying along clutching a bag of fish and chips. He was blocking our path so Idris did the smart thing and hopped into the road. I tried to dance around this drunken individual, who resembled 'Bluto' from the Popeye cartoons. He deliberately barged into me. "You tell me which way you want to go sunshine and I'll go the other," I said to him. With that he hurled his bag of fish and chips at me. Greasy food splattered onto my shirt front. I didn't have chance to protest. Perceiving I had insulted him he hurled himself at me. We tumbled to the pavement, where he rained an array of blows about my face. At first I was no match. Then this ogre started to falter. Somehow I rolled him onto his back and began giving him as good as I'd got. That was how the police found us.

As I was hauled to my feet another fellow dived in to the melee. He was obviously the drunken fish and chip eater's mate. "He started it," this equally inebriated Herbert lied, pointing an accusing finger at me. I denied this vehemently. The police were in no mood to listen. All three of us were bundled into a meat wagon that had pulled up next to the action. Idris, protesting my innocence, was warned he could have a ride to the station too if he didn't shut up. I shouted at him from the back of the meat wagon to get back on board.

When we got to the police station, remonstration at the unfairness of the lifting of my collar only made matters worse for me. "Were you fighting or not?" growled a desk sergeant. I had to admit I was but it had been in self-defence. He wasn't taking much notice. I was charged officially and escorted to a cell. Wisely, they separated me from my attacker and his mate, who I overheard were submariners. The policeman on duty down in the cells seemed quite sympathetic. "Are you in for fighting with that bloke in the next cell?" he enquired. I admitted I was. "What that great big bugger next door with the black eye?" I nodded. "Well I think you deserve a cup of tea lad."

The next morning very early, I was released and told to report to the Magistrates' Court in Portsmouth the next afternoon. When I got on board I had a pow-wow with Idris. He thought I should speak to the Reclaim's first lieutenant, tell him what had happened and ask him to be a character reference. I thought it was best to keep the Navy out of it if I could. It had worked with a Christmas tree, perhaps I'd be lucky over a fish and chip packet. Idris said he would come along with me and we'd try to get him up in the dock as a witness who would swear that I hadn't been drinking and I'd acted in self-defence.

In the event, Idris never got to speak. I didn't get chance much myself. After a charge of being 'drunk and disorderly' was read out, the policeman who had been the one to arrest me, drew out his notebook and gave a resumé of the night's proceedings. He told the magistrates that he was one of three policemen called to a fracas and that he "found the defendant (me) fighting on the pavement. I noticed his breath smelt of alcohol and his eyes were glazed." I snorted loudly and voiced my protest while this evidence was being given. I'm afraid that did me no favours. "The defendant will remain silent until it is his turn to speak," the chairman of the bench snapped at me. When it was my turn to speak I denied strenuously that my breath could have smelt of alcohol as I had not drunk a drop and I had a witness with me to prove it. I continued: "And if my eyes were glazed sir, then I think yours would have been as well, if you wore contact lenses and you had been punched in the face several times." I tried to explain that I had been provoked by a fish and chip packet. The beak nodded. He briefly consulted with his bench then said: "You have been found guilty of disorderly conduct (note the missing 'drunk and'). Conditional discharge. "

I was not happy with the decision but, as Idris pointed out, if I made any more waves it would have to go further and then the ship was bound to find out. I was supposed to be a head of department, after all.

I didn't even know whether or how to appeal, so I decided to let the matter drop. When I got home on long weekend the next night I related my escapade to Di and her parents. Ted was very sympathetic and said he was quite proud of his son-in-law for sticking up for himself. It moved me on a chapter or two in his good-books.

It was just as well nobody found out because a couple of weeks later I was told I had been chosen to take part in a leadership course. I embarked on a three-week long series of lectures, tests and physical training exercises. The most useful exercise in my book was being taught self-defence. It stood me in good stead one night many years later when I was a golf reporter.

We were sent to the New Forest on a survival exercise. That was old hat to me. However, my colleagues were a bit prissy. They wouldn't countenance camping out next to a pub.

Having passed the leadership course I knew I had a big decision to make. It was autumn 1971 and my 12 years' service was coming to an end. I had to decide whether to sign on and hope to go further than petty officer.

I decided to try for the 'S' branch of communications, the boys who did the secret listening jobs, mainly from submarines. After being accepted I then failed the medical before I even got to the diving-bell where emergency escapes from subs took place. My perennial ear problems and contact lenses ruled me out. So it was retirement for me.

The Navy was very helpful in guidance for what I might do on demob. I was told there were a variety of courses that might help me find employment. Nothing on the list appealed to me. I didn't want to be a painter and decorator, a bricklayer or a plumber. I did, though, fancy a fortnight learning to drive.

I arrived at the Naval driving school and found myself in a class of 12 people. Some had been driving for years and wanted an official driving licence; three of us had never been behind a wheel.

The course was split up each day. One half of the class would learn about the mechanics of the car in the morning and then have their driving lessons in Morris Minors in the afternoon and vice versa.

It was a little unfortunate for me that I did the driving part first. It would have been handy to actually know how gears and clutches worked.

"Right Mr Dabell, I want you to put the car into first gear and slowly move away from the car park."

"Erm, I can't drive."

"You know how to use the clutch and gears don't you?"

"No, that's why I'm on this course."

"Oh, I see." This final remark was imparted with eyes looking through the top of his head. I could read his mind: "We've got a right one here."

The instructor was gentle with me. He went through all the machinations of the Moggy. I don't know whether it was because of inheriting my dad's driving genes or what but within an hour I amazed myself and the instructor by quickly getting the hang of things. Me driving!

An afternoon of mechanical instruction then tied a lot of loose ends together. By the end of the fortnight I was driving confidently and without any need for my instructor to take over controls. Nights were spent swotting up on the Highway Code. My instructor had no hesitation in putting me in for my driving test on the Monday following the course's end.

It all went amazingly smoothly. I didn't funk any questions on the Highway Code, carried out my three-point-turn with aplomb, didn't reverse into anything, excelled on the open road, and parked the car competently when we arrived back at the school. I passed. Five out of the twelve on the course passed, including the three of us who had never driven before and hadn't picked up any bad habits.

I was jubilant when I got home on weekend and waved my driving pass in front of everybody. The only trouble was, I couldn't afford to buy a car. Every penny of my savings had gone towards buying a house. The car would have to wait.

I left the Navy on February 9 1972, ready for pastures new. I felt I'd enjoyed my years 'before the mast' (though rarely when I was up it). But then, you only really remember the good times, don't you?

Ends

Posing in my first sailor suit.

Our 'sparkers' class at HMS Ganges in 1960 which would go on to break the signal school record for results. I'm top left, standing above long-time pal Denis Lloyd. Mick Clifford, one of those who left me stranded on the mess roof, is fourth left, top row; Slinger Wood, my eternal partner-in-crime, sits third left, bottom row, alongside our instructor Tony Cokes.

Standing alongside Keppel Five Mess in my suit rather than my bottoms-less pyjamas.

HMS Ganges mast fully manned, complete with button-boy balanced precariously on top.

Slinger and I breaking the rules by lounging around the HMS Ganges quarterdeck. We were supposed to double-march across it, like the boys in the background.

The communications cadre of HMS Battleaxe, my first ship. Ever fastidious, I'm trying to resite my collar just as the picture was taken.

Time off from duties in the HMS Falmouth communicators' mess. My great mate Jim Sked is on my right and our friendly LRO Bungy Edwards on my left.

The crew of HMS Falmouth before we began our Mediterranean cruise.

Best man at my cousin and early mentor Robert Plant's wedding.

On the town, ready to hit Gibraltar. L to R: Flook Young, me in silly hat,
Johnny Vear, Jim Sked and Buster Brown.

Jim Sked, 'That is' Jones and Keith, 'Scouse', Grattan, the lad who was
left stranded in Aden following the frightening grenade attack.

Bearded wonder: In disguise still with Johnny Vear, not long after our escapades on the Thames and in Devonport Dockyard.

Christmas on the beach in Malta. Jim Sked is the one buried.

Sitting with our Filipina hostesses in the Sky Club in Subic Bay. Tom Mueller, who got his shoe shot off after going AWOL in Olongapo, is the tall American in the white sailor suit. Tom was killed in Vietnam about a year later.

Cutting my 21st birthday cake with Mum.

On the way to a date with destiny: Aboard the MFV on our way to
Tangiers.

A snap of Di taken at Albufeira on our pre-wedding honeymoon.

A publicity shot for the navy's all-singing-all-dancing integrated communications system. After learning how to use this sophisticated equipment, the radios on my next and last ship, HMS Reclaim, were out of the Ark.

My lovely, cuddly, stepfather Ray.